Prejudice and Race Relations

Prejudice and Race Relations

Edited with an Introduction by
Raymond W. Mack

A NEW YORK TIMES BOOK

Generously Donated to
The Frederick Douglass Institute
By Professor Jesse Moore
Fall 2000

Quadrangle Books
CHICAGO

THIRD PRINTING

PREJUDICE AND RACE RELATIONS. Copyright © 1970
by The New York Times Company. All rights reserved,
including the right to reproduce this book or portions thereof
in any form. For information, address: Quadrangle Books,
Inc., 12 East Delaware Place, Chicago 60611. Manufactured
in the United States of America. Published simultaneously in
Canada by Burns and MacEachern Ltd., Toronto.

Library of Congress Catalog Card Number: 75-78322

The publishers are grateful to the contributors herein
for permission to reprint their articles.

Mrs. Lee Bradford deserves my gratitude for both her patience and her efficiency. She did almost all of the basic library research which made it possible for me to edit this book. Her intelligence, good judgment, and competence made the task bearable; her wit and cheer made it fun.

Mrs. Jane Taylor nagged me to complete the book, inspired me to try to do it well, and took full responsibility for preparing the final manuscript. This page is inserted in the book at my request to tell both ladies how deeply I appreciate their brains, their professionalism, and their help.

If there is anything wrong with the book, that is clearly their fault. If the book is coherent and useful, I am willing to accept the credit.

R.W.M.

Evanston, Illinois
March 1970

Contents

5. Options Facing Americans: Paths to Separatism or Integration

Prejudice and Race Relations

Introduction:
A Decade of Change

THE HISTORY of America is in large part a story of social relations between the races. An account of the experiences shared by blacks and whites, of what they learned to believe about themselves and each other, of how they came to behave toward each other, and of the consequences of their beliefs and behaviors— such an account encompasses the major events of American history from the early exploration of the continent through the development of a plantation economy, its disruption by the processes of industrialization, and the massive dislocations of families and communities as the entire society has become urbanized. The constant reweaving of the fabric of American society can be understood largely in black and white terms.

The place of America in the larger perspective of human history will be defined principally by what Americans do about the conflict between their behaviors in the realm of race relations and their beliefs about democracy, equality of opportunity, and the brotherhood of man.

Race in American History

Negroes were among the first "European" explorers of North America, participating in the discovery of the Pacific Ocean with Vasco Nuñez de Balboa, the exploration of Mexico with Hernando Cortes, and of New Mexico with Francisco de Coronado; there were Negroes among the early French settlers of the Mississippi Valley. In 1619 twenty Negroes were sold for needed provisions by the captain of a Dutch ship to colonists in Jamestown, Virginia. Like indentured white workers, these Negroes were sold into service for a specified length of time. Not until white indentured servants stopped coming from Europe in 1688 were African slaves brought in large numbers to the North American colonies. By 1715 there were over 58,000 slaves in the colonies; by 1775 there were over half a million. Congress voted in 1807, at the request of President Thomas Jefferson, that no more slaves should be imported, but an illegal traffic continued nonetheless. By 1830 the Negro population was 2,300,000, and by 1860 it had reached 4,400,000.

The overwhelming majority, but not all, of the Negroes remained enslaved. Some slaves bought their freedom with money saved from their work; a few were able to purchase freedom for their families. Occasionally a slave was freed as a reward for outstanding work or devotion. By 1790 there were nearly sixty thousand free Negroes, comprising almost 8 per cent of the total Negro population. Free Negroes could buy land and own property, but their "freedom" was severely restricted. Throughout the country they were denied access to many churches and public amusement places, kept separate from whites in public conveyances, and denied access to many of the skilled trades. In the South, "free" Negroes were not permitted to vote, to intermarry with whites, to purchase white servants, or to give testimony in court cases involving white people. Too, there were considerable differences between being a slave and being an indentured servant with a set period of service. As a slave, a Negro could not vote, hold office, make contracts, move without permission, or even legally marry. Neither was he permitted by law to learn to read and write. He could be sold, given away, separated from his family, and in some cases even killed by his master.

By the time the colonies became a new country, slavery was quite unpopular in many quarters; the institution was not of overriding importance to the new nation's economy. All this was drastically changed in 1793 by Eli Whitney's invention of the cotton gin, a simple machine which made possible the quick mechanical separation of cotton seed from fiber. As cotton became a major crop, the value of Negro slaves for cultivating the fields increased greatly. As a result, the center of slavery moved from the Virginia tobacco fields to the cotton plantations of the Deep South, concentrated in South Carolina, Georgia, Alabama, and Mississippi. Slave labor became so desirable that Negroes were deliberately bred within the United States. The Negro population increased by 200,000 between 1790 and 1900, by 300,-000 between 1800 and 1810, and by more than 500,000 between 1820 and 1830.

The development of sizable plantation communities altered somewhat the distribution of occupational skills among black Americans. Although most slaves remained field hands, some were taught to become carpenters, spinners, weavers, nurses, bricklayers, blacksmiths, cobblers, painters, and mechanics. This development of a more balanced labor force in the plantation community created the possibility of occupational competition between blacks and whites once emancipation came, and led to much of the friction between working-class blacks and whites after the Civil War.

President Abraham Lincoln's Emancipation Proclamation became effective on January 1, 1863, freeing all slaves in states that were at war with the Union. On December 18, 1865, the 13th Amendment to the Constitution granted freedom to all slaves. These measures effected an enormous change in the formal social structure of the United States, setting free more than four million Negro slaves.

In 1868 the 14th Amendment to the Constitution was passed in order to penalize any state that restricted the right to vote, and in 1870 the 15th Amendment made it illegal to use race as a qualification for voting. With the large Negro population in the South, these amendments effectively placed much control of the government of the Southern states in the hands of Negroes during the decade following the Civil War. For a time Negroes controlled all Southern state governments except Georgia's.

Many Southern whites were violently opposed to these changes. After the Reconstruction period (1866–1876) the Negro governments of the Southern states were overthrown, and Negroes were prevented from voting by various means including terror and intimidation. The federal Civil Rights Act of 1875 prohibited the exclusion of Negroes from public conveniences and places of entertainment, but this act was ruled unconstitutional by the United States Supreme Court on the ground that it usurped the rights of the states. The protection of Negroes' civil rights was therefore left to the states, a decision which resulted in widespread discrimination in the former slave states. Sets of laws were passed requiring the separation of Negroes from whites in streetcars, trains, jails, hospitals, graveyards, and schools. Many states forbade intermarriage. Segregation was enforced by either law or custom in churches, libraries, hotels, elevators, and theaters.

For a time, Southern Negroes were prevented from voting by the "grandfather law," which denied the franchise to citizens if they or their ancestors had not voted before January 1, 1867 (very few would have been able to). Negroes were also denied the vote on the basis of their lacking certain qualifications. For example, if they did not own $300 worth of taxable property, or did not have a regular occupation, or had not served in the army, or had not paid the poll tax.

In summary, emancipation from slavery cannot be regarded as a single act that eradicated the consequences of nearly two and a half centuries of slavery. White Americans had learned through their history to regard black Americans as an inferior underclass. The legal awarding of freedom was not a sufficient tool for wiping out deeply ingrained attitudes and behavior patterns based on the assumption that black Americans live, and belong, at the bottom of the American social structure.

Race and American Social Structure

Negroes were slaves into the latter half of the nineteenth century. As such, they were assigned to the very bottom of the American social structure.

It is not sociologically precise to say that black Americans have traditionally been lower class in the United States. It is more accurate to say that they have been underclass, or beneath the class structure. In American society a lower-class person who achieves the requisite education, income, or occupational skills can work his way into the middle class. A middle-class white who fails to meet the educational, income, or occupational standards becomes lower class. But there is no such thing in American society as the Negro who excels in the achievement of education, income, and occupational status and is therefore promoted to white. Neither is it possible for a white person to fail so miserably that his fellow citizens demote him to Negro.

The traditional role of race in the American social structure, then, is that of an overriding factor. Race has been considered so important a characteristic in defining one's position that no amount of achievement can overcome its force.

Where an efficient segregation system minimizes one's exposure to members of a minority who do not conform to the stereotype, a culture of discrimination can flourish. As most of the Negroes with whom many white Americans deal conform to their stereotype of Negroes—that is, that Negroes are poor, ignorant, and subservient—it is easy for white Americans to think of the term "Negro" as a synonym for poor, ignorant, and subservient. If people are isolated from the mainstream of society, as many whites are in the Southern states, this culture of discrimination can become a norm in itself, further isolating its members from "outsiders" who do not share their belief in Negro inferiority, or do not share it with the same intensity and conviction. When discrimination is basic to the culture, when it is part of a people's "way of life," it is easy for them to think of it as a natural, even an inborn, trait. Thus people may justify racial discrimination as a consequence of the "natural human aversion" to differentness, rather than the learned behavior that it is.

Recently (in part, no doubt, as a consequence of what social scientists have taught to a generation of students), it has become fashionable to substitute culture for biology in racist arguments. Educated people know that all human beings belong to a single species. But nowadays educated people also know about socialization and culture. "If they're brought up in those dreadful slums without a father in the home and with crime and drugs all around, you can't expect them to be like us, can you?"

Culture is a congenial explanatory variable; while it assigns the dominant white society a measure of guilt, the guilt is ancestral, and hence bearable. At the same time it assures us that it's going to take at least a generation (newly socialized) to get us out of this, and hence racial justice is really our children's burden.

Black has been a synonym for underclass in the United States, and both black and white Americans for more than three centuries have grown up with the understanding that black means inferior. The extent to which this is true is evident in the use which many white Americans make of the word "exception" when discussing Negroes. When an American white person protests that he would not want a Negro to buy the house next door, one may ask him why he would object to having a successful black businessman such as John Johnson or a Supreme Court Justice such as Thurgood Marshall or a civic leader such as Whitney Young for a next-door neighbor. His most likely reply to any one of these suggestions is, "But he's an exception." He is obviously not an exception to being Negro. What is meant is that he is an exception to what white Americans learn to mean by Negro: he is not a poor, uneducated citizen at the bottom of the social structure.

The recent friction in American race relations stems less from black Americans' being "kept in their place" than from the fact that urbanization and industrialization have enabled so many Negroes in the present generation to work their way out of what has traditionally been their "place." Before World War I, 90 per cent of all black Americans still lived in the South, and most of them were farmers. During World War I, with foreign immigration cut off and an intense demand for labor, over 500,000 Negroes moved north. Many black families were exposed for the first time to participation in an industrial labor force.

World War II brought another great migration of Negroes out of the South to meet the demand for factory labor. Since World War II the increasing mechanization of agriculture has continued to provide an impetus for Negroes to leave the South. By now a majority of black Americans live in the North and almost all Northern Negroes live in cities.

The very fact that some black Americans have achieved so much in the past twenty years helps to account for the high level of dissatisfaction both among them and among their fellow black Americans who have not shared in their gains. To both groups, real access to real equality of opportunity no longer seems incredible. Rather, continuing delays in achieving equal access to opportunity are more and more frustrating. The situation is a paradox in which the position of some black Americans in the stratification structure has improved dramatically, but where the rewards for the average Negro remain well behind those for the average white. Measuring income in constant 1966 dollars, we find that 1.6 per cent of black Americans had incomes of $10,000 or more in 1950, and that sixteen years later the $10,000 or more category included 12.2 per cent of black families. In 1964 and 1965 the median income of nonwhites was 54 per cent that of whites; by 1968 nonwhite median income had increased to 60 per cent of the white median income. But the dollar gap between white median income and the income of nonwhites has widened since 1947, with nonwhite income increasing from $3,076 to $5,359, while the white increase was from $4,020 to $8,936.

The greatest gains black Americans have made in recent years in the American stratification system have been in education. The 1960's saw a considerable increase in the school enrollment of pupils above the compulsory attendance age. In 1960, 35 per cent of Negro youths eighteen and nineteen years old were in school, but by 1969 the figure had risen to 45 per cent. The proportion of Negro men who completed four years of high school or more rose dramatically during the 1960's, from 36 per cent in 1960 to 60 per cent in 1969. For whites the increase was from 63 per cent to 78 per cent.

The 1966 data of William Brink and Louis Harris (published in their book *Black and White*) indicate that black Americans recognize the recent improvements in their everyday lives, whether or not journalists and social scientists do. A set of questions was asked, all phrased, "Do you feel that you are better off today than you were three years ago, worse off, or about the same as you were then?" The individual items dealt with housing, pay, being able to register and vote, being able to eat in any restaurant, being able to live in neighborhoods with whites if you want to, and being able to have your children educated with white children. On all items except housing, more than half the black respondents said they were better off. In no case did as many as 10 per cent say they were worse off. The summary question was: "All in all, compared with three years ago, do you think things for people such as yourself and your family are better, worse, or about the same?" Sixty-seven per cent said "better"; only 5 per cent said "worse."

In short, most black Americans identify themselves as middle class. But most black Americans also identify themselves as black. The real question is whether white Americans will welcome blacks into the former reference group—middle class—or push them into the latter—black Americans.

Prospects for Achieving America

Americans profess a dedication to cultural ideals of equality of opportunity and the brotherhood of man. The question facing us is whether, in James Baldwin's fine phrase, we shall achieve America.

The 1950's laid the setting for drastic social change in American race relations. The 1960's were a decade characterized by alterations in the laws governing race relations, the role of race in politics, and even in economic relations between the races. By the mid-1960's the entire legal structure supporting racial segregation and discrimination had been destroyed. The beginnings of school desegregation have been made in every Southern state, and the federal government has exerted some pressure for more effective desegregation in both faculties and student bodies in Northern city schools. Black voter registration has increased greatly in the Southern states, and effective political organization and participation have helped to bring about the election of black mayors in Fayette, Mississippi; Gary, Indiana; and Cleveland, Ohio. By 1970 apprenticeships for Negroes in the building-trades unions were being negotiated in several cities.

Many Americans cherish the wistful hope that these gains achieved by black Americans will lessen the pressure for change. Because blacks are much better off than they were twenty years ago, the argument runs, it seems reasonable to expect less militancy, less friction, and reduced interracial conflict. From a social scientist's point of view, it makes better sense to predict increased pressure for equality, more widespread dissatisfaction with discrimination, and more insistent demands for access to the mainstream of American society. Revolutions, whether peaceful or violent, are made not by the most oppressed and downtrodden people in a society, but by those whose position has been improving and who find that access to further improvement is resisted or blocked. The United States became a nation when a revolution was organized by the thirteen best-governed colonies in the world. That revolution was followed by one in France made not by serfs or by an urban proletariat but by the bourgeoisie. The French bourgeoisie in the late eighteenth century had earned a position in some ways analogous to that of many Southern Negroes in the 1950's: they had achieved a higher status than the social order was prepared to recognize. The civil rights protest movement of the 1950's and early 1960's was led not by sharecroppers or by unskilled laborers but by clergymen, lawyers, and college students—people who had achieved the occupational and educational levels of middle-class whites but who were still treated as underclass because they were black. As T. H. Marshall says in *Class, Citizenship, and Social Development* (1964):

> Some people hold that social mobility affords a safety valve and helps to avert the threatened conflict. Although this is true up to a point, I think its importance can easily be exaggerated. Where individual mobility is automatic, or nearly so, class loyalty develops with difficulty. If every apprentice has a reasonable hope of becoming a master he will form his associations on the basis of his trade or profession rather than of his social level. Again, where a whole group can rise in social estimation and economic value, leaving no stragglers, the alliance of groups into classes is more difficult. This is no doubt the effect of the recent rise of many skilled occupations into the ranks of the professions. But where mobility is individual and not automatic, but depends on the results of competitive striving, I am doubtful whether the same result follows. When the race is to the

swift, the slow, who are always in a majority, grow tired of their perpetual defeat and become more disgruntled than if there were no race at all. They begin to regard the prizes as something to which they are entitled and of which they are unjustly deprived. They declare that no man ought to be made to race for his bread and butter, and the argument is not without force. Especially is this so when society shows itself indifferent to the condition of the losers on the ground that the road to better things is ever open before them.

Neither peaceful protests nor large-scale riots result simply from the existence of an oppressed class. It is true that we have in America both an oppressed class and a pattern of violence and protest. But the pattern of violence we have seen over the past three or four years and the pattern of protest which has developed over a period of nearly twenty years are both relatively new phenomena. The pattern of oppression, on the other hand, is older than the nation itself.

The protest and the violence involve a large, discriminated-against lower class, socially defined on the basis of race, a class whose median members are poor, overcrowded, poorly educated, discriminated against, and underprivileged in their access to political power, to economic opportunity, and to human dignity. But the protest and the violence are relatively new, whereas black Americans have been underprivileged and discriminated against for over three centuries.

It is indeed poor social science analysis, then, simply to say that the position of black Americans in the stratification structure is the cause of civil disorder. This is not to say that oppression is not a causative factor. But throughout most of our history, oppression has not resulted in militant protest or in widespread violence. We must ask as social scientists what other factors America has added to the pattern of oppression we have always practiced against our black citizens. American Negroes have been poor and discriminated against for over three centuries. What have we added to the equation in the past two decades that leads us to a National Advisory Commission on Civil Disorders?

Social scientists can identify four variables which differentiate black Americans today from their parents, grandparents, and enslaved ancestors: (1) marked upward mobility in that most critical of stratification factors, education, leading to (2) markedly higher expectations for equality of opportunity, for human dignity, for access to political power, and for economic payoff in the society's reward structure, leading to (3) social organization to protest the discrimination which serves as a roadblock in gaining access to these expectations, with all three of these occurring at the same time that black Americans have suffered (4) the dislocation of the mass migration which has removed them from their traditional rural Southern homes to the concentration of Northern urban ghettos.

All four of these factors stem in part from the social upheaval of World War II and from a social policy following it, the G.I. Bill of Rights, which had quite unintended consequences in the realm of race relations. World War II took millions of young Americans, black and white, removed them from the relatively parochial surroundings of their childhoods, and sent them across the country and around the world to meet new people and face new experiences. The poignant query of the World War I song, "How you gonna keep 'em down on the farm after they've seen Paree?", implies consequences in a host of attitudes and behaviors. After World War II a large proportion of these well-traveled young Americans used the G.I. Bill to acquire a college education. It is probably not accidental that the most effective early organization of black protest occurred in the Deep South, where for black Americans the discrepancy was most marked between the achievement of middle-class characteristics, such as a college education, and access to middle-class perquisites, such as respectful service in a restaurant.

One other massive change in American society has been of incalculable importance in fomenting changed patterns of race relations: the widespread dissemination of information through television. The commercials and situation comedies as well as the newscasts dispense the stuff of increased expectations. The advertisement for a new floor wax shows the housewife in a modern, gleaming, eighteen-foot-square kitchen. The situation comedy presents a set of role models—a well-dressed, well-spoken family in an expensively furnished living room. The television newscast not only reports a sit-in at a department store lunch counter, it shows before the viewers' very eyes a group of young black Americans standing up to white Americans, demanding their rights, and getting away with it.

What will the 1970's bring? All the factors that contributed to the ferment of the past twenty years are still with us. Many of them, such as amount of education and degree of urbanization, are with us on an increasing scale. For the first time America has a generation of educated, urbanized Negroes. These people are not a few "exceptions." They are the cadre of a social movement, and they have considerable support for their aspirations among a generation of young, better-educated white Americans. Unlike their grandparents, they were not reared to live in a caste society where one is taught to expect to stay in his place. They have been taught—by churches, by schools, by governmental pronouncements, and by the mass media—to expect the rewards available in an open, competitive society. They are unlikely to accept institutionalized race discrimination as a roadblock between them and those rewards.

In the coming years, then, we shall probably see among our black citizens increased education, wider participation in the economy, increased political participation, and increasing demands for equality of access to opportunity in all sectors of life. And perhaps we shall achieve America.

Part 1

RACE AND ITS CONSEQUENCES: BELIEFS AND ACTS

INDIVIDUAL HUMAN beings differ from one another in many ways: height, weight, ear size, finger length, hair color, and so on. When a group of people live together for a long time in relative isolation from other groups, they develop clusters of similar traits. These clusters are, however, minor variations within the species. From a genetic point of view, it is the unity of the species that defines it. Men all around the world, regardless of the curl of their hair or the color of their skin, have the same basic set of organs, the same kind of lungs, the same skeletal structure and nervous system, and the same sensory apparatus for seeing, hearing, feeling, tasting, and touching.

The variation within the human species is minor; the range of physical differences among human beings, for example, is not as great as that among black bears. But we human beings find the minor differences among us extremely interesting. When one group of people notices that another group is physically different and behaves differently, it is easy for them to assume that people who look "like that" behave "like that"—in other words, that racial differences cause differences in religion, or work habits, or emotions, or intelligence. The error in such an assumption is evident where members of several races participate in one society. By looking at a society, such as the United States, made up of people from various races and regions, one can see that people of widely divergent physical types can learn the English language, live in cities, participate in Christian churches, enjoy professional football, and eat strawberries.

The culture of any society is a set of learned behavior patterns. Normal human beings of any racial background learn the behavior patterns that are practiced where they are brought up. When we see differences between Italian-Americans and Irish-Americans, they are differences learned from Italian-American and Irish-American grandparents, parents, and friends in Italian-American and Irish-American neighborhoods, churches, and schools. The most efficient mechanism for perpetuating cultural differences in a multi-group society, then, is segregation. Many black Americans share some behaviors not shared by many white Americans. But those behaviors are not consequences of tightly curled hair, black skin, or a wide nasal index. They are consequences of the shared experiences of generations of black Americans and of the isolation in which those behaviors have been nurtured and transmitted.

The question of whether Negroes differ from whites in intelligence is more complicated than it appears. Black Americans and white Americans simply do not share a comparable environment. Even a black child attending a predominantly white school in a Northern city does not share the white child's environment. Most likely his parents had less formal education than the white children's, and what they received was of poorer quality. He probably lives in a poorer, more crowded neighborhood. Many of his teachers will expect less of him than of their white pupils —a critical environmental factor. The white students may exclude him from their evening homework sessions—perhaps at the insistence of their parents. Because the Negro lives in this environment of discrimination, it is impossible for social scientists to make firm statements about comparative racial abilities as if there were an experimentally controlled situation.

We do know that Negro draftees from Northern urban areas do much better on army literacy and aptitude tests than whites from Southern rural areas. We cannot conclude from this that Northern urban Negroes are a more intelligent race than Southern rural whites. We *can* say that where there are better opportunities, Negroes, like whites, benefit from them.

While we are unable to make positive statements about averages, we do know that all of the major racial stocks are represented throughout the range of human intelligence. There are Caucasoid, Mongoloid, and Negroid idiots, and there are Caucasoid, Mongoloid, and Negroid geniuses.

Given this range and what we know of the enormous impact of environment and of learned culture patterns on motivation and opportunity, we must conclude that social science research offers no evidence of any innate difference in ability between races. When we are interested in predicting motivation, social goals, or success, we can tell more from urban-rural differences, educational level, and parents' occupation and education than from race.

Chinese Have Bigger Brains Than Whites— Are They Superior?

by Robin Fox

WHAT IS THERE left to say about race? The anthropologist certainly feels weary at the prospect of repeating over and over again the known truths that should have been assimilated generally years ago. But it seems that the old truths must be constantly restated since there are still too many Bourbons in the world who have learned nothing and forgotten nothing. Prejudice is tenacious and thrives on ignorance. It was once beautifully defined as "being down on what you are not up on." Hence there is no substitute for persistent reiteration of the clichés.

And here I am talking of prejudice, not simply dislike. People are at liberty to dislike and avoid any identifiable social group whose culture offends them. They are not at liberty to attribute the offending characteristics to genetic "inferiority" in contrast to their own "racial purity." It is at this point that the anthropologist must step in and say at least "not proven," and certainly "not probable." People may hold what opinions of their fellows they wish, but no one should take liberties with the facts.

From the *New York Times Magazine*, June 30, 1968, copyright © 1968 by The New York Times Company.

There are, however, many unsolved and perplexing questions about the genetic diversity of human populations, and the only honest attitude toward many of these questions is open-mindedness. But to some liberals it is heresy to suggest that there is *any* genetic diversity of a significant kind within the human species. They regard it as tantamount to fascism even to *raise* the issue. One can appreciate their concern: once one admits diversity, it is also too easy to start *ranking* the diverse features, and since it is usually the Caucasoid imperialists who are doing the ranking, it is not surprising they come out on top. We should not, therefore, the argument goes, expend breath on the question since this may fan the flames.

But I'm afraid this is not an argument in favor of ignoring diversity. Rather we must examine the diversity and glory in it. We must point out that genetic diversity is an evolutionary asset to a species and should be capitalized on. We should also hammer home that any kind of ranking of attributes is not "given" in nature but depends on the values of the rankers. Even if it should be proved that the New York Chinese have, on average, bigger brains than the New York whites (which they undoubtedly have), I would not accept this as an argument for handing over the city government automatically to the Chinese.

I often put the following argument to people who argue that Negroes should stay underprivileged because their "intelligence" is genetically inferior to that of whites: Suppose it were proved beyond doubt that the opposite were true, that Negro intelligence was inherently superior to white? Would you then immediately hand over all white wealth, power, housing, etc., to the Negroes and move your family into the ghetto? If one can get one's opponents, purely for the sake of argument, to admit the premise—which is curiously difficult—they usually conclude that the answer is *no*. It would not be fair or just to effect such a reversal. It is even harder then to get them to see the inevitable conclusion, namely, that the present situation is just as unfair and has nothing to do with "inherent" intelligence but with many years of cumulative human action.

It is thus difficult to see quite what, for example, we are to conclude from the arguments of Dr. William Shockley—the Nobel

Prize winner in physics from Stanford—whose views on race caused a conference to be canceled for fear of "disturbances." He contends that Negro intelligence is inferior because of "evolutionary adolescence" (whatever that may mean). An objective diagnosis of this phenomenon, he says, would be "the greatest relief to the frustrated agony of black Americans." Presumably black Americans would, once convinced about their adolescent intelligences, simply throw in the sponge and admit that there was nothing for it but the ghetto, poverty and an eternity of discrimination. That any of these things would follow, *even if Shockley's contention were true,* is nonsense. Insofar as it is a highly debatable proposition—to the extent that it is difficult to attach any meaning to it —then it is even greater nonsense.

If Shockley confined himself to examining the differences between Negro and white performances and the possible genetic bases for these differences, then one could not quarrel. But like so many naive sages (and he did give us the transistor radio), he wants to make the leap to social policy, a leap which by definition involves the *non sequitur* we have already examined. Social and political justice has nothing to do with the chemistry of the chromosomes but with the interests and values of human groups and the distribution of power amongst them. Given Dr. Shockley's terms of reference, we could argue that Caucasoids have inferior brains to Mongoloids. Should we Caucasoids then relieve our "frustrated agony" by backing out of world influence and humbly letting the Chinese, North Vietnamese and what have you dictate whatever terms they chose to us? Over to you, Dr. S.

Here I should stress that the role of the anthropologist lies in this area of "inherent" inferiorities. If these are resorted to in racist arguments, the anthropologist can contribute. But there are many other aspects of the problem over which he must respectfully bow out to the sociologist, the psychologist and the historian. What, then, has the anthropologist to tell us about race?

First of all, we must admit that many anthropologists have stopped using the term as a scientific concept because, they argue, it is meaningless for any useful analysis of human differences. Those broad categories of "White," "Black," "Yellow," "Red" and various other areas of the spectrum are so full of internal diversity that one cannot use them as units of analysis at all. Between the two ends of the "Black" spectrum, for example, there may be nothing in common other than dark pigmentation, and in some cases even this may be less dark than the pigmentation of some "Caucasoids"—Hindus, for example. And here again we run into problems, for "Hindus" are not a race but a religion; the "British" are not a race but a nation; "Aryan" is not a race but at best a language family. All these varying categories, however, have at one time or another been dubbed races. The catalogue of races varies from a list of three to several hundreds and there are no settled criteria of discrimination.

Perhaps the broadest and least controversial of all definitions is the one proposed by M. F. Ashley Montagu and Loring Brace. They define a race simply as "a group of mankind, members of which can be identified by the possession of distinctive physical characteristics." But even this is a cultural rather than a biological definition. It depends on the *perception* of differences that are distinctive rather than on the actual genetic differences between the groups. Groups which look alike may have radically different genetic make-ups, in, for example, blood chemistry. And in "race relations" it is of course the *perceived* differences that matter.

There has been an attempt to substitute the idea of the "breeding population" for race in studying human variation. In zoology the concept has enormous importance, and many would regard the "population" as the unit of evolution rather than the individual. A breeding population is that group of animals which regularly mates within itself; the members of the population, that is, breed with each other much more frequently than with outsiders. Over time, certain genetic characteristics will become fixed in the population because of the inbreeding and eventually these may become so different from the characteristics of other populations that interbreeding between populations will be impossible and new species will have developed.

In this view, human races are incipient species. But the breeding-population approach has its own difficulties even though it is scientifically more useful than the rather slaphappy "racial" approach. The problem with it is that many of the crucial features that divide mankind into identifiable groups cut across breeding populations. Natural selection does not recognize breeding-group boundaries, and it produces dark pigmentation or crinkly hair or mesomorphic body form in many different groups which have no breeding relationships with each other. Hence these "racial" traits are not characteristic of particular populations and so the breeding structure of the populations is by no means the only clue to human variation.

What we are left with is this variation. Races, or populations, do not seem adequate units to explain it. What we have to do is to take each trait separately and try to account for it and its distribution. Here and there "clusters" of traits will be found that seem to hang together, and these give us those broad divisions of mankind with distinctive physical characteristics whose nature we wish to explore.

Why should there be variation at all within the species *Homo sapiens sapiens?* (The extra *sapiens* does not indicate increased wisdom but serves to distinguish us, the only surviving members of the genus *Homo,* from our close ancestors *Homo sapiens neanderthalensis.*) Why should we not all look alike? To this there are two answers which probably amount to the same thing, although much heat has been generated by their opposition. One says roughly that the species originated (i.e., became totally distinct from its nearest relatives) about 50,000 years ago, and then proceeded to differentiate as a result of adaptations to widely different environments. By roughly 30,000 years ago, distinctively "white" and Mongoloid types of skulls are in evidence; the earliest known American remains are distinctively Amerindian about 20,-000 years ago.

We can assume therefore that the original small stock of the ancestors of *Homo sapiens* gradually spread out over the globe (from where we do not know), changing and adapting as they moved into different ecological niches. The great factor that prevented them from "speciating" too far was culture. Man (as we can confidently call him by this time) did not have to wait upon the process of genetic change in order to adapt. A combination of genetic changes and cultural adaptations enabled him to exploit almost all known environments (exceptions being underwater and the highest mountains). He did not have to redevelop his hairy coat in order to survive in Arctic climes—he could invent clothes. But in any case, the races of man would on this theory be divergences from the common stock in response to environmental pressures.

Another theory would put these differences further back. It says that the major divisions of mankind are derived from distinct stocks with a much more remote common ancestor than is postulated by the first theory. One might not think this makes much difference, but it does. The proponents of the second theory maintain that the divergent stocks diverged before they reached the *sapiens* level, and that they crossed this Rubicon at different times. Thus rather than the present races of man being post-*sapiens* developments, they are pre-*sapiens* developments.

The chief argument against this theory is its lack of economy, and the unlikelihood of at least four different paths of evolution all ending up with the same result. The fossils from which the various races are supposed to be derived show more differences amongst themselves than do the present races! Such remarkable convergence in evolution is unknown and almost inexplicable. But even if it should be true, the end result is one species which interbreeds and produces viable offspring. And if it is true, then it simply increases the depth and range of diversity which we have already said is an advantage to the species as a whole.

However arrived at, then, the picture of our ancestors of, say, 30,000 years ago is one of small groups of hunters and collectors spread over a considerable part of the globe in a variety of environments and displaying recognizable differences in physical features. Some of these differences may have been largely due to chance. The relative isolation of the various breeding populations at this stage may have helped to fix certain characteristics such as nose shape or head size which had no particular advantage but which were not selected *against*. The accumulation of such differences may account for some distinctive features which are hard to account for on the grounds of adaptation.

Also, of course, despite relative isolation, there would have been considerable interbreeding as populations migrated and this in itself would have produced new and distinctive traits. The Polynesians, for example, are probably a result of one of these great intermixings. But ultimately, the test of all these traits was usually selection. Did they give some advantage to their bearers such that these left more offspring who themselves were successful in breeding, and so on?

With some of the traits we are more happy than others. Take the most obvious and seemingly the easiest—skin pigmentation. Why do some groups have very dark skins and some very light? Discounting the effects of suntanning on groups who wear few or no clothes (e.g., the Australian aborigines who are, in fact, "lighter" than constant exposure makes them appear), we can explore the readiest answer: that dark skin is a protection against ultraviolet radiation. The color of the skin is determined by an organic molecule called melanin of which you either have a lot or a little. Melanin in the outer layers of the skin absorbs ultraviolet radiation, thus mitigating its effect. A lack of melanin leaves one prone to skin cancer if exposed to excessive amounts of radiation. Hence dark skins are an advantage in the tropics.

But this has to be qualified. Dark skins absorb 30 per cent more heat than light skins, thus increasing the heat load of the body. In a hot dry climate, a black-skinned man would collapse from heat stroke much more readily than a light-skinned. Conversely, there is some evidence that in a hot *wet* climate, the darker skin would have a small advantage. In colder regions, however, it might appear that a dark skin would have an even greater advantage in that it absorbs heat, but this is offset by the awkward fact that the heavy pigmentation shuts out the vitamin D that would otherwise be taken from sunlight. In the temperate zones a light skin would have some slight advantage on this score. A gradation then could be expected of black skins in the hot-wet climes, brown in the hot-dry and white in the cold-wet. And indeed *very* roughly this follows for the distribution of man before the age of discovery reshuffled so many populations.

But it is indeed very rough, since many populations have shifted about a good deal. Many of the Negroes in the hot-wet areas are not native to them; indeed many of the peoples living near the equator are not very dark at all, as in Indonesia and South America. These migrations make a good deal of the speculation on the survival value of skin color very tentative. Many of these so-called advantages are marginal and it seems difficult to see how they could have seriously affected survival and reproductive success. Cancer of the skin takes many years to develop; people don't tend to die of it and anyway will have had their children by the time it becomes virulent. Vitamin D can be obtained from other sources than sunlight and clothes can protect against sunburn.

One anthropologist, Harold F. Blum, concludes that a really black skin could only reap *all* its advantages (from an adaptational point of view) on one of the snow-capped mountains near the equator. The "natural" color of the human skin—one that would be most advantageous in most circumstances, and the one from which the others are probably evolutionary divergences—is probably a pleasant medium-brown, tending towards *café au lait* rather than cocoa. But I can't help thinking that some elements of chance are at work in this matter of skin color. As one of my students said at the end of a particularly frustrating seminar on the subject, "For Christ's sake, skin has to be some color!"

The same may be said of hair: it has to be some shape. A mild clustering occurs here in which tight, black, curly hair is associated with dark skins and lighter, wavy hair with white. But this is a vague correlation. The classic Negroid features of curly hair and full lips are usually thought of as "progressive" features—in an evolutionary sense—in contrast to the more apelike straight hair and thin lips of other groups, such as Caucasoids and Mongoloids.

If we turn to teeth, then we can see how difficult it is to take races, however defined, as units of explanation. Teeth come in various sizes and shapes and no one can be in any doubt about their significance for survival. Let us take the simple dimension of size. The smallest teeth in the world are found in the peoples of Central and Eastern Europe and the Middle East, and the largest among the Australian aborigines. These large teeth also show a good deal of wear. Were they any smaller they would soon be worn down to the gums. Since the Australians use their teeth virtually as tools, the adaptive advantage of ultra-large teeth is obvious. And this seems to be the pattern. Where teeth are very much used, either as tools or in the consumption of tough food

—among many hunters, for example—they are large, and the masticatory apparatus and the lower face and jaw are large in proportion. Where this is less true, the teeth are small.

But if we plot the world distribution of tooth size and that of skin color, we find no correspondence. This is a perfect example of natural selection (or random genetic drift) being no respecter of races or breeding populations. If we wish to explain the variation within the species of these particular traits, we cannot start with races as units, since the variations cut across them in different ways. Tooth size and shape varies amongst the Negro peoples (Negroid race?) as much as it varies amongst the species as a whole.

We might do better with the nose in terms of "goodness of fit" with adaptational advantage. A high-bridged, long narrow nose is of advantage in two environments—very cold and very dry. In the former it helps to warm the air as it passes on its relatively long journey up the fine nasal passages; in the latter it helps to moisten the dry air during inspiration. On the other hand, it does not seem to have any particular disadvantage in hot humid climates; a flatter shorter nose is marginally preferable. (I write this in hot and humid southern New Jersey amidst a a sharp-nosed family devastated by various respiratory malfunctions, so perhaps I should be cautious.) A good deal of nasal form, however, is clearly related to the size and shape of the rest of the face, so this is a tricky subject.

With eye form we have at least one fairly clear example of adaptation at work. I allude to the epicanthic or Mongoloid eye fold. This is an example of adaptation to extreme cold. It goes along with shortness of stature, very flat nose and fat-padded cheeks. Some groups of Mongoloids (late developers from an archaic "white" stock probably) were trapped during the last glacial period—about 25,000 years ago—in northern Asia, and either adapted or froze to death. The eye fold is a brilliant protection against the effects of cold on the eye.

Adaptational response to extreme cold (up to -100 degrees F.) may also explain the relative hairlessness of this group, since moisture would freeze in a beard and hence freeze the face under it—as bearded Caucasoid arctic explorers have discovered to their distress. Beards are fine for subarctic winters where they warm the face but do not freeze. The classic Mongoloid face is best seen in the Eskimos, the Tungus of northern Asia and some American Indians. Other American Indians, the Malays and Polynesians and the Southern Chinese are results of mixtures between Mongoloid and other stocks—for example, the archaic whites of east Asia from whom the hairy Ainu of Japan and the Australian aborigines sprang. (Crosses between Mongoloids and Australian aborigines produce very Polynesian-looking offspring. The dark skin of the Australoids is probably a very recent—in evolutionary terms—adaptation.)

Another example of a variation that cuts across "races" is body build. Roughly speaking, human bulk decreases in the hotter and increases in the cooler parts of the globe. At one extreme we have the Eskimo—short, squat and heavy; at the other we have the Nilotes of East Africa—tall, slender and light. One can easily imagine the effects of reversing these body builds. Eskimos would melt in the dry heat of East Africa, while the Nilotes would perish in temperatures of —96 degrees F. This has to do with the loss and preservation of body heat. The ratio of body surface to body weight is what is at issue. Heat is lost from the surface of the body, so in a hot climate it pays to present as much surface relative to bulk as possible; in a cold climate, the opposite is true. While again this is not an absolute correlation, it holds pretty well, and again variations among, say, the Mongoloids are almost as great as variations within the whole species. The same is true for that old favorite of the taxonomists, the "cephalic index"—the classic measure of head shape. Except for very narrowly defined populations, head shape varies widely and does not correlate highly with other features. It is very difficult to see any adaptational advantages accruing from any particular head shape.

Variations in color and morphology, then, have some adaptive significance, but this is not "racial." To understand these adaptations, we have to take each trait on its merits, and the traits cut across the conventionally accepted racial classifications in different ways. Color, tooth shape, nose shape, build, hair form, eye form, etc., do not come in neat racial packages clearly distinct from each other. All we have are a sequence of clines, or graded series of differences, from one population to another.

But what about blood? Next to color, this has the most emotional significance, it seems. "Mixed blood" is looked on in some circles with horror, while "true blood"—or even for some reason "blue blood"—expresses metaphorically the worth of a person, and "red blood" his relative virility. But despite our love of ranking, one thing remains true: no blood is better than any other in any absolute sense; it is just different. As with all these evaluations, we have to ask: Better for what? There is no intrinsically "bad blood," but if you are group A you had better not have a transfusion from someone of group B, and if you are a rhesus-negative mother, you had best avoid giving your child a rhesus-positive father.

Most of us know about blood groups and how they are inherited and we know that all groups are present in the American population. Most groups, in fact, are present in most populations—with some interesting exceptions; what differs is their distribution within the populations. Thus they are like other physical features, and, like these, their distribution is not "racial." A high incidence of group O, for example, is characteristic of both Celts and most American Indians, while group A, which is high among Western Europeans (non-Celtic), reaches its highest incidence (83.7 per cent) among the Blackfeet Indians. The Rh (rhesus) negative group has a high incidence in northwestern Europe (40 per cent) but is also present in some Negroid populations and is rare or nonexistent in other parts of the world. Similarly, Negroes and Europeans share the subgroup A2 absent in East Asia, Oceania and America. Thus it is perfectly possible that a white American and an American Negro should have much the same blood group series, but it is unlikely that the parent populations would present the same distribution of types.

Some types are found exclusively in some populations, which is not surprising, since blood groups are inherited and hence relatively isolated breeding populations may develop characteristic differences. Indeed, blood groups give very important indications about population movements and the relationships between populations in the remote past. But again it must be stressed that these characteristic distributions are characteristic of breeding popula-ions and they in fact *define* the populations. One cannot prejudge the issue of where one population starts and another stops; one must simply plot the distributions of the groups and see what happens. Here again there is no neat correlation with shape of nose or color of skin or size of skull. For sorting out the dense "networks" of genetic material that are breeding populations, however, blood groups promise something more definitive than morphological features. One thing is certain: there is no "white" blood that is incompatible with "black" blood. White blood of group A is compatible with black blood of group A but incom-patible with white blood of group B. And there it is.

But what is the significance of these differences in blood chemis-try? If they are just another example of human variation, then they should be explicable on evolutionary principles in terms of their adaptive value. A start in this direction has been made but the findings are tentative. Clearly blood is directly affected by disease; therefore the most plausible explanation for the differences lies in differential resistance to disease. Given the typical distributions within whole populations, it also follows that it is epidemic diseases that are most likely to be involved; that is, diseases that affect whole populations at a time.

It has been suggested, for example, that the relatively high in-cidence of group A in Western Europe and B in India might have been caused by selection due to plague and smallpox epidemics. B in fact is probably a relatively "new" group and may have de-veloped late in human history. It is high amongst the Mongoloids —one of the last stocks to become differentiated. Persons with the "ancient" blood groups—O and A—seem more prone to peptic ulcers than those with B, and it has again been suggested that this is due to their inability to take stress resulting from overcrowding. These blood groups evolved, as it were, to cope with the diseases of relatively free-ranging animals, and their bearers break down under more civilized conditions. This is strengthened by the associ-ation of the A-B-O system with diet. The various blood-group types may well differ in their capacity to cope with varying amounts of fat, protein and carbohydrate. This research is in its infancy but is obviously very suggestive and makes sense. It also makes blood into something very unmysterious and puts it in the same class as nose, shape and skin color so far as explanation is concerned.

Thus far, then, we have seen that human variation is the response of the species over time to a variety of habitats and ways of life. A number of small genetic adjustments plus a great deal of cultural ingenuity has enabled *Homo sapiens* to people the globe and dominate all other forms of animal life. We have been dealing with morphological rather than behavioral characteristics (not that the two are separable), but surely the same arguments should apply to features of human behavior? Factors such as motor ability, temperament and intelligence are "adaptive" in the same way as skin color, so should they not also show characteristic distributions?

Here, however, we are not dealing with quite the same kinds of units. "Intelligence" is not a concept of the same order as "tooth size." It may, for example, be quite obvious why the Australian aborigines have large teeth and white Americans small ones, but it is not clear that it takes more intelligence to survive in America than it does in the Australian desert—probably the reverse. It may be true that hairlessness is an advantage in arctic and hairiness an advantage in subarctic climes, but again it is not clear that greater intelligence is needed to survive as a Viking than is needed to survive as an Eskimo. Different skills are involved in each of these cases, and there may well have been some evolution of different abilities in different directions, but much the same intelligence is needed to perform one lot of skills as the other. Similarly, it is highly likely that differences in temperament might well have evolved in different populations to cope with very different conditions. But much the same range of temperaments has been found in all human societies and it is almost impossibly difficult to sort out the genetic "givens" of temperament from the results of training.

The problem with differences in intelligence and temperament is that they are not discrete and measurable differences like those between blood groups, and they depend heavily on evaluation of what is "basic" in any skilled performance. Tests, for example, only test what the testers want to test, and there is no way of knowing whether the skills tested are in any sense basic or are themselves very specialized. It is entirely plausible, as I have said, that differences exist between various populations with regard to their capacity to execute certain skills, just as differences in stature and blood chemistry exist. But the same amount and kind of mental energy is being exerted in each case: the human brain is uniformly of the same structure throughout the species.

To start ranking these abilities is like saying that, although exactly the same engine may be powering an automobile as a motorboat the automobile is better than the motorboat. The particular adaptations of the boat engine make it suitable for the water, and those of the automobile for the land. If all the land were submerged, where would the automobile be? Every race in fact has demonstrated its capacity to learn anything produced by any other race, and this, like the ability of any race to breed with any other, is the crucial factor, for it demonstrates the universality in the species of the learning ability that is its characteristic. This is the brilliance—if you will forgive the nonscientific word—of the process of "raciation" in *Homo sapiens:* It has allowed genetic diversity without speciation, which means that the developed differences can be pooled and re-pooled. Common breeding and common learning can take advantage of these undoubted differences in genetically based abilities whether mechanical, esthetic, verbal or whatever, and recombine them both physically and culturally.

Thus it seems to me that the so-called differences in intelligence are a total red herring. Certain differences in capacity for the solving of certain kinds of problems exist between individuals and between populations. What a group lacks in one kind of ability it always compensates for in another, and the same kinds of mental processes are involved in the execution of different skills. There is no race (however defined) that is not capable of developing high civilization, even if it has not bothered to do so. This is more a matter of motivation than ability. Harsh or lush environments may inhibit any tendencies to elaborate civilization. Lack of easy communication or dense settlement prevents the diffusion of new techniques and ideas, the cumulation of which is the basis for civilization. Many of the so-called "lower races" of today are themselves the descendants of groups which produced high civilizations. And the same was true of them as it is of us. It was not the qualities of the "race" which produced these advances but the exertions of a few geniuses who crop up in all groups. When we speak of the great advances of the "white" race, what do we mean? We mean the cumulative efforts of a tiny handful of outstanding men and women on whom the dim multitudes are totally parasitical.

When was the last time you, gentle white reader, made a significant breakthrough in scientific or artistic advance? And if you did, how much of it was in fact attributable to the cumulative efforts of past generations? The fact that, for a variety of reasons, various ethnic groups have not produced the same kind of technological civilization that you have pales into insignificance beside the fact of their ability to take over and operate successfully whatever you produce. You may, in fact, have exhausted yourselves in producing material for them to take over painlessly and use against you. This is perhaps the biggest practical joke that an unkind God has played on his chosen people.

Yet again, we must stress that even if these differences in specific ability exist (and we have no reason to suppose that they do not), they are very difficult to correlate with morphologically defined "races." To take the simple case of motor performance: this is as variable amongst, say, Negroes, as it is amongst whites, and the variations between these two groups significantly overlap. The same is true of so-called intelligence, even when measured by tests almost totally oriented towards white western European values of what constitutes basic skills in problem solving—skills which would often fare very badly in the desert or tundra. While, not surprisingly, "white" *averages* tend to be higher than "black," there is considerable overlap in the total range of performances. You, white reader, are certainly worse than *some* blacks even at your own rigged tests. On the other and more neutral tests, you are undoubtedly worse than most members of various ethnic groups. Once we really know how to estimate human abilities, then similar kinds of distributions will undoubtedly crop up as we find in blood groups. Like blood groups, some kinds of abilities will have slight advantages over others in specified circumstances. But every population has practically the full *range* of abilities in it in the same way as it has most of the *range* of blood groups. There may be some marginal exceptions to this as there are with the rarer blood group series. The leaping ability of the Watusi of Rwanda, for example, is probably unique.

So, as with the distribution of blood groups within populations, the distribution of genetically based abilities will differ, and some populations will be high on some things and low on others.

But in the same way that all populations have blood, all populations have intelligence; and as blood is blood whatever its group, so intelligence is intelligence however manifested. In the same way as there is no *absolute* ranking of blood groups—although some may have marginal advantages in some circumstances—so there is no absolute ranking of different manifestations of intelligence. In the same way that we can shuffle around blood types by interbreeding them, so we can any other inherited features, to the benefit of all concerned. To do this *within* populations, as we do all the time, is no different in principle from doing it *between*.

Race, as one biologist put it, is an evolutionary episode. It should be seen against the time scale of human evolution. During the earlier and more precarious years, it was necessary for the basic stock to differentiate genetically in order to spread and survive. This has taken, in evolutionary terms, a relatively brief time and has got the species to where it is now. At present the differentiation is not so necessary. (Unless we spread out into the solar system where genetic specialization might well be useful to us again.) But, because the specialization has not produced new species, and because a common capacity to learn extensively is shared by all members, there exists a magnificent pool of genetic diversity on which the species as a whole can draw.

Genetic diversity within a species is the finest instrument it can possess in meeting the varying challenges of the environment. (And those who think the human species is not constantly being challenged to make the necessary adaptations are living in a fool's paradise that could be dangerous.) What we should do now, therefore, is take maximum advantage of the diversity and crossbreed the various specifications to produce new combinations. In doing so we would still produce diversity, but it would be a more meaningful diversity for our future evolution than that produced by specialized adaptation to natural habitats. The advantages may only be marginal, but they are worth exploring.

As a species, the process of raciation is no longer much use to us now that we dominate the globe. It should therefore be eliminated by vigorous interbreeding in order to reap the benefits of this remarkable evolutionary episode and move on to better things. Even if all we achieved was the abolition of peptic ulcers and a permanent suntan for everyone, it would be worth trying. It might, incidentally, solve a few other problems on the way, but this is where the anthropologist bows out.

jensenism, *n.*
—the theory that I.Q.
is largely determined
by the genes

by Lee Edson

BERKELEY

FOR MOST of the last 10 years Prof. Arthur Robert Jensen of the University of California, one of the nation's leading educational psychologists, has lived the generally quiet, cloistered existence of a scholar, burying himself in statistics, standards and students. If the Free Speech Movement, the People's Park confrontation or any of the other well-publicized blowoffs of Berkeley student unrest penetrated the Education Building on the west corner of the campus (where such egg-yolk institutions as Agricultural Extension, Life Sciences and Home Economics are clustered), it was hard to tell it from Jensen. A tall, almost somber figure, addicted to dark attire, he strode through the corridors with aloof dignity. He seldom cracked a smile, fraternized with colleagues or engaged in small talk. He was a very involved, very serious professor's pro-

From the *New York Times Magazine,* August 31, 1969, copyright © 1969 by The New York Times Company.

fessor who had no time for hanky-panky and insisted on keeping himself free of the academic maelstrom. "It's incredible," a colleague once remarked after leaving his office. "Jensen is so absorbed he doesn't realize he's on top of a volcano."

Then on Feb. 15 the volcano erupted. The Harvard Educational Review, a 30-year-old scholarly journal published by Harvard graduate students, came out with an article by Jensen entitled: "How Much Can We Boost I.Q. and Scholastic Achievement?" The detailed scientific paper, the longest ever printed in the review, begins with an appraisal of the alleged failure of compensatory education programs such as Head Start, a project to help preschool ghetto youngsters overcome years of cultural deprivation in order to catch up with middle-class youngsters in school readiness. The article goes on to state that these programs seek, in effect, to raise children's academic achievement by increasing their I.Q.'s. Jensen then examines the entire concept of the I.Q.: "what makes it vary from one individual to another; what can change it, and by what amount." In the process he says that Negroes as a group—as opposed to any single individual Negro—test out poorly compared with whites or Orientals on that aspect of general intelligence that involves abstract reasoning and problem-solving. And he adds that this ability (which he equates with the ability measured by I.Q. tests) is largely inherited, a matter of genes and brain structure, and therefore no amount of compensatory education or forced exposure to culture is going to improve it substantially.

Jensen emphasizes in his article, that the "particular constellation of abilities we call 'intelligence,' and which we can measure by means of 'intelligence' tests," is only a part of the whole spectrum of human abilities—and that it "has been singled out from the total galaxy of mental abilities as being especially important in our society mainly because of the nature of our traditional system of formal education and the occupational structure with which it is coordinated." He points out that, "as far as we know, the full range of human talents is represented in all the major races of man." But such statements did little to lessen the impact of the article's conclusions about I.Q. and race. The magazine had hardly hit the academic mailboxes when a sound truck manned by members of the Students for a Democratic Society roared through the Berkeley campus, blaring: "Fight racism. Fire Jensen." Jensen's normally sparse scholarly mail grew fat with hate literature. He was accused of being a fascist, a white supremacist, of having black ancestry and hating it. He received postcards emblazoned with the Nazi swastika; one had a single hand-scrawled word: "Death." A group of aroused left-wing students invaded his classroom and he had to lecture in secret locations; crank callers engaged him on the phone, and he was forced to summon the Berkeley campus security forces to protect his files from being raided. At night the lights burned bright in his office to discourage looters. One fearful assistant quit her job.

In the academic and political worlds the furor has become ever more intense. Not since Darwin's theory of evolution, as one writer put it, has so much fiery discussion and violent opposition been generated over a treatise. A Congressman put all 123 pages of the article into the Congressional Record, and segregationists took to citing the article in court as the word of science. Lengthy reviews of the article were printed almost everywhere in intellectual circles. At Columbia University's Teachers College the article became required reading in some classes, and at the University of Minnesota a psychology professor, in as irrelevant a reaction as one could find, offered $100 to anyone who could predict a man's intelligence by looking at his features.

At the University of California a number of Jensen's professional colleagues sought to have him censured, and he was in effect summoned before a specially organized symposium which at first had the tone of a modern witch trial—perhaps the first time in recent academic history that a professor has had to defend a scholarly paper before his assembled colleagues and the videotape cameras. Since then word has filtered down that the article was distributed as "must reading" by Daniel Patrick Moynihan to members of the Nixon Cabinet. An educator in San Juan was forced to resign when he quoted Jensen in a talk opposing Negro violence. And The Wall Street Journal started to speak of "Jensenism" (though one colleague informed Jensen that he should "wait till they print it in lower case before you think you've made it").

The extent to which some critics have gone in denigrating Jensen was illustrated by a paper distributed by a University of California psychologist, John G. Hurst. It cited a study which found that among 24 leading psychologists, the 12 who generally favored environment over heredity were radical and liberal in their political point of view and largely included people who had come from poor environments and worked their way up; whereas the other half, those who believed in heredity, were conservative in politics and came from the conservative middle class. Hurst argued that Jensen fits the latter category. This attempt to establish Jensen's guilt by association helps point up the problem social scientists have in dealing with uncomfortable findings in an emotionally charged social environment.

The affair has caused the 45-year-old, mild-mannered Jensen some severely trying moments. A contract he held with the Berkeley Unified School District to evaluate the effect of busing and integration in the city has been canceled. His home life, according to his wife, Barbara, hasn't been the same since the article appeared. "Our house in Orinda was turned into a mad office," she says. "I bought a special IBM typewriter to answer the bushel of letters and we still have files marked 'kookie mail' where we throw all the threats and nasty remarks." Friends with a sick sense of humor inquire whether the Jensens are taking out double-indemnity insurance. "We always remember what happened to that professor at San Francisco State," Barbara Jensen says with a shudder. (Prof. John Bunzel's car was smeared with paint and he narrowly escaped injury from a bomb placed outside his office door. He was attacked by radical students as a symbol of establishment liberalism.) A lesser impact, she adds with a quick smile, is on the family dog, a Rhodesian ridgeback who seems to growl more fiercely than ever at male visitors to the Jensen home. "However, it may be genetic," she says, "since the Boers used to train these dogs to like women and attack men."

This reaction to Jensen's views—amounting to a kind of intellectual overkill—is a measure of the deep tensions that run through the heart of American life today. The nature vs. nurture controversy is an old one, and most observers agree that Jensen has added little that is new. Yet the attacks on him have been vicious, notwithstanding the fact that he is not an ideal target. He has no connection with the South and no history of racial intolerance which the enemy might seize upon. He opposes segregation and declares himself to be a political liberal or—"at worst"—a moderate. A registered Democrat (a colleague calls him an "unconcerned Democrat"), he voted for Eugene McCarthy in the primary and later switched to Nixon in the Presidential election because "I felt that Humphrey was just giving us more of the same Johnson bankrupt policy."

As a leading educational psychologist and a former Guggenheim Fellow, Jensen's academic credentials are impeccable. In addition to his professorship in Berkeley, he holds degrees from three universities and is one of the founding fathers of Berkeley's prestigious Institute of Human Learning. He maintains membership and some high posts in the leading psychological and educational research organizations and has written a book and more than 90 scientific papers in education and educational psychology.

Many of his co-professionals find it unforgivable that a man with this formidable background should rock the boat. They blame him, in the words of columnist Joseph Alsop, for "speaking the unspeakable" and "mentioning the unmentionable." In the early days of psychological testing, educators spoke freely of the hereditary base of intelligence, just as they spoke of the inherited maladaptive traits of the Jukes and Kallikaks over six generations, but in recent times, as Federal funds have poured into the education of preschool slum children, educators have kept silent on such themes. Many of the critics are traumatized by the memory of the Nazi genocidal insanity and lash out at anyone who hints of racial differences. "The incredible consequences that arose from Nazi theory," says a professor, "make every liberal with historical memory blind to any opinions in this area."

But there is more to it than that. The liberal egalitarian point of view is tied up with the romantic anthropological wish that all races should be equal—that all men should be born with a kind of *tabula rasa*—a clean slate on which everyone can write his own destiny. This notion of the unlimited plasticity of the human brain is pervasive in social science circles and in Government position papers; on the wall of one university researcher I found a sign reading: "We're all different—sorry about that." "Scientists drop their cool on this one," says a prominent educational psychologist. "They don't want people to be different in the area of intelligence, and attempts made to find differences are quickly put down. The ascendancy of the sociologist, anthropologist and psychologist over educational theory has blocked any consideration of nonenvironmental forces as contributing to the spread of ability throughout the population. One Harvard anthropologist wrote a 700-page book on the origin of the races but left out all information on brain differences. To these people there is only one race—*Homo sapiens*—and that's that. Jensen scrapes a raw nerve when he keeps using science's own statistics against an entrenched point of view, and they can't stand it."

Jensen says his case is based, "not on a single definitive study but on a preponderance of evidence pointing in a single direction, like the theory of evolution." Geneticists have long agreed, for instance, that intelligence has a genetic base. Studies of matings between cousins of normal I.Q. reveal that they produce larger numbers of retarded offspring than are produced in nonfamily, random matings. The link between retardation and heredity is very direct.

Jensen's most telling argument, he believes, and the easiest to grasp, proceeds from studies of identical twins—siblings whose genetic inheritance is precisely the same, since they have developed from a single fertilized egg. Psychologist Sir Cyril Burt and geneticist J. A. Shields studied 100 pairs of identical twins in England who were reared apart from each other. It was found that the separated twins were, on the average, only six points apart in I.Q. By contrast, any two people in the total population, chosen at random, will be on the average 18 points apart. Nonidentical siblings reared in the same household are on the average 12 I.Q. points apart.

"If you look at studies of adopted children," Jensen says, "you find that their intelligence relates more closely to their natural parents than to their adoptive parents. And if you add this to 100 other twin and kinship studies over the last 25 years over four continents and a wide range of environmental conditions, you have a strong body of evidence for the heritability of I.Q. In short, the closer people are related, the more similar are their I.Q.'s."

The second line of evidence of the heritability of intelligence,

Jensen says, comes from the studies of the relationship between intelligence and socioeconomic status dating back to the work of Alfred Binet 70 years ago. We know that people in the upper classes generally have higher I.Q.'s than those in lower classes. Some people like to read an environmental cause into this. But, in fact, studies indicate otherwise. Regardless of the social class in which an adopted child is reared, for example, the child's I.Q. will correlate better with that of his natural parents than that of his adoptive parents. If a child's natural parents have high I.Q.'s, it is most likely that he will also have a high I.Q. even if he is raised by low-I.Q., lower-class adoptive parents. The environment is not the deciding factor.

How does all this evidence tie up with racial differences? "First," Jensen says, "it should be noted that race is not an abstract Platonic essence—it is actually a 'breeding population,' as the geneticists term it; the population is not closed, but there is a well-known probability of greater mating within this population than outside it. As a result, the frequency of genes for white skin or dark skin differs in the different groups. It is true that there are extremely few if any Negroes of pure African descent in the United States today; but this doesn't change the genetic analysis of a particular population or affect the opportunity to study it by methods that have worked in other genetic fields."

Social scientists have been studying racial differences for many years, Jensen says, citing some 400 major studies. "All of them point out—unhappily perhaps—that in the standard distribution of I.Q. throughout the population the Negro is 15 points lower than the white. Only 3 per cent of the Negro population exceed an I.Q. of 115; in the white population 16 per cent exceed 115. In the white population 1 per cent exceed 140; a sixth of that exceed 140 in the Negro population. A similar percentage prevails at the lower end of the distribution. In fact it may even be worse in the retarded area. A long-term study by researchers at Johns Hopkins, conducted in one rural county of Maryland, showed that 31 per cent of the Negro males tested between the ages of 40 and 44 were mentally retarded—that is, they had I.Q.'s under 70. This was true of only 1.5 per cent of the tested white males of the same age."

Jensen asks: "Is this genetic in origin or caused by environment? I think it must be genetic to a very large extent. When you control samples of white and black population for social class differences, you still have major differences in I.Q. between them—from 15 points on the average to 11 points over the various social classes. In other words, across the same occupational category and income bracket, you still find this striking fact—children of Negroes in the highest income class of our society will average lower in I.Q. than white children of the lowest class; this is backed up by a great deal of data, including that obtained in studies conducted by the Federal Government. You couldn't predict such results from purely environmental theory, and it would be highly improbable to assume that the entire influence was due to subtle factors of early prenatal and postnatal environment. It is more likely—though speculative of course—that Negroes brought here as slaves were selected for docility and strength rather than mental ability, and that through selective mating the mental qualities never had a chance to flourish.

"In the famous Coleman study, the American Indians come out lower on all environmental indices than do American Negroes; yet the Indians score higher on I.Q. and scholastic achievement. So do disadvantaged children of the island of Taiwan. In fact, they do as well as children of white middle-class parents in the United States.

"Remember—we're talking of populations here, not of individuals. There are Negro geniuses, and certainly many greatly talented figures among Negroes, and race should not stand in the way of hiring, promotions or providing awards. But in large groups, one is compelled to say that on the basis of these studies improved environment is not likely to change the fundamental intelligence of large groups of individuals to a substantial extent—no matter how romantic the environmentalists want to be."

Jensen grants that some extremely deprived children can have their I.Q.'s raised by markedly changing their environment. He mentions the classic and dramatic case of Isabel, studied by Kingsley Davis of the University of California. An illegitimate child, she was reared for her first six years in a dark attic by a deaf-mute mother. When found, she was unable to speak, and tests showed that she had an idiot's mentality. But in two years in a good home with lots of attention her mental age jumped up to the average of her age group, and she could perform normally in school. But, as Jensen points out, her I.Q. didn't increase further than this average value. "You can boost an I.Q. in an enriched environment, but once its genetic potential is achieved—once the threshold environment capacity is reached—you cannot improve I.Q. any further. I am afraid there is nothing you can do to create an Einstein without the right kind of genes."

Against this skein of evidence the more rational critics of Jensen in anthropology, sociology and psychology have retaliated with a barrage of their own evidence and argument, picking their targets in virtually every aspect of the Jensen case. The I.Q. test, on which Jensen relies for a good deal of his data, has, for instance, come under probably the severest attack in the last few years. New York and Washington, anticipating pressure from minority groups, withdrew I.Q. testing from their school systems some years ago, but as a result of the Jensen article, the momentum of antipathy to testing has increased. This year, under pressure from Negro groups, the Los Angeles City Council voted to eliminate I.Q. tests from the early grades of the public school system; in Philadelphia, a similar change is being considered. One of the ironies of this movement is that the uneasiness that I.Q. testing generates among ethnic groups is shared by ardent right wingers such as the Birchites, who regard such testing as an instrument for Big Government brainwashing.

Many social scientists who once accepted I.Q. tests as predictive tools of school success and never thought more about it now slip into silence and leave the field to those who question whether there is even a definable quantity known as "g," or general intelligence, separate from interaction with environment. Some in fact argue that I.Q. tests are culturally unfair—loaded with factual material that only certain groups in our society could know or respond to.

Then there are those who attack the reliability of the tests on other grounds. In the case of the highly tested Sirhan Sirhan, for instance, his first test score was 89, and a second test score some months later was 109. Did his intelligence increase or was there something wrong with the tests? Teacher expectations are also said to contribute to scores. An experiment performed by Harvard's Robert Rosenthal and Lenore Jacobson showed that if the teacher persuaded a random group of subjects to believe they were superior, they actually did better than a group not told anything. "If all this is so," the argument runs, "then intelligence tests tell us nothing. They're even dangerous because they lead one to believe that mental ability is fixed at birth and nothing can be done about it."

Jensen is not convinced. "I am afraid," he says, "that the long history of the I.Q. test cannot be overcome by these bursts of criticism. The reliability of the Stanford-Binet test is 95 per cent, with a 5 per cent error, due to such things as the subject's not being up to par when he took the test. This test is more reliable than TB diagnosis based on chest X-rays.

"I.Q. predicts scholastic performance better than any single factor or personality trait. The higher the I.Q., the higher the performance. Below 75 he will not get a high-school education (though he might get a diploma), and below 90 it is doubtful. A good I.Q. is necessary for school success, and this in turn stands at the heart of our technological civilization, which in its simplest terms depends on the ability to manipulate symbols and reason abstractly from them. Not all people with high I.Q.'s succeed in school or in life, of course; other qualities are also needed. The I.Q., however, as a thermometer, explains why children differ in school, and there is no better measure, when used properly, to indicate the factors involved in these differences.

"As for the argument that the I.Q. is culturally unfair, psychologists have tested children in a variety of cultures and have eliminated as many items that relate to one culture and not to another as they can. While you probably can't make an entirely culture-fair test, we do find that in these specially devised, cross-culture tests, Negro youngsters score lower on abstract questions.

"As to teacher expectations, I am afraid that too much publicity in the popular press has been given to the book by Rosenthal and Jacobson, 'Pygmalion in the Classroom.' As a study, it is not regarded highly by professionals. Drs. Robert L. Thorndike and Richard Snow, for example, two psychologists who reviewed the book recently, state categorically that the book does nothing to raise standards of educational research. 'If there is such a bias as teacher expectation, the authors have not demonstrated it,' says Thorndike, and Snow adds that 'by publishing prematurely and inadequately they have performed a disservice to teachers and schools, to users and developers of mental tests, and perhaps worst of all to parents and children whose newly gained expectation may not prove quite so self-fulfilling.' "

Critics: Bruno Bettelheim and Benjamin Bloom argue that environment does have an effect on children's I.Q.'s, citing studies in Israel. They found that deprived Oriental Jewish youngsters from the desert raised in the kibbutzim showed higher I.Q.'s than those raised by their parents. And what about the Army qualification tests which showed that the scores of draftees in World War II were higher than those in World War I? Wasn't this caused by the general improvement in education—an environmental factor?

Jensen: "Bloom's and Bettelheim's argument would be more convincing if Negroes were to be raised in kibbutzim (as Bettelheim suggested recently to Congress) to see whether they improved greatly. In any case some deprived youngsters would get adequate nutrition and possibly the right adult models to identify with. This is a study worth pursuing. But as it stands conclusions drawn from the Israeli work are rather wishful.

"Social scientists who raise the environmentalist flag over the Army Alpha tests are also drawing too much from the data. After all, an Army Alpha test is not an I.Q. test; it is a knowledge test. The Army wanted mainly to know what the draftees knew, and thus the test correlates highly with the number of years of schooling. Moreover, to clinch this argument, a national survey in Scotland in which all the youngsters were given the I.Q. test a generation apart shows that the gain was a mere two to four points."

Critics: Could the I.Q. be determined at a very early stage of life, before or soon after birth, when it might be affected by a lack of proper nutrition? Perhaps many Negroes are shortchanged in intelligence because of inadequate diets.

Jensen: "Nutrition is undoubtedly important in early development. But one would have to prove malnutrition in a majority of Negro youngsters who have taken the I.Q. tests. Herbert Birch of

Albert Einstein Medical School, one of the leading researchers in this area, says he cannot find malnutrition in marked degree in Harlem and had to go for his studies of deprivation to Mexico and other Latin-American countries. The Indian youngsters, who came out higher on the I.Q. tests than the Negro, are much more malnourished than American Negro youngsters. So are the children of the poorest untouchables in India, but they got approximately the same I.Q. scores as the Negro youngsters in California public schools.

"I am in favor of studies of early environment, particularly the prenatal environment, and I have been analyzing data from California school children in this regard. I am studying two groups of half-brothers and half-sisters. The brother and sister live in the same home, so the environment is a common factor. However, they have different parentage. The members of one group have the same fathers but different mothers. Those of the second group have the same mother. The question is, are the children with different mothers less alike in I.Q. than those with the same mother. In other words, will the difference in their prenatal environments affect their I.Q.'s? I think the answer could help reduce the heredity-environment uncertainty, at least insofar as the prenatal aspect of environment is concerned."

Critics: The argument has been raised in the Harvard Educational Review and elsewhere that you cannot separate black genes from white genes, so how can you tell which produce high or low intelligence?

Jensen: "That is a silly question. There are no 'black' genes or 'white' genes; there are intelligence genes, which are found in populations in different proportions, somewhat like the distribution of blood types. The number of intelligence genes seems to be lower, over-all, in the black population than in the white.

"As to the effect of racial mixing, nobody has yet performed experiments that reveal its relative effect on I.Q. If the racial mixture weren't there, it is possible that the I.Q. difference between blacks and whites would be even greater. I think such studies should be done to lay this uncertainty to rest once and for all."

Critics: Even if the evidence suggests a genetic difference in racial intelligence distribution, is science really in a position to separate experimentally the effects of environment from heredity? Surely the factors are too complex, our tools too imprecise, and it would take generations to work out the interactions.

(The National Academy of Sciences underscored this viewpoint in their reaction to William Shockley, the Nobel physicist, who called for research into the genetic aspects of Negro intelligence. The academy declared that "there is no scientific basis for the statement that there are or are not substantial hereditary differences in intelligence between Negro and white populations. In the absence of some unforeseen way of equalizing all aspects of environment, answers to this question can hardly be more than reasonable guesses.")

Jensen: "This is true of a good deal of science. Take air turbulence, for instance—my engineering friends tell me that we don't really know all the factors in it, and we have no precise law of turbulence, but engineers design many devices to take it into account.

"I think we can set up experiments to decrease the heredity-environment uncertainties. I referred earlier to Bettelheim's suggestion—place disadvantaged Negro children in kibbutz-like set-ups and see what happens. I think this is preferable to throwing money into the entire school system, hoping for the best. I believe science is capable of creating techniques to cut through the complexities, if given a chance. Social scientists should be scientists, not ideologists."

Critics: Isn't it terrible and self-defeating to make people think they can never break the bonds of their genes? Why raise the specter of invisible disadvantage to an already disadvantaged group? Right now the Negro is coming into his own. Why allow others to use a weapon against him at such a critical time in history when he needs everything to give him a sense of uplift?

Jensen: "I don't think one gets uplift from hiding from truths. Social scientists are annoyed because I am showing them that they must be loyal either to their science or their longings."

Thus the flames of this bloody social-moral-scientific debate leap ever higher, and Jensen has begun to take on the aspect of a professorial Joan of Arc. His square jaw seems more stubbornly set, and his deep-set eyes flash with the light of battle. In the cause (if one can call it that) he takes time off from a busy program to write his critics long, well-argued rebuttals. Though inherently a reticent person, he accepts interview sessions on popular television shows such as an upcoming David Susskind show. He has turned down offers that obviously are directed toward intellectually tarring and feathering him, but he says he is willing to match wits with opponents who will debate the subject without overtones of circus and politics.

One of Jensen's strongest characteristics, according to friends and colleagues, is his single-minded intensity and his extraordinary capacity for work. A friend recalls the day when Jensen left a building and took a seat in his car, his mind caught up in a problem. He waited there some minutes before it occurred to him he was supposed to be driving the car. As is often true of men given to such mental absorptions, Jensen's breaks for relaxation occasionally have a weird, childlike aspect. His wife recalls that he was once so overcome with joy after leaving a theater that he broke into a jog and skipped down the street, flapping his arms like a modern-day Icarus trying to reach the sun. A police car pulled up and Jensen had to explain that nothing was wrong. Jensen says he was inspired by Nureyev, the Russian dancer, who followed a similar routine once when he was overcome by the tall buildings in New York. "Moving one's arms," Jensen says thoughtfully, "helps the sense of momentum."

Jensen has always been dominated by an ascetic approach to life though he has somewhat mellowed in recent years. He still doesn't smoke and seldom drinks. An old friend claims that as a young man Jensen didn't even use after-shave lotion because it seemed impure. Yet Jensen seems always to have been captivated by men of power and charisma. He was terribly attracted to Norman Thomas because of his great magical skill as an orator; and he once became so intrigued with Gandhi that he wanted to run off to India to write a book about him. For one six-month period he was an avowed vegetarian—possibly under the influence of another of his god-heroes, Bernard Shaw.

Arthur Jensen (known as Bob to his family) was born in San Diego, the only son of a Minnesotan of Danish stock who owned a lumber supply business. He recalls that his mother, who is now 80, traveled by stagecoach. One of his earliest memories is of the neighborhood magic shows he used to organize. He himself gave free mind-reading performances, a bit of small-boy fraud that depended upon exchange of secret signals.

Friends recall that Jensen grew up a loner. As a teen-ager he became enamored of orchestra conductors and wanted to become one. Working day and night, he achieved his ambition at the tender age of 13, when he took the baton of the Bonham Brothers Band, a private orchestra of 100 pieces that played at Sunday night church gatherings.

Although in time Jensen concluded that he could not become a great conductor—"I couldn't quite believe in my own infallibility"—over the years he has continued to worship the orchestra conductor, and every chance he gets he tries to crash rehearsals. On one occasion he was thrown out of a rehearsal by Pierre Monteux, though Jensen says he felt better about it when he learned that Otto Klemperer once suffered the same fate.

"Conductors are great brains," says Jensen, his eyes flashing. "They believe in themselves and they're marvelously undemocratic about art. The great conductor has a clear picture of what he wants and how to get it. He internalizes everything and the orchestra follows him like a slave if it's convinced he's touched with genius. The conductor uses all of himself; the scientist uses only part."

Today Jensen still works up musical scores as though readying himself for the call. He reads and remembers virtually everything he reads about his heroes and their music. In London he won a B.B.C. contest by identifying Sibelius's Fifth from hearing just the last two notes.

Jensen's interest in psychology may have been a natural consequence of his fascination with powerful and awe-inspiring individuals. He recalls that an aunt gave him a book on I.Q. when he was in high school, and from that moment on he haunted the San Diego Public Library, reading such works as the great John B. Watson's book on behaviorism and trying to find out why people are different from one another.

In 1942 he enrolled at Berkeley, majoring in psychology, larded with such hard sciences as physiology and biology. After graduation he returned to San Diego and accepted a teaching appointment at Hoover High School while he continued on for a master's degree at San Diego State College. Then he served a brief stint in the Social Welfare Department of the city interviewing applicants for old-age assistance.

In 1952 Jensen enrolled at Columbia University for his Ph.D. in psychology and then went on to the University of Maryland, where he did a comparative personality study of three types of adolescents—delinquent aggressive boys, nondelinquent aggressive boys and "shrinking violets." The boys were asked to respond to a series of pictures. Jensen found some relationship between aggression and sex (as others had found before him), particularly in the delinquent boys, and he published these and related findings in 1961 in his first book, written with Dr. Percival M. Symonds of Columbia and entitled "From Adolescent to Adult."

Jensen moved on to the University of London, where he came under the influence of Prof. Hans Eysenck, a pioneer in behavior therapy, or as he describes it, "the application of Pavlov to neuroses." Jensen was impressed with Eysenck's efforts to find objective, quantitative approaches to psychological testing.

In 1958 he accepted an appointment in Berkeley as assistant professor and devoted himself to his current interest—the relationship between behavior and intelligence. At Berkeley he met a black-haired, vivacious girl named Barbara DeLarme; the daughter of an airline pilot, she was studying psychology. Barbara describes the courtship very simply; "Bob's approach to women is like his approach to everything else: direct and candid. He stared at me for two weeks, followed me to the laboratory and proposed, and I accepted. What else could I do?" They were married in 1960.

Jensen concentrated at first on individual differences in verbal learning in college students, but in 1962 he became interested in testing children. He developed a series of tests which could be used in any language, directed at discovering how fast children learn. He tested Mexican-American youngsters and then went on to test Negro and white children in Oakland, Richmond and other Bay Area cities. He found that he was measuring two different sets of learning abilities—what he now calls Level 1, associative learning, and Level 2, conceptual learning and problem-solving ability. The first ability involves simply the retention of input and the capacity to repeat it; the second involves the student's ability to manipulate and transform material.

For example, one of Jensen's Level 1 tests is made up of a series of pictures of common objects (or the objects themselves in miniature) which the child is asked to recall by name after they're shown one by one and removed from sight. Negroes and whites who may differ in I.Q. by as much as 20 points score equally on this test. In a Level 2 test, the examiner groups the different objects in categories—say, furniture, animals, clothing and food. Then he mixes them again and they are presented in random order, one at a time. After the child has seen all the objects again, he is asked to name as many as he can remember. This is done a number of times. The white children catch on and soon recall the objects by their categories; they call them off in groups and thus remember more individual objects. The Negro children by and large don't do this, or they group the objects on a functional basis; they relate apples and horses for instance. They fail to make use of the group concept as a memory device, but call off the objects more or less in the order they saw them, and they don't remember as many.

In the first and second grades there is no significant difference in the amount of recall or in the amount of "clustering," as it is called, but in the fourth and fifth grades the difference appears and Negro children in general start to fall behind white children as the conceptual material gets more difficult. In short, Jensen concludes that Level 1 ability is distributed about equally in all races while Level 2 is distributed unevenly. Jensen contends that for Level 2 abilities to develop requires not merely learning ability but also certain inherited neural structures in the brain. "Without them, the learning of abstract concepts doesn't develop," he says.

Jensen drew this conclusion slowly. In the tests themselves, he made sure that the children knew the names of each object and each category. He also investigated the role of motivation and found that both Negro and white children do better when well motivated but not enough better to change the scores significantly.

(Oriental children, incidentally, stay the same; they are apparently already motivated to do their best.)

Jensen found that scores on the category lists correlated with I.Q. differences among the youngsters. He concluded that Level 2 is "pretty much what we mean by I.Q."

Then Jensen reviewed all the published papers dealing with genetic differences. He found Burt's study on twins and was amazed at the lack of attention given to it by social scientists in America.

Even major geneticists had not heard of it—largely, Jensen believes, because of the built-in environmental bias which had led most social scientists in the field to forgo their usual examination of opposing studies.

Jensen's first paper on the heritability of intelligence was published by the National Academy of Sciences in 1967; in it he expressed the belief that 80 per cent of the variability in intelligence could be attributed to inheritance, the other 20 per cent to environment. He did point out that this estimate was based on tests in Europe and North America and could not be generalized to other populations, and he is amused today by those critics who cannot bring themselves to believe in the figures but refuse to examine the test data. Jensen gave a talk on the subject in San Diego suggesting how educational policy might be geared to this finding through schools catering to diversity of mental ability rather than to sameness and returned to Berkeley to find himself headlined: "UC Prof Urges Diverse School for Minorities." He didn't know it then, but the article inspired a confidential memo circulated in Berkeley educational circles hinting that Jensen was "racist."

In April, 1968, Donald Moore, then editor of the Harvard Educational Review, invited Jensen to write an article based on his report in San Diego. The editors outlined the article, and Jensen wrote it, as is his custom, in longhand on airplanes. He says several geneticists had a chance to review his draft and concurred with his basic analysis, if not with all his conclusions. His opening sentence ("Compensatory education has been tried and apparently has failed"), which caused a storm all its own, was put in, Jensen says, because he learned from a high-school English teacher always to start an article with a strong statement.

The editors cut some 15 pages from the original manuscript, and though Jensen says he never saw galley proofs, he admits to being pleased with the final results, even though there were some printing errors in text and figures. The editors then sent a copy of the article to The Boston Globe, whose reporter telephoned Jensen to check it out. By an odd coincidence, George Jones of U.S. News and World Report was in Jensen's office when Jensen took the call from Boston. Jones immediately sensed a good story, and the result was an interview in the magazine which unleashed some of the torrent of controversy.

The Harvard editors, taken aback by the storm they had raised, reacted at first in a confused manner. For one thing, they refused to send out reprints of the article, even to Jensen. He had to reprint the article himself, paying the costs out of his own pocket. A protest was lodged with Harvard President Nathan Pusey by University of Buffalo psychologists, and reprints became available. Then a comedy of errors developed over who said what and did what to whom. The Review editor, for example, insisted he'd never asked Jensen for material on racial differences, but apologized when Jensen waved aloft his letter outlining the article.

While the furor over his article continues to mount, Jensen has been giving some thought to the practical implications of his findings. His own visits to schools in the Bay Area and elsewhere have convinced him that educational policy requires a complete overhaul. "Everywhere I saw children failing to learn at all," he says. "In New York City children in the 12th grade are at the sixth-grade level. In one classroom in Berkeley I found a group of Negro youngsters who were going to class but not learning to read; I tested them and found that they did as well on the test as did white youngsters doing well in school in another neighborhood. What happened? I think that teachers reward only signs of conceptual brightness but not things learned by rote. So without a sense of satisfaction these youngsters get turned off on school. Both sets should be rewarded."

Children arrive in first grade lacking intellectual readiness, Jensen says. "It is important for a child to have a perception of his own growing mastery and to see himself approach a goal. If the child doesn't get this, he fails to get reinforcement and he responds by failure to learn. I once tried to teach my daughter Roberta how to play chess when she was 5 because I heard that the great Capablanca learned it at 4.

"Some psychologists say that the child can learn anything if he or she has each prerequisite step under control. I don't quite believe this. In the case of chess we started with simple categories like black and white and then worked up to the names and moves of the pieces. She found it was fun—learning is fun, and kids do it naturally—and she quickly learned how each piece moved, but she couldn't put it all together in a game. She made bad moves; it wasn't fun any longer, and she turned off. So I learned 5 was too young for her. Her capacity was not yet developed. So I finally dropped it and taught her how to play checkers. At 6 she went back to chess and now plays reasonably well.

"Our schools ignore this simple lesson. Intellectual activity is not simply a function of prior experience; it is prior experience plus maturation of the brain. An average child of 5 cannot draw a diamond; it takes a child of 7 to accomplish it. A 4-year-old can copy a square but cannot copy a square which has a diagonal in it. The long and short of it is this: you don't teach before the organism is ready, or what is learned will be learned with inferior mechanisms to the detriment of the individual in later life. Teachers need to recognize readiness and adapt their teaching to differences among children and not, as they do now, teach everyone with the same program and the same sequencing of materials."

In effect, Jensen says, the school system must set up a diversity of programs that match the abilities and readiness of youngsters. "Some children will be happiest and most productive learning by rote alone. Others, who have conceptual abilities, should be in classes where they can make the best use of them. If this results in a racial imbalance in classes, so be it. You don't do a service for the child who has a mental age of 5 if you treat him as though he were 7."

In his article, Jensen emphasizes this concern for individual differences: "Whenever we select a person for some special educational purpose, whether for special instruction in a grade-school class for children with learning problems, or for a 'gifted' class with an advanced curriculum . . . we are selecting an *individual*. . . . It is unjust to allow the mere fact of an individual's racial or social background to affect the treatment accorded to him. All persons rightfully must be regarded on the basis of their individual qualities and merits, and all social, educational, and economic institutions must have built into them the mechanisms for insuring and maximizing the treatment of persons according to their individual behavior."

Jensen acknowledges, however, that "whether we like it or not," our educational system serves to sort out children to assume different levels in the occupational hierarchy. Intelligence tests and academic performance have become occupational screening devices. But since I.Q. "is not the whole of human abilities," Jensen says, "there may be some fallacy and some danger in making it the *sine qua non* of fitness to play a productive role in modern society." He suggests that such hiring requirements may be irrelevant for many jobs, and that they should be re-examined. Educational programs to train people to meet the actual requirements of a given job, he says, may be more worthwhile than efforts to raise I.Q.'s or academic performance.

As a professor, Jensen still operates from the cool objectivity (he hopes) of the university, but he is closer to the great social debates than ever before. With racial alienation rising, his ordeal, one realizes, is only beginning, as it is for the rest of America.

They Are Not So Much Anti-Negro as Pro–Middle Class

by John Finley Scott and Lois Heyman Scott

THE RECORD of programs for social reforms shows, alas, frequent unintended and undesired results. Reformers are usually quite clear about the nature of the evil they want to end, much less clear about how to end it. One reason for this is the premise that an evil is always caused by another evil, never by anything good. But analysis usually shows that an evil condition is more complex than such a purely moral perspective implies. And this suggests that a simple cure will be unlikely and raises the further question of whether any cure will be worth its cost. Analysis of such social "evils" as illegitimacy, crime or social inequality shows each to be linked to other conditions, both good and evil.

In the 13 years since racial segregation *de jure* was outlawed by the Supreme Court, the problem of segregation *de facto* has proved stubborn and complex. Millions have been spent to integrate American schools, but the results so far are discouraging.

From the *New York Times Magazine,* March 24, 1968, copyright © 1968 by The New York Times Company.

Militant advocates now call for redoubled effort, and they are joined by the President's National Advisory Commission on Civil Disorders with its recent recommendations for "sharply increased efforts to eliminate *de facto* segregation in our schools." Yet in the present situation, plans to integrate schools are likely to fail in proportion to the resources marshaled behind them, and to cause more segregation and worse education for subordinated racial groups than would otherwise occur.

The problem is that the evil of *de facto* segregation is sustained by a number of factors, at least one of which—parents' concern for what they judge to be the welfare of their children—is conventionally regarded as an important social good. Because programs for integration are part of a highly moral crusade, the implication of this parental concern is overlooked. But when it is analyzed in connection with other factors, it appears that the drive for rapid integration will fail, and that the means for improving education for black Americans within the context of *de facto* segregation deserve more attention. They deserve it not because they are more just, but because they are more likely to succeed.

Americans are racists. They persistently and invidiously distinguish among groups on the basis of genetic traits that evidently have nothing to recommend them except ready observability. American racism is, to be sure, relatively mild (especially compared to what it was in 1900) and highly variable within the society. But it is a widespread attitude and one that Americans share with most of the world's technologically advanced societies —including many that did not share in the Western European conquest of various nonwhite populations. No program for improving the lot of subordinated racial groups in America will succeed if it depends on the notion that racism is not a popular attitude but only the prejudice of a small and conspiratorial minority made up of Southern Senators, suburban school boards and metropolitan policemen. For the Senators voice the virulent racism of several million Southern whites, the school boards represent millions of white parents who fear that integration will compromise their children's education, and the policemen nicely express the sentiments of the strongly rooted urban groups from which they are usually recruited.

The hope for more egalitarian race relations in this country rests more securely on the fact that American racism is qualified and limited. Americans who are racists in some areas will support racial equality in others. A man who opposes "open housing" legislation because he fears for his neighborhood may still support antidiscrimination measures in voting or employment. White voters have recently helped elect Chinese Senators and black mayors.

Most racial antipathy in America is not "pure" racism but derives from the disdain of higher classes for those below them. The tragedy of race in this country (and many others) is that visible genetic differences, superficial in themselves, have become generally reliable clues to a person's class position—his education, his income, his manners. The present low position of black Americans is a legacy of centuries of living under a most extreme and brutal form of slavery and of strenuous efforts since legal emancipation to contain them socially as a subordinated caste. Events of the last 20 years have done much to modify the legal and political aspects of this subordination, but the more general social effects of the past remain: black Americans are disadvantaged and poor, and their culture—so much a "culture of poverty" —is offensive to more affluent classes.

Advocates of integration frequently note that interracial contacts in housing and schools are less strained when both racial groups are reasonably well educated and "middle class," and they suggest that this provides the key to successful integration. But the number of middle-class blacks, though growing, remains small, and as Christopher Jencks, of the Institute for Policy Studies in Washington, has pointed out, there just aren't enough of them to go round. Since the majority of whites today are broadly in the middle class, this means that most programs for quick integration by race must also involve integration by class. And the long-run problems of achieving genuine educational integration by class are vastly greater than those of genuine integration by race.

It is possible today to marshal evidence that racial attitudes are changing rapidly. But these are highly imperfect measures of behavior. It is the concrete action of white parents that will cause school-integration campaigns to succeed or fail, not what they say about the abstract rights of black Americans when their own interests are not at stake. People learn fashionable circumlocutions far faster than they change their habits. New York mothers exist who recite liberal platitudes in one breath and in the next declare that "New York City schools are simply impossible," which is why they are moving to Scarsdale. They remain tactfully vague about *why* the schools are impossible. In some respects racist sentiments may have hardened. Open-housing legislation, which not long ago had widespread support, is today something that few local candidates for public office can afford to endorse. Although the Senate has now included open-housing provisions in the new civil-rights bill, they are largely ineffectual or unenforceable for most housing, and the final legislation as it ultimately clears Congress probably will accomplish even less.

In the long run, American racism is probably waning. But the impatience of antiracists with ancient injustice, the penchant for provocative and dramatic confrontations—in education and elsewhere—may ironically give the old myths of racism a new lease on life.

The special difficulty in programs for school integration is that they affect members of the dominant white groups in a most sensitive part of their lives; that is, they affect the family, especially in its universal function of defining the social position of children. In Western societies all members of a family are commonly judged to occupy the same social class, regardless of age or sex. Parents desire to pass on to their children a status at least as good as their own. This makes the family the most conservative of all social institutions, the slowest to change in an otherwise rapidly changing society. In America today we may have parents who are liberals, yet a "liberal parent" is almost a contradiction in terms.

The behavior of professors as parents illustrates this well. Often strong advocates of equality, in the case of their own children they want what Everett Hughes, the Brandeis University sociologist, has called "equality—plus." They generally do what they can to give their children an élite education of the kind their own occupation requires, and this proves difficult in class-heterogeneous schools. Academic parents become distressed when sons learn hot-rod culture and neglect physics and English composition and when daughters threaten to marry angry young men who show no interest in college. The ideal is a small, homogeneous and "sophisticated" school, where liberal values are taught in the abstract, with exemplary but token integration of students and not enough real heterogeneity to interfere with the learning of skills essential to an educational élite.

American society, like all industrial societies, is rapidly changing, so that new opportunities for social advancement are constantly created and old élites deposed. Social change is the greatest enemy of familial inheritance and increases the burden of parental responsibility. Thus families concentrate on providing their offspring with training that will give them an advantage in the otherwise relatively open competition for valued positions in society. This is why the class position of a child's family is such a good predictor of his score on any standard test of "educational achievement," as a recent United States Office of Education report by James Coleman, entitled "Equality of Educational Opportunity," showed on a very large scale.

As competition for valued positions becomes more and more open, the selection of environments and schools that will aid in establishing status becomes more and more important. The middle-class white parent's fear of the impact of interracial contacts on his children's training does not depend simply on an unlettered racist belief that black children are "inherently" stupid or immoral, although this may play some part. He is fearful mainly because society is stratified, because parents are anxious to pass on their stratified status, and because most black children are poor.

One good place to learn about the behavior of Americans (rather than their verbal professions) in regard to integrated education is in the housing market. When we study attitudes we often end up recording platitudes. But in the housing market money does the talking. Money is very sincere, and a visit to a real-estate broker's office can be highly informative.

In the broker's office the walls are usually covered with maps. These show city streets, land-use zoning and school districts. Though many are colorful and expensively printed, they are not there because they are decorative. They are there because they provide needed information. The builder of speculative apartments, for example, wants to know where the zoning law permits their construction; the parents of school-age children want to know the boundaries of "good" school districts.

Because such parents constitute the large majority of all buyers of single-family residences, the character of the school that serves a given residence becomes an important part of its value. This becomes quite clear after the most cursory interviews with real-estate brokers and a comparison of prices. As one broker we interviewed put it, "You don't just buy the house, you buy the school district." In cities with a Catholic school system, the broker will need two sets of school-district maps, public and parochial, for each map serves a different market. Houses that cannot be sold to Protestants because the public school has "too many" black students can still be sold to Catholics, who will send their children to the parochial schools. It is true that the church welcomes black Catholic children to its schools, and in some cases non-Catholic black children as well, but in most places there are very few of them to welcome.

Two cases illustrate the effect of school districts on white housing demand. In Seattle, residential districts are remarkably heterogeneous, mainly because of a complex geography that provides many lakefront and scenic sites. Some prime locations are in largely black school districts; others in white ones. Two areas belonging to a largely black school district contain well-sited middle-class houses, but prices for these are substantially lower than the prices of similarly sited houses in a third area where the lots are smaller and upwind from a garbage dump. The difference is that the third area belongs to a lily-white school district with (in the words of a district mother) "lots of children of professional people for our kids to associate with."

A recent proposal in Berkeley, Calif., to transport black children from "flat" to "hill" schools not only sparked a school-board recall campaign but noticeably softened the demand for residential property in the "Berkeley hills"—the home of most of the conspicuously liberal faculty of the University of California. Across the municipal (and school district) border in El Cerrito, in similar locations, there was no softening of demand. El Cerrito has the advantage for anxious white parents of being "all hill" and "no flat." Most of its homes are priced beyond the financial capacity of black parents.

The amount that white buyers will discount otherwise attractive houses in "polluted" public school districts tends to be limited by the cost of alternate private-school tuition for their children. This pattern is well-established in neighborhoods of expensive older homes in Eastern cities and is very clear in New York City's tight housing market. In Seattle one of the highest-income residential areas is near the most integrated public high school, but its affluent parents send their children to conveniently situated (and thriving) private schools.

Residential segregation is linked to school segregation through the "neighborhood school." Before educational policy became preoccupied with integration, the system of neighborhood schools eliminated the problem of transportation. With schools widely dispersed, children could get to them by walking short distances. It was, and is, a practical arrangement, economical for schools and popular with parents, quite apart from the fact that neighborhood schools reinforce the class system.

Because of its key role in *de facto* segregation, militant integrationists have attacked the neighborhood-school concept and have discovered that it commands widespread social support. For one thing, integrationists have tended to assume that segregated neighborhoods produce segregated schools. But in view of the strong white demand for status-reinforcing schools, it is also true that segregated schools produce segregated neighborhoods, not because black families are simply barred by covenants from buying in certain neighborhoods (although they certainly were barred in many cases until 1948, when the Supreme Court nullified racially restrictive covenants to property titles), but because demand by the vastly more affluent whites bids up prices in many areas beyond what all but a tiny minority of blacks can pay. Insofar as white parents have made substantial investments in property partly because they presumed their children would attend a particular school, they are disposed to defend existing arrangements with political craft and power.

Changing the distribution of students among schools has proved to be difficult enough within individual school districts and municipal jurisdictions. It is much harder when whole school districts become the units of segregation, as they are indeed becoming in many metropolitan areas composed of white suburbs and a largely black central city.

Often the suburbs are Balkanized into a patchwork of small municipal governments, each jealous of its petty sovereignty, proud of its middle-class residential character, resistant to involvement in problems affecting the metropolitan area as a whole. This resistance is widely regarded as a major problem of American government, and if those who recommend interdistrict integration are to succeed, they will have to overcome it where many far less controversial programs have failed. Where concrete proposals for merging metropolitan and suburban school districts or for busing more than token numbers of black children have been presented to the suburbs—in St. Louis and elsewhere—they have been resoundingly rejected.

Most advocates of integration have recognized the difficulty of getting effective governmental support at the local level, and they now place more hope in national programs. These are often administered by persons committed to integration, and their discretion in granting Federal funds constitutes a potentially powerful sanction. But so far Federal agencies are long on plans, "pilot studies," "demonstration projects" and speeches that will inspire disheartened integrationists to further effort—and short on tangible results. Why has so little been done?

One reason is that Federal agencies are accountable to elected officials, who, in turn, are accountable to the electorate, and the electorate is not particularly keen on school integration. An instructive case was the attempt in 1965 by Francis Keppel, then United States Commissioner of Education, to enforce Title VI of the Civil Rights Act of 1964, prohibiting disbursement of Federal funds where state and local agencies practiced discrimination in their use. Funds were withheld from the Chicago schools after a redrawing of school district lines increased segregation. In response, Benjamin Willis, the Chicago superintendent of schools, decried Keppel's move as an attack on the "neighborhood school" and local control of education. Meanwhile the engines of political influence began to turn, and Chicago got its money about two months later. The combination of factors that operated in the Chicago case may not be present elsewhere. But it is understandable if Federal administrators grow cautious after a few episodes of this nature. Much of their apparent discretion in the exercise of Federal sanctions really resides with the people who appoint them or vote them funds, and these people in turn must stand periodically for election. Many Congressmen from Chicago came strongly to Willis's defense in 1965.

Most arguments for large-scale school integration presume that white parents can be outmaneuvered by paired schools, "educational parks" and squadrons of school buses. But this presumption is unrealistic, for it is the parents rather than the schools that have the greater strategic flexibility. Whatever strategy of integration confronts white parents, they will calculate an effective defense against it—a defense that may not be carried out (because their racism is not unlimited, and because any defensive strategy will have manifold costs and effects), but that many of them have the means to implement whenever they judge integration to constitute a sufficient peril for the welfare of their children.

The whites' main defense against integration is to move, and the general movement is to the suburbs. The desire to avoid racial integration is not the only motive for suburban living. A desire for newer houses or for "rural life" (at least till the next subdivision is built) doubtless plays a part. In America the rich have been abandoning the central city to poor newcomers for generations, and the current flight to the suburbs, powerfully stimulated by Federal subsidies to housing and highways, merely continues an old trend. But the racial integration of schools does seem to produce short-run accelerations. In the last 15 years more than 215,000 whites have left Washington, D.C. But 40 per cent of them left in the three years following the desegregation of Washington's public schools in 1954, and today 91 per cent of the city's public-school students are black.

Most people who move from a given central city to its suburbs are members of a family with school-age children, while the whites who remain in or move back to the city are disproportionately single, childless or old. By selecting among the wide range of suburbs available, the prospective buyer can find a neighborhood at the limit of his ability to pay, suitable to his aspirations and remarkably free from contaminating heterogeneity.

Because suburbs are so well-adapted to the maintenance of class distinctions, they are ill-adapted to many other activities (which accounts for the continued attraction of central cities for the childless), and they are usually expensive. Commuting costs, in money and time, are dear. Property taxes are high (no contaminating industry to bear the bulk of the tax load), but these go mainly to support a school system equal to parents' expectations. The popularity of suburbs with parents shows that they are generally willing to pay the costs involved.

Many of the people who remain in the city do so because they are too involved to leave. They include those who work for municipal agencies (which often require local residence), those enmeshed in a web of neighborhood kinship, those with incomes so low or families so large that they cannot raise the cash for a newer house in the suburbs, and those with strong roots in an ethnic community or parish. All these qualifications apply well to urban Catholics. Recent events in Boston, Milwaukee and Chicago suggest that they are the most vocal (and sometimes violent) opponents of neighborhood and school integration, but this is not necessarily because their racist sentiments are stronger than those of Protestants and Jews who leave the city. The latter tactfully bury their racism in a multiplicity of "other reasons" for moving; only the immobile Catholics are left to stand and fight.

In a study of the political supporters of Louise Day Hicks, the Boston School Committee's champion of the neighborhood school and *de facto* segregation, it was noted that those most likely to support integration are also least likely to expose their own families to it. The authors of the study observed that Mrs. Hicks had been roundly denounced by white liberals in the Boston area, but these critics lived in the suburbs and could not vote against her. Here lies the problem in trying to assess public support by verbal professions. The Boston liberals have given their most sincere judgment by the residential location of their own families: they have voted with their feet. White parents who eloquently profess liberal opinions in the abstract live in Boston's suburban

Newton, in El Cerrito and Mercer Island, but, in the case of one's own children, who says parenthood says conservatism.

More than anything else, the response of large numbers of white parents who are anxious for their children is likely to confound attempts to integrate schools. Families can move across school district and municipal boundaries far faster than integration plans can. Fathers can commute longer distances than school children can be bused. Sites for new schools can be "strategically chosen" (although sometimes so much controversy attends site selection that school districts simply stop building new schools), but by the time the school is built, the white exodus is well under way, and shortly after it opens, the new school is as segregated as the one it was built to replace. Much the same is likely to prove true of the attempt to outflank parents with large-scale "educational parks." To keep up with the volatile white families, the buildings of the grand new park would have to be a fleet of house trailers.

When white parents withdraw their children from the central city, more is lost than students alone. With them go a significant source of tax revenue and, most important, community leadership in programs for good public education. The parents who typically provide this leadership campaign for bond issues support good teachers and new programs, and generally exercise their influence in ways that will benefit all children in the schools. But they do this because they live in the community and because *their* children will benefit, too. American public education, with its exceptional degree of local control, offers as much as it does to the lower classes (when it offers them very much of anything) not because of a passion for equality among professional educators—whose "life adjustment" curriculum is perfectly compatible with a caste system—but because community élites with a vision of education as an agent of social improvement have sought to apply their own standards to communities as a whole. When these groups finally decide that community schools are "past redemption" and withdraw their support, they produce a situation that is well and truly past redemption.

There is more than a loss of leadership. All over the nation, communities that for decades have passed every proposed school bond issue are now defeating them, and new dissatisfactions triggered by integration campaigns are probably partly responsible. It is not always possible to remedy this situation by raising taxes on industry. Modern factories put as little as possible into unrecoverable investments in land and buildings in order to be free to move where over-all costs are lowest—which is not likely to be a central city with many poor school children and no middle class.

At this point integrationists again resort to the Federal Government. We hear that "Federal bread will feed the urban schools." Will it? Federal grants usually come as programs to which local agencies apply for funds. The Federal guidelines are complex, and preparing applications to comply with them becomes a specialized skill of its own. Just as rich universities hire the best specialists for this purpose, so do rich suburban school districts. An even greater advantage falls to rich districts through the common Federal practice of supplying "matching funds." In short, as more Federal money is allocated to education, there is good reason to predict that affluent white school districts will continue to get their share and a little more besides.

The Office of Education could attempt to counter this by special dispensations for "integrated" (which is coming to serve as a euphemism for "black") schools, thus regressing to a racist criterion. But no Congress elected in the next decade or so is likely to pass effective legislation and funds for such a program. The sociologist Thomas Pettigrew, generally an advocate of school integration, has recently reviewed the provisions of the Federal Elementary and Secondary Education Act and warned his fellow partisans that it contains little that can be used to further integration. Indeed, whatever the legislation, Federal and local education agencies must act within a narrow range of nice distinctions, because many programs to improve the education of black children involve the unequal allocation of resources to students on the basis of their race—the very policy that moved the Supreme Court to its historic decision in 1954.

Even if, against all odds, some strategy for integration of the public schools is devised from which whites cannot escape, there remains the alternative of parochial and other private schools.

Apart from differences due to over-all regional prosperity, American public education is by most measures worst where community élites have forsaken public schooling for their own children and sent them to private schools instead; best where most élite children attend public schools and private schools are uncommon. Anything that motivates prosperous white parents to withdraw support from public education and to transfer it to private agencies weakens education as a force for social mobility and thus favors a more rigid class system, the very system integrationists oppose.

All of these arguments depend, of course, on probabilities and debatable interpretations, and their conclusions are not inevitable. The racism of American whites may change, parents may lose interest in maintaining status, competition among urban governments may disappear, Congress may demand that the United States Office of Education and the Attorney General apply stronger sanctions for integration, white fathers may tire of commuting, public education may be Federalized and private schools outlawed. But it seems more realistic for those who hope to improve the educational opportunities of black children to abandon the premise that integration must come before all else.

The effort to redress racial wrongs can be applied in principle to many different areas of social life; in practice it has concentrated on public-school integration. As Oscar Handlin, the Harvard historian, has remarked, "Because segregation enforced by law was long an instrument to oppress the Negro, integration became the primary objective of Americans concerned with equality." But this objective is a poor choice. So much energy has been put into the difficult pursuit of school integration that little remains to plan for more practical improvements within the framework of *de facto* segregation, which is likely to persist anyway.

The assumption is widespread that the only way to help black children is to put them in the same schools as whites. But cannot at least some of the presumed advantages of white schools be transferred—probably much faster than through militant integration? The President's Commission on Civil Disorders recommends this also in its call to "improve greatly the quality of ghetto education." Today many black slum schools are understaffed simply because teachers refuse regular assignments to them (often preferring the wider choice of schools available to substitutes). Premium pay for hazardous and extreme duty (which involves first admitting that it *is* hazardous and extreme duty) might help here. More use might be made of citywide schools with an élite curriculum and admission open competitively to all.

Although a metropolitan school district may have less money per student than suburban or private schools, it still has more in total, and some of its funds might be used to buy facilities and recruit personnel to attract white students. Special élite programs might be housed in ghetto schools. Some small degree of integration would result, with the white students attending the schools a few hours a week, and the programs would also be readily available to black students. High-school scholarships for the disadvantaged might induce some potential dropouts to stay in school who now have (at least in the short run) every economic reason to leave. Large cash prizes for the demonstration of reading ability in high school would be cheap compared with the later social costs of adult illiteracy.

The advocates of integration often appeal to impending crisis. We are told that the damage done to black children through segregation is so terrible and costly that any means of eliminating it is justified, and that rapid integration alone affords relief. But there has always been much in social life that is terrible and tragic. Rational social action must derive not simply from moral outrage but also from possible means of redress. One might claim with equal fervor that the damage done to the minds and souls of middle-aged women because they have grown sexually unattractive to men is so terrible and costly that any means of eliminating it is justified, and that a redefinition by Federal fiat of nubile appeal alone affords relief. After all, notions of sexual attractiveness, like notions of racism, are mere cultural artifacts.

The facts are that short of truly dictatorial authority over the education of white children, we lack the means to produce widespread school integration so long as white parents do not favor it. This is not to deny that integration benefits black children, but to argue that a concentration on integration programs risks losing many of the more general benefits that public education—even segregated education—can provide for them. It is to be wished that more black children could be exposed to the opportunities of the middle-class world, but the more immediate and prior goal is that many more of them learn to read. Pressing on with integration against all odds may simply eviscerate the public schools and produce more illiterates among the urban poor.

It is still hard to argue against integration. For one thing, it puts one in the bad company of traditional racists. Most of integration's critics have been conservative but highly literate Southerners, who use a graceful homiletic style filled with obsolete references to "human nature" and parochial appeals to common sense. The integrationists thus have their reply cut out for them: they refute the tired old saws of prescientific racism with fresh new facts from modern social science. It thus becomes difficult to criticize integration without appearing to be unfashionably prescientific.

This essay must risk that appearance. Its object is not to profess what it is currently fashionable to profess, but to explain what moral men only want to condemn, and to predict what will happen as a result of what they propose to do now.

Part 2

RACE RELATIONS IN DIFFERENT SOCIETIES: A COMPARATIVE PERSPECTIVE

IN 1970, the Israeli government is entangled in litigation about who is a Jew. At the same time the government of Great Britain debates whether an Asian resident of Kenya with a British passport can be prohibited from migrating to England.

If a man abandons the Judaism of his forefathers and becomes a convert to Presbyterianism, is he still a Jew? Are black, English-speaking descendants of African slaves in Trinidad English? Trinidadian? African? West Indian?

When is race the deciding factor in defining the boundaries of groups? When is race irrelevant? People are willing to sacrifice their lives for their group, but what determines what is their group? During World War II, German-American soldiers fought

Germans in Germany, and Italian-American soldiers fought Italians in Italy. In Italy, too, Japanese-American soldiers fought the white Christian enemies of their white Christian fellow Americans during the years when their parents were imprisoned in the United States because of their race. An American Indian veteran of the Vietnam War was honored as a war hero and then was refused burial in his hometown cemetery on the ground that he was not white.

Race is often central to group identification. Race becomes socially meaningful when the social structure causes race to be associated with social positions that are rewarding or punishing. Race makes an important difference or becomes a meaningful label where biological characteristics correspond to social characteristics deemed especially desirable, such as a high income, or especially undesirable, such as a menial occupation.

Group boundaries are maintained by social rewards and social punishments. People try to affiliate themselves with groups in which membership promises them rewards: families that will improve their status, neighborhoods that will convey prestige, colleges that will educate them, fraternities that will help them find jobs, clubs in which they will find friends, unions that will increase their wages, business associations that will increase their profits, the religious denomination that promises the inside track to salvation. Just as people seek rewarding situations, they attempt to avoid punishing ones. They decline the invitation to the ineffectual business association, the low-prestige country club, and the dull party. A man may study, but reject, the erroneous theology just as he may date, but not marry, the girl from the wrong side of the tracks.

People try to protect their reward-conveying groups by denying membership to the wrong people. Churches excommunicate heretics; sororities blackball candidates who "won't fit in"; colleges discriminate against applicants with low test scores; neighborhoods organize to exclude people who might lower property values.

When something that is rewarding or punishing, such as social class, is correlated with race, then race becomes a convenient social shorthand for specifying the boundaries of groups. Since black has meant "slave" throughout most of American history, and still means "underclass" to most white Americans, it is customary in the United States for whites to try to exclude black Americans from their most cherished group affiliations. For most white Americans, it is undesirable to have Negroes as neighbors and unthinkable to have them marry into the family.

Similar systems of race-related group boundaries exist in other societies. They are similar in their sociological patterns, and they vary according to what group has been on the bottom and what group exerts its present power to maintain its preferred position.

What Place for the White African?

by Tom Stacey

NAIROBI, KENYA

THE OLD Rhodesian stood among the beloved apricot trees and pomegranates, avocados and lemon trees of the poor, dry acres that bore the achievement of half his life, and broke our long silence. His vehemence was startling.

"The munts [Africans] can take over—I'll stay. *They* won't get me away from here. They'll get me away to bury me, that's all. I've told everyone, even the inspector [of police], *they* won't get me away. Nobody's going to take my rifle away, same as they've done in the Congo. The man that's going to come to take my rifle away is going to take me with him. If I shot one native— or two—not my brother can come and catch me. I'd blow his brains out.

"All can go. *I* won't go. Not out of Rhodesia I won't go, boy."

Their land is growing dark for them, and what they are composed of—the bones of their Government and the sinews of their society—is discovered to have the fatal disease. The inexorable agent of destruction of their body is recognized by the white Africans from the Highlands of Kenya to the banks of the

From the *New York Times Magazine*, June 10, 1962, copyright © 1962 by The New York Times Company.

Limpopo: the terrible desire to survive is confused with the death wish; and those who would fight for their society and the future they had presumed for their race in Africa would almost as soon die in the struggle.

People of British stock do not usually like to express anguish by violence. The brief shadow life of the so-called Rhodesian Republican Army cannot earn comparison with the O.A.S. in Algeria. No one can yet forecast whether one grim day relations between Westminster and Salisbury might not fatally rupture, and Sir Roy Welensky's jest that the British Government will put him in the Tower for defending Britain's interests in the depths of Africa might not turn into some kind of agonizing reality. But for the time being, the white Africans can *actively* express their anguish only by leaving their treasured country.

Last year, 1961, was the first year in which more white men left the Rhodesian Federation than arrived. In Kenya, the trend is established; probably more than one in ten of the white farmers have already gone, and the rate of departure grows. In some areas of Kenya like Eldoret, where the Afrikaner settlers centered themselves, about three out of ten have left. Late last year the Kenya "Convention of Associations"—whose members comprise all the country's 2,600 white farmers—conducted a private poll among all their members through the mail. The result showed that 79 per cent were intending to leave Kenya as soon as they could dispose of their farms for anything like a fair price—or else were leaving anyway.

Of the 21 per cent who said they were intending to stay unless compelled to leave, four out of five were over 60. Much the same ratio is considered to apply to that majority of settlers in business, or the professions, or retired, who own their own houses and other property in the towns or suburbs. Virtually all property in Kenya, whether land or houses, is unsalable. In Nairobi, scores of European houses stand blind and vacant, rank weed and high grasses re-establishing themselves—homes which the absent owners would jump at selling at half their pre-1960 values. Farms, of course, are not abandoned so easily. Even without the existing law of confiscation of an abandoned farm by the Government, there is nature to act as confiscator.

The old 'uns, that 21 per cent who will stay anyway, possess the fortitude of resignation. They have more to lose of the past than of the future. One couple, about 65, had taught in schools in East Africa for nearly forty years. When they retired, they bought a creeper-covered cottage and fifteen acres at Limuru, a few miles from Nairobi.

Walking home through the evening sunlight of that clean and smiling landscape, rolling and green and fertile—"like Somerset," she said: "After forty-five years in Africa we just can't leave now." Inside, the cottage was neat and snug and full of relics of their lifetime in the country. Two armchairs, with their antimacassars, were drawn up before the brick fireplace; and there, in two paper bags beside the arm of each chair, was the only evidence that this was not Somerset but Kenya, where, as independence approaches and security weakens, nocturnal gang attacks on European homes become more frequent, such as that in which an old widow had died a few months before within a mile of their cottage.

"Walter had a slight stroke about six months ago, and he doesn't feel he could manage a gun properly. So," she said, amused at herself, "we always have our bags of pepper beside us at night. Mind you, there's nothing unusual about us for you to write about, young man."

The steady deterioration of security is often the reason for leaving Kenya given by young people with small children; yet I always felt it only a fraction of the whole reason, which is too profound, too intricate, for themselves to explain. The white Africans express their anguish in many ways—in terms of love, in terms of hate; in persuasion, and in passion. The feeling floods out in words.

On Kenya's Kinangop plateau at 8,300 feet, Europeans have carved farms out of the cold heathland which the Africans never favored. The somber barrier of the Aberdare Mountains, barren no less from the parching sun than from the cold, forms the limit on the north, and the steeply falling escarpment of 3,000 feet into the Great Rift Valley is the limit to the south. The third side, to the east, is encircled by the black rim of the forest, secretive and most silent of all the forests of Africa I know and, all these years after Mau Mau, still the refuge of the hunted and the hunter; for beyond it lies the traditional land of the Kikuyu.

Jim Hughes, though vigorous, fit, and without a gray hair, is 66 this year; and even if he and his wife were not too old to "begin again," he loves his 503 acres against the forest too well not to go on fighting for the Kenya he believed he and his friends and their predecessors had been creating ever since Lord Delamere first staked out a farm in the vacant uplands three generations ago.

Hughes had saved most of his life up to 1938 to buy such a farm, and he earns from it what a farmer would earn with half the acreage in Sussex or New England—that is to say, not much. He had served in East Africa with the King's African Rifles and then worked on a sisal estate. The British Colonial governor had signed his 999-year lease in the name of King George VI. But now, talking to me in his isolated home up there on the South Kinangop, he admits he is beaten at last.

"We feel just as anyone would normally feel here—that we've been thoroughly betrayed by a lousy British Government, and that there's no more to it; and that when we can get our chips for the farm we'll go off, and we'll throw in our allegiance with somebody who's not always prepared to pull the bloody flag down. That's all."

Jim Hughes will not mind my describing him as a man of contrasts. When he is speaking of his farm, he is gentle and absorbed; the voice, still with its trace of Welsh that survived his father's service with the British Army in India, is that of a craftsman telling of what he had made.

"I came in this 1933 model Ford. There were no roads. So we went across country and we got here and I bought this piece of land. That's all there was then, a piece of land. And I started to find a means of plowing it and cultivating it.

"The first thing I built after the bamboo shack we lived in was that house—it's got three rooms, a kitchen and a bathroom. We first planted cereals, wheat. It did well until it got susceptible to numerous diseases—black stem rust and others; and then we found this wasn't a suitable place for wheat. But oats and barley, we found, did very well. Oats, barley, pyrethrum, potatoes."

Jim Hughes' small farm is the best-ordered I have seen anywhere in the world. He was offered £35,000 ($98,000) for his 503 acres five years ago; today with approaching *uhuru*—independence—he could not give it away. He himself makes most of the equipment he uses—from farm wagons to his own perfectly finished padlocks.

It was as we were strolling around his farm buildings that the "other man" unexpectedly came forth. He was saying: ". . . then we built this new house. We got the stone from the forest. I taught them how to cut it. I taught them how to use a square— they didn't know what a square was, they went round in a circle with it. We carried our own cement. We carried every bloody thing; we cut every single mortal thing from the forest and brought it here—there was nothing here. We have done our own doctoring, our own veterinary work."

It was now the voice of an old man who believed he had been fooled into wasting his life; in its bitterness it was savage.

"It's just the politicians responsible for starting up racial animosity. The African responds to being continually told the land was his. How can we stay after independence? What do you do if cattle are driven across your land and trample down your crops and you telephone the police and they say: 'That's a bloody shame, isn't it, but don't you surely realize, Mr. Hughes, that's independence, that's *uhuru?*'

"What do you do if they come and squat on your land and you ask them politely to get off and six witnesses go down to the police station and say you insulted some African and it's your word against half a dozen of them? What d'you do?"

After we had visited a neighbor who was leaving for New Zealand that week with his wife and young family, we returned to Jim's home-made bungalow farmhouse. Darkness fell rapidly. With nightfall, it seemed, he gave way completely to his grief and bitterness.

In the dim lamplight, his face all at once became a patch of violently contrasting colors—scarlet, and ashen white, and his hair and jaw black; and he himself became all gestures and voice in an unstoppable tirade against the British Government, against the British people, and the Africans, and the police and civil servants . . . "the lousy, stinking British Government. The politicians out there are like a bunch of bananas—they stick together, they're yellow, and there's not a straight one among 'em.

"An elderly couple farming here went to Tanganyika for a vacation three weeks ago. They come down to breakfast in their hotel the first morning. There's an African, union man, at the next table, playing his transistor radio as loud as it can. They ask him to turn it down, politely; and when he doesn't, they go out to the veranda for their coffee. And this African follows them, and begins dancing about, snapping his fingers in their faces.

"They decide to leave, of course. And when they go to their car, they find all the windshield smeared with filth. And they expect us to stay here!"

This silenced Jim. But his wife's chin buckled; and her fingers pressing into her cheek could not stop the momentary tears.

In that dark little living room, its deep brown furniture made by its owner, the carthorse brasses around the fireplace, and the Kikuyu houseboy lingering over his laying of the dinner-table at the far end of the room, straining to overhear what was said—in that dark brown room without children was the whole story.

It was told me in countless ways from the Highlands of Kenya to the southern borders of Rhodesia, but the themes were always the same: the British betrayal; the treachery of liberals; the settlers' struggle in building up the country; the generic backwardness of the native, his uncleanliness, his natural subservience; fears for security, impending chaos, the imminent collapse of "standards"; the interference of politics—concocted overseas—into a perfectly contented paternalist relationship between white and black.

Southward, in Southern Rhodesia, the whites perceive with a horrified incredulity the rapidly approaching threat to their position, but are not yet overwhelmed by it, as in Kenya.

Perhaps the most simple and moving expression of what is regarded as betrayal by Britain was given me by a large, warm-hearted farmer of Afrikaner origin living in Southern Rhodesia. Yapi Jacobs very well exemplifies Churchill's description of the Afrikaner farmer—"an unusual blend of peasant and squire."

"Well, sir, I used to be a very loyal man; so is my father. The old man has fought three wars for Britain, including the South African war. He's lost one of his legs. And I myself, I joined from the beginning in 1939, and I must say all my comrades will think exactly the same, very surprised that Britain wants to sort of sell us.

"They don't seem to care a damn for what we've done. As far as we're concerned, she'll just let us go, even if we're cut up, or strangled. As far as I'm concerned, a very, very poor show. It was the white man who fought for the freedom of these people, and now it's the white man who is being given over to them."

For a more considered opinion, I quote the welfare officer of a Northern Rhodesian copper mine which is run on enlightened principles. The speaker himself was a studiously liberal person.

"If you could do what the Russians do—take all these Africans, take all their parents, and put them in the labor camp and bring up their children in a completely new society, a new cultural background—in one generation you would have a different sort of person; in two generations you would have as good as any in the Western world. But, basically, we have not yet changed their outlook."

European society in Central and East Africa is the youngest of its kind in the world; and in its youthful lustiness it was quite unaware of its extreme vulnerability.

When, with great suddenness, the realization of the danger struck—in the case of Kenya in a single month, January, 1960, and in the case of Rhodesia over the past two or three swift years —it indeed reacted as might a young man who on the threshold of adulthood was apprised by his parents that he had an incurable disease and not long to live.

I do not believe it is sensible to say to the whites:

"You must contentedly accept that this country, which you thought was yours to make, is not yours, but theirs; that these Africans of whom you thought you were the masters and protectors are now *your* masters; that this land, which you believed was yours to possess and render fertile, belongs not to you but to them, on whose sufferance you might perhaps continue to cultivate it; that this wealth you have created, these institutions you have formed, this peace, this justice, this faith, these ideals, this nation you foresaw—a new America, a new Australia—these are not yours, and in them you shall have no significant part. You must accept contentedly that unless your society becomes part of their society, absorbed within it, subject to its control and strange passions and movements, there is no place for you in these territories."

I do not believe it is sensible to say that to the white settlers of colonial Africa, because in all experience I do not believe it possible.

The Africans have suffered deeply: called upon to exchange an African, tribal *possession* of life for a European, conscious *understanding* of life, they have been haunted by a sense of loss and obsessed by a fear of inherent inferiority. So far as African osmosis within European life is concerned, it has been readily acknowledged that the "culture gap" has been far too great.

It has been fashionable for us, who are not personally swept up in the situation, to espouse solutions for our fellows in East and Central Africa which we express with a conviction quite undisturbed by our failure to define them: multi-racialism, integration, partnership, and so forth. I do not believe I am expressing an opinion but a fact when I say that *on both sides,* on the spot in Africa, it is accepted that "it is either them or us."

That is to say, Kenya and the Rhodesias must each be either a "white man's country" or a "black man's country" in which the white settler will have no permanently tolerated place.

Some of the modes of expression I have quoted are not attractive. Some even suggest that the minds of the speakers have already become misshapen from the strain of their dilemma. Many —if not most—of the views expressed have little basis in fact: the "natural" subservience of the African, for example, or his "uncleanliness."

I have attempted in this article to perform two things—to describe the mood of the white Africans in East and Central Africa, and to place the reader in a position where he can feel a little of what the white African feels, however unfair and illogical his attitudes might appear. When we know what a man thinks, we may condemn his view; but only when we know why he thinks it may we condemn him.

Where 78% of the People Are the "Others"

by Joseph Lelyveld

AN HOUR before your big international jet lands at Jan Smuts
Airport outside Johannesburg, the French, Belgian or American
hostess comes down the aisle, her big international smile mo-
mentarily contracting into murmured apologies as she hands out
the oversized forms of the South African customs authorities.
One of these documents bristles with warnings about the terrible
things that can happen to you if you are caught with concealed
poppy seeds, firearms or pornography. The other asks a lot of
ordinary questions, a few not so ordinary and one that proves
to be as decisive as it is inescapable. Put a cross, you are told, in
the appropriate box: "White——, Asiatic——, Others——."

The white foreigner clucks to himself, enjoys a few highly
moral thoughts, then draws the "x" that enlists him in South
Africa's privileged minority for a few weeks or months. In his
preoccupation with his own declaration of whiteness, he probably
doesn't notice the only really odd thing about this entirely to-be-
expected bureaucratic rite. Is there any other Government in the
world that could so casually announce to foreign visitors that
78 per cent of the population it rules rates only as "others"?

From the *New York Times Magazine*, June 19, 1966, copyright © 1966 by
The New York Times Company.

Most white South Africans—if they put the question to themselves at all—strenuously deny that they oppress blacks. Sometimes their denials can be remarkably convoluted and theoretical. More often they are exasperated and angry. What business does a foreigner have to make a snap judgment? The problem is more complex than he can begin to realize.

"I won't have any outsider who has been in this country a couple of months telling me how we should treat the Bantu," a white official in Windhoek, South-West Africa, said to me emotionally, almost angrily only several hours, as it happened, before I learned that the Government was giving me a week to get out of South Africa. "What can any foreigner hope to know about the Bantu?"

That official wasn't assailing me or contradicting anything I had said. On the contrary, he was practically pleading with me to believe that he was a sincere man, capable of taking a humane interest in the black people under his jurisdiction. "I've worked with them for 15 years. I speak three of their languages," he said. "And I *know* they're not fit to live with us."

Most white South Africans claim the same sort of expertise in a complex social problem. Even those who have never bothered to learn the names of the black people who work for them assure you that they *know* the Bantu. Usually what they know is the racial caricature of a simple, childlike, cheerful creature who, mysteriously, is given to primitive, uncontrollable lusts and violence. Keep him simple and he stays happy.

One young Afrikaner told me I had no right to write about his country until I had been there a full year. (I lasted only 11 months so I still don't have that right.) He suggested I spend that year in African villages in the reserves. Then he proceeded to explain to me the racial problem in the United States, a country he had never visited.

As a foreigner I was regularly asked whether I had found myself discarding the "preconceived ideas" that, it was assumed, I had carried to the country. I would carefully reply that I had found its problems far more intricate than I had anticipated, that I had never been aware of the positive achievements of Afrikaner nationalism, that the land itself was a discovery in its rugged, compelling beauty.

But those answers would never do. They were considered non-committal; properly so, they were. For I knew that what the question really meant was whether I had learned yet that South Africa's whites do not deserve the opprobrium that has been heaped on them, that apartheid does not mean racial oppression, only self-preservation.

There must be a point at which the word "oppression" ceases to stand for an impression or a value judgment and becomes a fact; whatever that point is, it was passed long ago in South Africa. In its operation, as distinct from the thinly veiled rationalization that is its theory, apartheid is not merely a system of racial segregation or the denial of political rights to a majority group. That is only the beginning. Consider that there is no black man in South Africa who has a firm right simply to be in a "white" area, who cannot be expelled by a simple, irreversible administrative action. Consider that the "white" areas account for more than 86 per cent of the land, and that about 70 per cent of the black population lives in them. Then you begin to get a glimmering of the weirdly fantastic legal structure that has been erected in South Africa to keep the white feeling safe.

"Apartheid," Alan Paton remarked when I visited him, "is the finest blend of cruelty and idealism ever devised by man. The idealist stomachs the cruelty because of the idealism. The cruel man stomachs the idealism because of the cruelty."

The idealism is in the preachments about "Bantu homelands" where African peoples are free "to develop on their own lines," preserved—almost like wildlife—from the traumatic breakdown of their traditions that comes with urban life. The breakdown is real. But are a man's values preserved by thrusting him into a strange, dynamic environment, then making it impossible for him to come to terms with it? The answer is in the faces of black domestic servants window-shopping late at night in fashionable white suburban shopping centers. They're not yearning for thatched huts.

The cruelty is in the Bantu Affairs Courts, where 1,000 Africans are tried for pass-law offenses every day, convicted almost automatically in trials that can be measured in seconds instead of minutes, then jailed and returned to their "homelands," which are mostly overcrowded and arid.

The white South African indulges himself in the idealism, and blinds himself to the cruelty. But the cruelty is everywhere, smoldering on the surface of South African life, avoidable only by an act of will. Thus on one day last April The Johannesburg Star published two letters from white citizens. One asked whether it was legal for a maid's husband to spend the night with her in the servants' quarters, considering that the maid could not possibly get home for the night because of a lack of public transport for nonwhites in her employer's suburb. The other asked whether a black servant could keep her infant child with her on her white employers' property until it was weaned. In both cases, according to Johannesburg's Non-European Affairs Department, the answer was no.

"What is this society we are building," asked The Star, in an editorial intended less as a challenge to the Government than an expression of moral stupefaction, "that denies thousands of human beings what are basic rights the world over, and we remain unmoved?"

Or there is this advertisement for stationery that runs regularly in the nonwhite press. " 'I'll never be a stranger to my family,' says Jane Maepa." Under that testimonial is a series of photographs that tell, in comic-strip sequence, the story of Jane Maepa who "a few years ago left home and came to the city to earn money for herself and her children. While she is away, Jane writes each week to her family on Croxley paper . . ."

The photos show Jane ironing in her white madam's kitchen, then Jane writing to her family, then Jane's mother in the reserve reading the letter to Jane's children. ("Here's another letter from your mummy, children. She never forgets us." A little boy smiles broadly and exclaims, "Look what pretty paper mummy writes on!") Once a year, the ad continues, Jane goes home on her holiday. Her children crowd around her. "They remember me," she thinks, "because I remembered them." A happy ending to one of apartheid's success stories.

But if Jane displeases her madam she may have to go home sooner. There is a little green card that the madam is required to fill in and return to the authorities as soon as she decides to "let her girl go." It is called a "Notification by Employer of Termination of Employment of Female Bantu Worker." Once that is received by the "influx control" officials, Jane is almost sure to be "endorsed out" of the white area. This means she can be fired without explanation, but doesn't dare quit.

The effect of apartheid is to reduce the black man to a unit of menial labor. It tells him not only where he can live but where he can work; a black man in Johannesburg cannot leave his job because he has heard of a better opportunity in Pretoria, only 35 miles away. And it tells him what work he can do.

The only possible security he can have is that he do his work to the satisfaction of his employer. If he loses his job, he must apply to the Government for "a permit to seek work." Without that permit and a bewildering variety of stamps in his reference book—the passport all black men must carry in "white" areas— he is lost in a legal limbo from which there is no escape except by the hard-won mercy of the state.

Under the country's labor laws, no black man can ever earn the legal status and rights of "an employee." So anonymous is the market on which his labor is traded that most employers record only the Christian names and reference book numbers of their "boys," who are never asked whether they have family names, any more than they are asked whether they have families, or where.

As time goes on, simply by pressure of numbers, black men in the industry rise higher. But they never rise higher than the lowest whites who, almost invariably, receive smart pay increases to mollify them after every black advance. The result is that progress by blacks actually serves to increase, rather than to narrow, the ever-widening gap between black and white.

Does the system work? If you mean, does it promote the "separate development" of the races in virtual independence of each other, then the answer is obvious. It doesn't. Nothing makes this plainer than the finances of South African education. Less than two-fifths of 1 per cent of the national income is spent on the education of Africans, roughly one-tenth of what is spent on the education of whites. About 4 per cent of the national income is spent on all education, but little more than 2 per cent of what the Africans themselves contribute to the national income is spent on the education of their children. Of every 14 white students, one reaches the university level. The proportion of black students who get to the state-controlled black colleges is one in 762; even more telling is the fact that only one in 28 black students reaches secondary school. (Neither of those proportions takes into account the more than 30 per cent of all black children who never even reach school.) Not surprisingly, then, the educational gap also keeps widening.

But if by asking does the system work you mean, does it succeed in pulverizing multi-racial activities in any sphere without damaging the steady supply of cheap labor necessary for South Africa's booming industry, then the answer must be that it is working wonderfully well. It doesn't even matter that there are tens of thousands of black workers in "white" areas without the proper papers: they are under control.

Above all, the black man must be careful. Every township is full of African informers working for the security police because of threats or money, or both. The result is that politics becomes as intimate a subject as sex, only more so. No black man in South Africa today will easily allow himself to be lured into a discussion of politics unless he considers everyone in earshot a trusted friend. Even then conversation is guarded, heavily shaded in irony, habitually inexplicit.

One African friend of mine assured me that it was often easy to distinguish the informers. "They are the people," he said, "who try to strike up a conversation about the A.N.C. or the P.A.C. [the African National Congress and the Pan-Africanist Congress, the outlawed black nationalist movements]. No man would do that to a friend. It's too dangerous."

Almost as much as the Group Areas Act, which fragments families, the use of informers corrodes all human relations in the black townships. Mutual confidence between two friends becomes a dangerous luxury. Look at Port Elizabeth's township, New Brighton, which was once an A.N.C. stronghold. For three years the relentless state security machine has been working its way across New Brighton in search of active A.N.C. sympathizers, as methodically as a thresher in a wheat field. The result has been an almost endless series of political trials (at the last tally, 529 persons had been sentenced to 2,666 years in jail).

No doubt most of the accused are "guilty" of seeking "to further the aims of a banned organization," the crime with which they are charged. At the same time, it is obvious to anyone who watches these trials that the state cases have been trumped up. (Few people watch: the public is barred from the trials and the press usually neglects them.) What makes the trumping up obvious is the prodigious detail in which all the witnesses for the prosecution are normally able to recall distant events; with whom, for instance, the accused shook hands, and in what order, on arrival at an illegal meeting held four years before.

New Brighton calls these state witnesses, who are almost all former A.N.C. members, *"impimpis,"* a word with a Xhosa prefix and suffix and an English root. All of them still live in the township; though their names cannot be published, they are widely known. How come, then, none of them has yet been way-laid on his way home from a beer hall at night? "To do something like that," one New Brighton man replied, "you would want at least two men, wouldn't you?"

In what I indicated was an exercise of the Socratic method rather than an incitement to violence, I pointed to the man's best friend, the only other person in the room. There was a moment of embarrassed silence, then the man asked, "How do I know he's not an *impimpi?*"

Under the circumstances, it is hardly surprising that there is no sign of significant black resistance now. But considering what it took to achieve this quietus, there is something indecent about making the deduction most white South Africans make when they argue that the absence of opposition after the removal of "agitators" demonstrates that the masses are satisfied.

The white man knows very well how he would feel if he were treated the way he treats the black man; he simply assumes that the black man isn't capable of those feelings. The result is a debasement of language as well as feeling. It isn't considered strange that black students in Sharpeville study a text that takes the history of their country up to 1963 without mentioning the Sharpeville shootings of 1960, when the police fired into a protesting crowd of unarmed Africans. It isn't even considered strange that the text states: "South Africa is a democratic country, governed according to a Constitution."

I asked a teacher from another township what he did when he reached that sentence. A black man, like all who now teach black students except at the highest levels, he said he read it hurriedly and hoped that none of the students would ask him questions. Did they ever ask questions? Yes, he said, there was one boy who had asked why the pass-laws were necessary. "I said they were necessary to keep out the criminal element. Then he said, if that were so, why was his father arrested? I didn't dare say, 'Because the laws are unjust.' So I said, 'Probably he stole something.'

"I felt sick as soon as the words were out. If I was a real teacher I would have been teaching him to doubt the system. Instead, I taught him to doubt his father. That's how helpless we are."

It may well be that white South Africa feels justified in not fearing that sort of frustration. That is a question of power. But it is not justified in denying its existence.

"We know the Bantu," say the whites. But that proposition becomes increasingly dubious. The black townships are not even indicated on the country's maps. Highways don't pass through them. Most whites rarely see them, and never enter them. What do they know, then? One or another set of abstract rationalizations about what is really happening in their country, which is all, evidently, that they want to know.

"They're so smug and self-satisfied," an Indian woman remarked. "Our children know more about this country than they do."

The overwhelming majority of whites can deny that South Africa is a police state in perfectly good faith. No one reads their mail, taps their phones, follows them or tosses them into jail. Living on Easy Street, they say what they think and go where they want, for they think the Government well-advised and they don't want to go to the townships. So long as their privileges aren't spoiled for them by feelings of guilt and anxiety about the condition of the unprivileged majority they are unlikely to believe that they live in a country where people are oppressed.

Certainly the Government doesn't think of itself as tyrannical. The leading Ministers genuinely appear shocked when they are accused of being intoxicated with power. Turning back the accusations, they reply that they are simply applying necessary antidotes in order to preserve South Africa. They don't need to explain that the words South Africa denote not the territory indicated on the map but the aggregate of whites who live there.

The trouble with the theory of the necessary antidote is that it could not be applied without building up the enormous security machine. But the machine, once built, is not easily dismantled; it continues to churn out its weekly production of restrictions, only now the people who are "banned" under the Suppression of Communism Act from all social as well as political activities are no longer black nationalists and Communists, types that are in short supply. They are moderates who are immoderate only in their willingness to stay with a cause after their hopes have died.

The white South African, in his beautiful land where labor is cheap, enjoys a notoriously comfortable life. Heavy physical labor is almost excluded from his experience. Even the postman has his "boy" to haul the mail he delivers. Still, however glib it sounds, there are grounds for arguing that the whites are making themselves the real victims of apartheid.

This is so in trivial ways that the foreigner quickly notices; for instance, when he is waiting impatiently for a bus—and one pulls up marked "for nonwhites only."

I happen to have a great appetite for curries that I eagerly looked forward to indulging in a country full of Indians and Malays. I was disappointed, not because the Indians and Malays don't make good curries but because the good curries they make are served where whites aren't supposed to go. The curries the whites get are pallid imitations, not worthy of the name.

I also like jazz. The best jazz musicians in South Africa are Africans. The best place to hear them is in the townships at night, but my pass to the townships expired before sundown. It was legal for black musicians to play to all-white audiences—

and most of them needed the work—but the white audiences preferred white musicians. There was only one show by blacks for whites in Johannesburg while I was there. Its promoters discovered that to sell tickets they had to boost the cast as "World's Fair Dancers." That they had been to Flushing Meadow made them an attraction. As black South Africans, doing exactly the same show, they had nothing to recommend them to most whites.

More than a political strategy, apartheid is a defensive attitude toward life. Very occasionally its advocates seem to recognize their loss. At the International Court of Justice at The Hague, where South Africa's title to the vast territory of South-West Africa is being challenged, the rector of Pretoria University, Prof. C. Rautenbach, was asked whether apartheid, in the fullness of its days, would permit social contacts between the races in order to deepen mutual understanding.

In visionary terms the rector replied: "There would be wining and dining together, visits to the opera together, speaking together. I dream of that." He didn't explain where the wining and dining and the operatic forays would take place. Not in South Africa; there are no restaurants and theaters that would permit it. Nor did he explain why the future of which he dreamed was unthinkable in the present.

Under apartheid, the whites plainly have the upper hand, but somehow they always seem to be cringing. They don't hate, they fear; what obsesses them is race, not a doctrine of racial superiority. This means they must continually detach themselves from the reality around them, blocking the normal workings of their imaginations. There is a premium on not seeing.

In a Durban courtroom I heard a young prison warder testify that it was not cruel to place a man in solitary confinement in a cell seven feet by seven feet for a month, forbidding him to talk and withholding all reading matter except the Bible. Why wasn't it cruel, asked an incredulous lawyer. Because it gave him "an opportunity to review his whole life," the warder replied, and gave trained observers like himself an opportunity to assess the prisoner to see how his rehabilitation might best be achieved.

"How can you assess a man by exposing him to the unnatural conditions of isolation?"

"That's the method we use."

"Do you recommend such conditions for people outside prisons?"

"Their conditions are different. It's not necessary for them."

"How would you like it if someone locked you up for 30 days and prohibited you from talking?"

"I can't imagine myself in such a position." That last answer seemed to me crucial.

The white South African—the Afrikaner especially—bravely claims to be risking his privileges in order to preserve his values. He should not be judged hastily; in a simpler setting his values would seem neither cruel nor archaic. That they so often seem so now is the result of unlucky circumstances that reverse the formula, insidiously tempting the white to risk his values in order to preserve his privileges.

But knowing that his power is inherently insecure, the white becomes grimmer, tougher, more deliberately determined to be strong. This is a private as well as a public fact. The 400,000 whites of Johannesburg, it has been reckoned, own more than 100,000 guns. A statistic like that measures fear as well as strength.

All the time, apartheid goes on working and happening, deliberately tearing up whatever threads of understanding there were between blacks and whites. It is easy to see what is happening to the whites, more difficult to see what is happening to the blacks, but plain enough that what is happening to both groups is not making an eventual accommodation between them easier. South Africa's future is as clouded as that of any country in the world. Demographers say that in the year 2000 there will be 42 million South Africans; only 6 million of them will be whites. A 4-to-1 ratio will have widened to 6 to 1 and, what is more important, most of the nonwhites by then will be urbanized. It is far from impossible that a high proportion of those 6 million whites will blame their fathers for not having sought a compromise in 1960, when compromise was relatively simple.

They may even quote to each other what the African leader Nelson Mandela said two years ago to the court that sentenced him to life imprisonment for sabotage: "It is not true that the enfranchisement of all will result in racial domination. Political division based on color is entirely artificial and, when it disappears, so will the domination of one color group by another. . . . I have fought against white domination and I have fought against black domination. I have cherished the ideal of a democratic and free society." But in South Africa today it is a crime to quote those words.

Not the smallest part of the price the white South African pays for apartheid is his inescapable awareness that it has made him a pariah in Africa and the world. A white South African outside his country who receives a kind word can be inordinately grateful; he doesn't get many.

The Afrikaner finds compensation in a carefully tended mystique of a chosen people fighting to survive in a pagan world. The central figures in his chronicles of that people are white-bonneted matriarchs and sturdy *Voortrekkers,* the pioneers who abandoned the Cape of Good Hope in the eighteen-thirties to evade British authority and safeguard the principle of "no equality in church or state."

The fact of the long Afrikaner past, as opposed to the mystique, could be decisive. These people aren't colonists. There is no obvious place for them to go, so they cannot and won't contemplate leaving. After the worst imaginable disaster there would be at least a couple of million whites remaining in South Africa. Even if a solution were sought in a drastic partition of the land, those whites would always remain a minority, wherever they were deposited. Thus, if no permanent settlement can be found in apartheid, the only answer left will be multi-racialism.

The events that will test such possibilities are almost certainly remote. There is no power inside the country or on the African continent that the whites, for the present, need fear. The only danger they face is outside intervention, which could never get very far without the determined support of the United States and Britain.

But the United States makes more than $150 million a year in South Africa; Britain makes more than $400 million a year there. Britain has a problem with the pound sterling and the United States has a war in Vietnam. Prime Minister Hendrik F. Verwoerd is a careful man. He says he is counting on "the common sense and sane judgment" of the United States and Britain to "guarantee the safety of the whites in this country." He is probably not miscalculating.

So you are left with the taut South African present, which daily becomes more inward, more fragmented, more dreary. In the nineteen-fifties the white-black conflict was in the open. Now it is hidden, and a glacial silence, broken only by the self-assuring boasts of the whites, has settled on the land. And that silence thickens.

Whenever I drove out of Johannesburg on my way to Pretoria, the route I followed took me through a highway underpass where on one pillar I would see, in faded black paint, the letters "A.N.C." and on another the enigmatic words "Torture the end."

Did they mean that torture was proving the end of some members of the African National Congress? Or of the whole movement? Or of its policy of nonviolence? Or, Cassandra-like, were they intended to prophesy some dreadful future for the land? That scarcely seemed possible, especially once I had put the city behind me, where the present was bad enough, and was driving through open country under cloudless skies. But, then, Cassandras are never believed.

"Aloha" for the Fiftieth State

by James A. Michener

AMERICA, IN accepting Hawaii as the fiftieth state, is much like a man who finds himself married to a picture bride. He does not really know her, but as he starts living with her he discovers that she is beautiful, intelligent and gifted with a dowry.

Physically, Hawaii is exquisite. Palm trees bend into the wind and glistening lagoons tempt the eye. Across one of the islands (Kauai) runs a deep geological gash as colorful as the Grand Canyon; it tells, in layer after layer of dazzling rock, the story of how the islands sprang from volcanic origins. On another island, Hawaii, active volcanoes rise to snow-covered peaks nearly 14,000 feet high. Waterfalls are so numerous they are not named and cliffs that drop 2,000 feet into the sea are common.

It is a land of flowers, so brilliant that they are difficult to visualize. They blossom all year round: orchids, torch ginger, plumeria, hibiscus and bird-of-paradise. There is the beefsteak plant, with leaves the size of platters and startling red. There is the lowly croton, a winsome shrub whose iridescent leaves cover

From the *New York Times Magazine,* April 19, 1959, copyright © 1959 by The New York Times Company.

a spectrum of more than twenty colors, dominated by gold and purple and rust. This is my favorite.

But most of all, Hawaii is a land of people, an amalgam of many types. Two per cent are full-blooded Hawaiians, brothers of those Polynesians who inhabit Tahiti and Samoa; 16 per cent are part-Hawaiian, and this segment is growing; 25 per cent are ordinary mainland white Americans, and since immigration from Asia is halted while, with statehood, movement from the mainland will increase, this is the fastest-growing group; 2 per cent are Puerto Ricans; and 1 per cent are from European countries. That leaves 54 per cent as having come from Asia: Filipinos, 12 per cent; Chinese, 6 per cent; Koreans, 1 per cent; and Japanese, 35 per cent, which makes them the largest single ethnic group.

The most important fact about Hawaii is that these varied peoples live together in harmony. There is practically no race discrimination. The Governor of Hawaii is a handsome Irish Catholic from St. Louis. The President of the Senate is a Chinese, the Attorney General a Japanese. The powerful Mayor of Honolulu is part-Hawaiian, and the strong man of the legislature is Chinese-Hawaiian. This pattern is maintained throughout island life. However, many Caucasians and Orientals prefer to live strictly within their own communities, and there is no great flood of intermarriage. A Caucasian boy who wants to marry a Japanese girl may have a very tough time, indeed—mostly from the Japanese family.

Two common rumors about Hawaii must be rejected. First, Hawaii is not going to be submerged in an Oriental tidal wave. An educated guess would suggest that today the economic control of the islands is vested as follows: white Americans, 70 per cent; Chinese, 20 per cent; Japanese, 10 per cent. Second, Hawaii is not governed dictatorially by the "Big Five," the informal combination of sugar factors who once ruled the island in a benevolent feudalism. The Big Five are still strong, capable and conservative, but they are not major landowners and they do not control the Legislature nor do they exercise a veto power over much of anything. Commercially they are an asset to the islands, and in their junior offices one begins to find smart young Chinese and Japanese.

Credit for the amazing manner in which so many diverse people live together so easily must be given to three groups. First, the gentle Polynesians who inhabited the islands originally were by nature inclined to accept other races, and the dominant spirit of Hawaii has always been *aloha,* gracious welcome. Second, the missionaries who stamped the islands with their rigorous concepts were liberal Congregationalists from New England who believed in fellowship, education and the immanent presence of God. Hawaii's heritage derives from New England, not California, and Chinese immigrants were not abused in the islands because the missionaries would not tolerate such behavior. It has been said, "These missionaries did not love Chinese and Japanese, but they did love justice." On this basic Christian justice, Hawaii was founded.

But the *aloha* of the Polynesians and the rectitude of the missionaries would have accomplished little if the next wave of immigrants had been unequal to the occasion. Chinese and Japanese in large numbers were imported to work the sugar fields and after indentures of ten years were supposed to go back to Asia. Instead, they saved money, kept out of trouble, and soon owned either stores or lands. They were admirable citizens and built themselves securely into Hawaiian society. Their major characteristic was an overwhelming passion for education, and in the early days it was not uncommon for a Japanese field hand making 77 cents a day to send five children through high school and university. The ablest son might even go on to become a lawyer at Michigan or a doctor at Penn. Among the best-educated people in America are the Chinese and Japanese of Hawaii.

Five additional assets help make Hawaii a fine state. The population is young and vigorous. Of a dozen political leaders, eight will be under 40. The average age of the islanders is lower than that of any other state in the Union.

Hawaii is a wealthy state. It pays enormous taxes to the Federal Government. People live well. There are no extensive slums or depressed areas. Citizens save money and invest in the future. If one considers only the financial balance sheet, America got a great bargain when she accepted Hawaii.

Contrary to the popular image, men in Hawaii work hard. Hawaii was not originally suited to sugar and pineapple, for there were deficiencies in the soil and never enough water. Clever men corrected the soil and dug for water—deep wells and miles of tunnels through the hearts of mountains. If Hawaii is a paradise—and I think it is—men made it so.

Hawaii is by far the most advanced state culturally that has ever been admitted to the Union. It has a famous preparatory school dating back to the eighteen-forties, a strong university, fine churches, interesting newspapers and televison stations. Its historical libraries are immensely rich, and its symphony and theatrical groups strong. But the intellectual glory of Hawaii is its pair of museums: the Bishop is about the world's best in Pacific lore; the Academy of Arts owns one of the finest collections of oriental art.

Finally, Hawaii is a forward-looking state. Its labor laws are more liberal than those of many other areas. It spends a high percentage of its income on education. Its health services are first rate and the proud citizen is apt to say, "We have the best hospitals and the poorest jails in America." Hawaii prefers it that way.

I could continue for many pages listing the virtues of Hawaii, but on this eve of statehood I think it might be more instructive to explain some of the problems that face the islands.

Land. No large area of the United States is more limited by land shortage than Hawaii. On Oahu, the site of Honolulu, population density is 835 per square mile, a figure comparable to Belgium's and exceeding Indonesia's. At every point this lack of land inhibits growth. Men cannot find land for either their businesses or their homes, and one of the principal reasons people leave Hawaii is the complaint: "We couldn't find a place to live."

The problem is exacerbated by the fact that what land exists is held in large parcels by a few. The six principal owners control 26 per cent of all available land. Sixty owners control 80 per cent, and since they have been able to prevent their holdings from being properly taxed, that burden falls upon personal income.

In Honolulu a man doesn't buy land by the acre. He buys it by the square foot, and a reasonable figure for a good lot would be $2.50 a foot, or about $110,000 an acre—provided he could find one. Choice land runs about $1,200,000 an acre. What the homeseeker does is to lease a plot for fifty-five years with the understanding that each ten years the terms of his lease may be re-negotiated upward.

Many businesses seem reluctant to launch major projects on land they cannot own and on which they face upward renegotiation every ten years.

Taxes. Since land is not adequately taxed, income has to be overtaxed, and Hawaii is one of the most heavily burdened areas in the world. Personal income taxes quickly rise to the 9 per cent level, topped by an across-the-board levy of 3.5 per cent on any business activity. This makes retirement of people with middle incomes to Hawaii rather unlikely. Artists, writers and musicians should also think twice before fleeing to paradise; they, too, must pay 3.5 per cent on their business activity. And because Hawaii has such a youthful population, much of which earns no income, personal taxes will probably rise rather than diminish.

Economy. Fifteen years ago Hawaii was in a rather more precarious position than now. Then island income depended upon military expenditures, sugar and pineapples, in that order, and a disruption in any one could have plunged the island into depression. Today the economy rests on five pillars. The military investment, represented by sixteen major installations, including Pearl Harbor, Hickam Air Force Base and Schofield Barracks, with 50,-000 uniformed personnel, 50,000 dependents and 20,000 civilian employees, accounts for 38 per cent of the islands' income or $327 million yearly; then come construction ($185 million), sugar ($145 million), pineapples ($412 million) and tourism ($100 million).

It seems likely that the last category will ultimately rise to second place, for there are few areas in America more appealing than Hawaii. But this introduces a major problem: as tourists increase, the natural facilities that attract them diminish. The physical appearance of Waikiki has slipped in the past decade and those responsible seem to lack both the vision and the ambition to correct the drift. New resort hotels in less developed areas are needed and such projects are being actively pursued.

Labor-management relations. Hawaii has not yet achieved a mature attitude on the interlocking responsibilities of labor and

management. Because the Big Five long refused to permit union-
ization, labor leaders find it profitable to revive old bitterness in
a manner that became unfashionable on the mainland twenty years
ago. And because some leaders of the longshoremen's union were
at one time communistically inclined, management tends to casti-
gate all labor as extremely radical. However, the smart young
executives who are now assuming leadership of the great corporations are finding it possible to work with labor.

Bloc voting. A constant fear in Hawaii is that the various races
may begin to vote in blocs, Caucasians voting only for Caucasian
politicians, Orientals only for Orientals. But a study of voting records fails to show that this has so far happened. Governor Bill
Quinn, an astute politician, guesses: "Hawaii will probably become a lot like Boston. If a Japanese voter doesn't know anyone
on the ticket, he'll naturally vote for a Japanese, the way the Irish
vote Irish in Boston, on the grounds that 'he's one of us.' But I
have found that if any of our voters know the men running, they
pick and choose with great intelligence."

Imbalance among the islands. Hawaii's second permanent head-
ache, after land, is the fact that, while the island of Oahu grows
richer and gains in population, the neighboring islands, which are
in many respects more attractive, grow poorer and lose population. Thus Oahu, with only 9 per cent of the land, produces about
80 per cent of the income and houses 79 per cent of the population. Legislating thus becomes a dogfight between Oahu and the
rest of the pack. If tourists could be lured away from conventional
Waikiki to the neighboring islands, part of the necessary corrective
would have been undertaken; but since this seems difficult to do,
the imbalance will probably worsen.

Lack of support for culture. The fine cultural institutions which
I have praised have been largely created and supported by the
private charity of the great missionary and industrial families, but
the time has come when these older families should not be expected to continue this burden. Yet replacements have not been
found. Rich Orientals have not discovered that Uncle Sam, through
generous provisions in tax laws, makes it prudent to give money
to public institutions.

For example, on the mainland a man who graduates from Harvard may express his mature gratitude with the gift of a chair, but this does not happen in Hawaii where the lack of support suffered by the university is a scandal.

The "da kine" plague. An unnecessary handicap faced by Hawaii is its addiction to pidgin English, a barbarous *lingua franca* derived from bad English, Hawaiian, Chinese, Portuguese and Japanese, all delivered in an incredible sing-song. The phrase "da kine," from "that kind," is used in everything. A man who wants to tell his friend that a sandwich costs too much will sing, "Eh, blalah! Da kine sammitch pipty cent takai too much!"

Sensible parents try to combat pidgin, but it remains a damnable burden. Entire schools succumb to it and occasionally even teachers take the easy way, so that one generation after another hampers itself by addiction to this folly. However, some firms are beginning to reject young people who speak pidgin and the university is trying to stamp out the barbarism.

Lack of a name. A minor, but serious, problem is that there is no name for the people who inhabit Hawaii. A man who lives in Texas is a Texan and is proud of it. I used to be a Pennsylvanian and for a while a New Yorker. But what am I now? I can't be called a Hawaiian, because that name is reserved for the Polynesians. Possibly we will all become "Islanders," but in the meantime the fact that we have no common name perpetuates old cleavages.

Discrimination. Since Hawaii is famous for the fact that all its people live together in enviable harmony, it is regrettable that a few major institutions still practice racial segregation. There are clubs where Orientals are not permitted, fine residential streets where they are not welcome to live. (On the other hand, Orientals have other clubs to which Caucasians are not admitted.) With the passage of years such customs seem bound to vanish. In the meantime they do little harm and do not deter me from stating that people live together more harmoniously in Hawaii than in any other area I know.

Striking a balance between strength and weakness, it is obvious that Hawaii is going to be a strong state. It is young, progressive, adventurous. It is able to pay its way and to contribute richly to American life. Its major contributions will probably be along these lines:

Vacation land. In addition to its great natural beauty, Hawaii has an almost perfect climate. It never gets as hot as New York does in summer. It never gets cold. About ten days a year, when the northeast trade winds fail to blow, things can get a bit sticky. For the rest of the time there is probably no place in the world with a better climate. Hawaii is thus an ideal vacation land and, with jet aircraft, is practically next door to places like Chicago and St. Louis.

Leadership in internal problems. It is not yet clear what kind of men the islands will send back to Washington. I would be proud to support either the Republicans or the Democrats who have so far been mentioned. Possibly one or two will be Oriental, for Hawaii has a wealth of able Chinese and Japanese who would grace any legislative assembly in the world. But whoever goes to Washington will embody the Hawaiian spirit of *aloha,* and will be well grounded in American principles. Such men, or perhaps women, will lend our national leadership a breadth of experience which will be good for America.

The United States faces grave internal problems arising from race relations. In the next decade states like Alabama, Mississippi, Georgia and South Carolina will undergo trying experiences in which the tensions of Little Rock may be repeated many times over. America is going to be pleasantly surprised at what Hawaii will be able to contribute to the relaxation of such tensions.

Hawaiian Senators and Representatives are going to be men of the most conciliatory character. They are not going to shout and bellow. By their quiet precept they will encourage all who seek logical and unemotional solutions. They will be proof that conciliation is possible.

On the other hand, agitators and men of ill will can no longer cry, "It can't be done!" In Hawaii, quietly and without anger, we have done it.

Help with foreign problems. One of America's major concerns is its relationship to foreign powers, and we are trying to assure uncommitted or wavering nations that they ought to trust in our good intentions. A serious bar to our efforts has been the bad publicity stemming from Little Rock. The Communist Chinese and Russians have abused us severely on that issue.

But with the admission of Hawaii, the Communist propaganda line collapses. Congress has demonstrated anew our historic attitude toward other peoples. We have shown that we can accept men of varying colors. Russia claims, "Americans hate Orientals." We do not, and we have proved that we don't.

Let me put the significance of Hawaiian statehood this way: Today the job of every State Department official in Asia and Africa has become a little easier; the words of every U.S. Information Service man have become a lot more persuasive.

But the greatest boon to America will be in the realm of the spirit. For sixty-one years our nation held in the middle of the Pacific Ocean a group of islands to which statehood had been implicitly promised. Over the years, because we feared distance and skins of different colors—and perhaps because we feared the responsibility of taking a new step—we failed to fulfill that implied promise. Then, one by one, the reasons against statehood vanished until at last the nation was faced with one simple moral problem: Were we willing to redeem an old pledge?

Those of us in Hawaii well appreciate what a bold step America has taken in extending statehood to the islands. That Congress chose to do so is a supreme joy to most of the islanders, and we are determined that America shall never regret that daring decision. And for its part, the United States today is a little stronger, a little more secure, a little more courageous. To me it looks like a great bargain all the way round.

Part 3

IMPLEMENTING DISCRIMINATION: THE INSTITUTIONAL IMPACT OF PREJUDICE

WHEN RACE becomes relevant to defining group boundaries in a society, then those defined as the inferior category will be excluded from full participation in the social order.

Once discrimination against a racial category becomes institutionalized—that is, once discrimination becomes part of the everyday life of the society—everyone participates in and is affected by it. Even those who are consciously opposed to the system do not remain untouched by it.

A person may be unprejudiced and still discriminate. A barber, for example, may say he is not prejudiced against Negroes; but he knows that if he allows them to patronize his shop, white clients will be offended. Nonetheless, a person's claim that he is free from prejudice cannot always be accepted as evidence that he has been "pressured" into discrimination. His behavior must be analyzed in the context of the power of the majority in a society to set normative standards. What does it mean when a white homeowner says that he himself is not prejudiced and would sell his house to a Negro but for the fact that others in the neighborhood would make life unpleasant for the Negro tenant and for him, the white owner? If most other white owners in the neighborhood say the same thing, it becomes obvious that the owners and the neighbors are actually the same group. It is certainly possible to discriminate without being prejudiced, but it is not the most likely combination.

In cases such as this, whites are reacting to a stereotype of the Negro which has developed through centuries of institutionalized discrimination in American society. Social typing is extremely important and often necessary in modern urban society: we associate with so many different people in an ordinary day that we don't have the time to get to know each of them intimately.

Stereotyping is a special form of social typing. It is the classification of a whole category of persons as particular social types. Instead of responding to the individual characteristics of intellectuality or cynicism, American whites see intellectual Negroes and cynical Negroes. In a word, no matter what the Negro does, he is seen first of all as a Negro and only secondarily as the perpetrator of a deed. This is stereotyping. It is the use of a category as invariably relevant. How powerful the role of racial stereotyping is is indicated by the fact that whenever a Negro is not seen as conforming to the stereotype, he is still regarded not as a clean, meticulous, erudite, and responsible man but as an "exceptional Negro."

Such a well-learned and strongly held set of beliefs enables us to maintain power relationships that control access to highly desired positions. In the American occupational structure, we find the preponderance of Negroes in occupations of service and semi-skilled and unskilled labor. Persons in the power positions of ownership, of hiring and firing, are predominantly members of the dominant white group. It is an integral part of discriminatory social systems that the privileged maintain their own position by thwarting the access of the less privileged to the most desirable positions. In a well-developed system of discrimination, this will include behavior ranging from a distortion of history to what

R. K. Merton has called the self-fulfilling prophecy: if enough people believe a doctrine of racial inferiority for long enough, the doctrine itself will have consequences whether or not it is factually true. If Negroes are inferior, it is a waste of money to try to educate them at the same level as whites. If one believes this, then it is sensible to allocate less money to Negro schools and to be satisfied with inferior facilities, teacher training, and curricula. The vicious circle is closed when the products of this inferior educational system turn out to score lower on I.Q. and achievement tests than white students. The end product of the prophecy that Negroes are inferior becomes evidence for the inferiority of Negroes. The prophecy becomes the condition.

The Absent Father Haunts the Negro Family

by C. Eric Lincoln

UNDER PRESSURE of law, public opinion and Negro militancy, progress in civil rights has reached the point where many Americans assume that the practical end of discrimination is only a matter of time. But even the end of formal discrimination falls short of the distant goal: full integration of the Negro into American life. Nor can true integration be achieved until the nation— and the Negro—solves a crucial and immediate problem: how to "Americanize" the fragile, fractured Negro family.

The Negro in America was never a "black Anglo-Saxon," though sometimes he tried to be. He was never simply "another ethnic group" to be assimilated into the mainstream. His family structure is unique in American society.

The U.S. family is primarily patriarchal. The husband and father is the chief breadwinner, carrying the responsibility for his wife and children. Even in families where husband and wife supposedly share equally in making decisions, our society regards the male as "more equal." The law defines this relationship; custom supports and rewards it. But the majority of Negro families do not

From the *New York Times Magazine,* November 28, 1965, copyright © 1965 by The New York Times Company.

follow the U.S. custom and are appropriately penalized. Because women have assumed primary responsibility as head of the family, the matriarchal Negro household is at a distinct disadvantage in competing for its rightful share of benefits offered by American society.

About 25 per cent of Negro families are headed by women who have no husbands. These are families where the male is absent because of divorce, separation or desertion, and do not include families with illegitimate children which have never included a male parent.

The easy explanation of the shattered Negro family puts the blame on the Negro male, caricatured as shiftless and lazy. A more socially acceptable reason attributes the matriarchal family structure to superaggressive females. In fact, the blame rests on the horrors of a slave society which stripped the Negro male of his masculinity and condemned him to a eunuch-like existence in a culture which venerates masculine primacy.

There are no discontinuities in history. Negroes today (like any other people) are largely the product of yesterday. And American slavery, the "yesterday" of the American Negro, ended only 100 years ago. For 250 years before emancipation, slavery ordered the lives, the thinking and the behavior of white people in one way, and of Negroes in quite another.

American slavery was a different institution from contemporary slavery in South America, Portugal, Africa, or from ancient slavery in Greece and Rome. It developed its own institutionalized values uniquely designed to promote its own ends. Its peculiar impingement upon the Negro in America inescapably conditioned his values, his behavior and his future.

When Negroes were slaves, neither the law nor the slave owners recognized marriage between slaves. Males of prime physical condition were mated with females, like so many cattle. Children were left with the mother, giving the Negro mother an early, exclusive interest in the family and forcing upon her full responsibility for its care. In those instances where a male and female were permitted to live together longer than necessary for procreation, the Negro father (he could hardly be called a husband) had absolutely no control over his family or its fortunes. Children were seized and sold. Often the father himself was sold away from his family, never to see them again.

The psychology of castration was viciously applied in other ways, too. No Negro man was given a title of respect, a practice which continues in much of the rural South today. A Negro man was simply "Sam," "Jim," or frequently "boy," no matter what his age. He was never "Mister." If he was "living with a woman" —the nearest thing to marriage—he was known as "Hattie's Sam" or "Mandy's Jim," again denying him a position as head of the family. And if the white man wanted Hattie or Mandy for himself, the Negro male had to step aside; interference as a "husband" meant severe punishment and, not infrequently, death.

When the Negro was freed from bondage all the laws Congress could muster were not effective in wholly transferring him from the category of slave to the category of citizen.

The slaves were freed without any provision for their economic or social well-being. They were almost totally uneducated, for to have educated a slave was a criminal offense. They had no money and no homes. And they were concentrated in a politically and economically distressed society hostile to their presence as freedmen. Even those who made their way to the North quickly found themselves unwelcome, for as indigents with low skills they threatened to glut the unskilled labor market and become a burden on the tax-paying citizenry.

Because of her peculiar relationship to the white woman as a servant, and because she was frequently the white man's mistress, the Negro woman occasionally flouted the rules of segregation. Her impunity was by no means absolute, but because she often reigned supreme in the white man's kitchen and nursery she could, in times of crisis, "talk to the man" and get concessions that made life a little more bearable for herself and her children.

The practice of sending the Negro woman to do business with the white man became quickly established in the Negro-white pattern of relations. In the ruptured economy of the postwar South, Negro women were frequently paid more than their menfolk and they could ordinarily find jobs in domestic service while their men walked the streets looking for work.

"Freedom" did not improve the image of the Negro male or give him a sense of security as head of the family. He remained a semi-slave, and his slavery was rooted in the centuries he had spent in America.

If you want to understand his hatreds, his resentments, his castration as a husband and father, look back 100 years. And if you ask why in 100 years he has not overcome the past, it is because the past has never died: every day, every hour of that 100 years of semi-freedom has had to be rewon day by day from the prejudice which still promotes, openly or covertly, the old ways of slavery. The Negro did not earn rewards for being manly, courageous or assertive, but for being accommodating—for fulfilling the stereotype of what he has been forced to be.

We may note, in the interest of keeping perspective, that some stable Negro families with male heads existed before and after slavery. Before the Civil War, some free Negroes in the South and the North maintained family structures and customs as closely analogous to those in the prevailing white culture as circumstances would permit. A few upper-class Negro families, mostly along the Atlantic Coast, have an unbroken tradition of more than 100 years of social stability and cultural progress. And in the Deep South a handful of Negro families that date to slavery, or the first decades after emancipation, testify to the Negro's determined attempt to overcome the scars of thralldom.

The symptoms of the Negro family's enduring sickness are everywhere evident today.

The Negro crime rate is higher by far than the national average. The rate of illegitimacy is higher—regardless of the inconsistency of reporting procedures—and may be as high as 25 per cent. Negro drug addiction, especially among juveniles, is much higher than among whites—dramatic evidence of the attempt to escape the rigors of living in a society which for them bears little promise of a better future. The percentage of Negro high-school dropouts, again far above the national average, reflects the same sense of Negro hopelessness.

This is social sickness of epidemic proportions, and it spreads with the steady deterioration of the Negro family.

As the basic unit of socialization for the young, the family needs the presence of both parents if children are to learn the values and expectations of society. But socialization is a continuing experience which affects not only children, but parents as well. A "family man" is much less likely to lapse into criminal activity than one without ties and responsibilities.

The absent father has not been, until recently, a particularly disturbing factor among Negroes themselves (except for educated Negroes who were particularly sensitive to the white man's blanket charge of racial immorality). Any male in the average Negro family might function as a father-figure: uncles, older brothers, grandfathers, even cousins. Similarly a grandmother or aunt was frequently "mama" to a brood of children not biologically her own.

Television has been one factor in sensitizing the Negro child to the fact that his family is different. Another increasingly important factor is the integrated school. In their association with white children from complete families, Negro kids learn early that something is different about their households. This awareness is sharpened even further by white teachers who have Negro pupils for the first time. As a Negro teacher in a newly integrated school explained it: "My white colleagues get *so* frustrated when they ask little brown Johnny, 'What does your father do?' and Johnny says he doesn't know. Then they ask, 'Well, Johnny, what does your father look like? Is he big and tall?' and Johnny says he doesn't know. And finally they say, 'Well, all right, Johnny, what is your father's name?' And Johnny says he doesn't know."

The divorce rate among Negro families is 5.1 per cent, compared to 3.8 per cent among whites. But divorces are expensive, and the rate of desertion—the poor man's divorce—is even higher. In many cases, the psychological strain of being a member of a family he cannot support because of unemployment or lack of skills is too much for the Negro husband, and he simply disappears. More often he "deserts" so that his family may become eligible for relief payments, since the family is often better off on relief than depending on the uncertainties of a job. In any event, only a minority of Negro children will complete high school in a two-parent home.

Among middle-class Negroes the battered male ego is frequently a factor in divorce or separation. The Negro professional is in actual or vicarious contact with the American mainstream. He knows his white counterpart is the chief breadwinner and head of the family in *his* home, and the Negro is acutely sensitive to the possibility of his own failings in these respects.

As tangible goods accumulate, and increasingly important decisions are made, most Negro men become restive and uncomfortable if they are married to women who outearn them, and who assume the prerogatives of family leadership as a corollary to their earning power. In Atlanta, for example, I asked a young Negro woman, a teacher, "Who is head of the family at your house?" She thought for a moment, then answered: "Well, Jack is now, but when I get my raise, I'll be head, because I'll be making $27 more than he will."

The problem is considerably more formidable than such naiveté, I assure you. The Negro female has had the responsibility of the Negro family for so many generations that she accepts it, or assumes it, as second nature. Many older women have forgotten why the responsibility devolved upon the Negro woman in the first place, or why it later became institutionalized. And young Negro women do not think it is absurd to reduce the relationship to a matter of money, since many of them probably grew up in families where the only income was earned by their mothers; their fathers may not have been in evidence at all.

Even in middle-class Negro families where the husband earns more than his wife, the real cement holding the marriage may be status and "appearances" rather than a more fundamental attachment. The Negro wife who grew up in a matriarchal home finds it difficult to assent to male leadership in the family; the Negro husband with a similar family history may be overanxiously insistent on male prerogatives in order to align his family in what he conceives to be the American tradition.

I know a prominent professor in Atlanta who has taught there for 15 years while his wife works as a teacher in her hometown several hundred miles away. They see each other at Christmas and for a brief period at the end of his summer term. This respectable arrangement obviates, or at least postpones, the problem of who will be head of the family—at the price of maintaining a one-parent household.

The task of giving the Negro husband and father a status in keeping with the larger society requires a basic change in established patterns of Negro education, training and employment.

More Negro women go to college than men, just the reverse of the white educational pattern. Six per cent of all female professionals are Negroes, while just a shadow over 1 per cent of all male professionals are Negroes. Negro females do better in school too, probably reflecting the low incentive of the Negro male who frequently feels that even if he graduates, he still won't be getting anywhere.

The long tradition of educating the girls in the Negro family is rooted in the system of segregated employment which limited sharply the Negro male's prospects of finding a job commensurate with college training. In the typical Negro family the boys leave school and go to work early, frequently pooling their earnings for the education of their sisters. The process inevitably produces a pronounced imbalance in the ratio of educated women to educated men, reinforcing the disproportionate power and prestige of the Negro woman in the family.

Having to "marry down," if she marries at all, is a common experience of the Negro woman and one which perpetuates the matriarchal pattern while fostering dissatisfaction, desertion and divorce. For that reason, certain Negro colleges are famous as hunting grounds for eligible men, and the tuition of many an indigent medical school student has been paid by the doting parents of aspiring daughters.

The ratio of Negro college men to women is changing slowly as employment opportunities for Negro men are broadened. In time, the existing disparity as a distinctive feature of Negro life may disappear, but not until Negroes can try for success in fields closed to them for so long, and not until the incentives of Negro youth can be sharply increased.

The problem of education is, of course, interwoven with the question of jobs. Since 1930, the ratio of Negro unemployment to white unemployment has hovered steadily at about two to one.

The working husband of any race is usually the key to family stability; when the husband loses his job it represents the point at which the family may begin to deteriorate. His loss of self-esteem, the inability to support his family, dependence upon some social agency or the wife's earnings—all these factors generally presage more difficult problems to come. In the case of the Negro family, with its historic weaknesses and the tentative nature of male leadership, a prolonged period of unemployment can be disastrous. The family may break up completely and in the long run society has to pay.

The problem is far larger than the individual Negro family; it is bigger than the limited resources of the Negro lower class, which is most affected. The Johnson Administration, using the pioneering report on the Negro family by Daniel P. Moynihan as a point of departure, has recognized the dimensions of the crisis and inaugurated the most comprehensive series of social rehabilitation programs ever designed by the Federal establishment.

Even that will not be enough. The Government can make available better schools, better housing and better opportunities for employment. It can enforce the laws protecting the franchise and the right to public accommodations. But the Government cannot establish a pattern of family relationships which will foster the values needed to make all this meaningful and effective. Only the Negro can save his family. The substantive help of law and the Government is essential, of course, but the incentive, the motivation which can transform the Negro predicament into a shining achievement of the Great Society must come from within the group.

The white man destroyed the Negro family and kept it weak by preserving the psychology of slavery, thinly disguised as racial discrimination and prejudice. But the white man cannot give back the values he took away.

For years, myopic but well-meaning whites have been challenging the Negro to pull himself up by his own bootstraps, even though the Negro didn't have either boots or straps. The white man was looking at his own boots and imagining the Negro owned a pair, too. The "straps" of the Negro's family problem are not encouraging, but he must work with what he has.

The Job Gap

by Herman P. Miller

THE UNITED STATES is now well into the sixth year of uninterrupted economic expansion. This is the longest upsurge in our history and the end is nowhere in sight. Unemployment is below the 4 per cent level and economists are predicting a near-record growth in the national income this year. The President did not exaggerate when he told Congress in January that American incomes are higher than ever before, profits are bigger and jobs are better. "Our nation's industries, shops and farms," he said, "prosper today far beyond the dreams of any people, any time, anywhere."

How has the Negro fared in this growth? Prosperity may be unrelated to some of the Negro's major complaints against this society—segregation, discrimination and the denial of basic rights. But it is closely related to the demand for better jobs, higher pay and greater regularity of employment.

There can be no question that the economic status of Negroes has improved during the past few years, though the *gap* between whites and Negroes has not changed much, if at all. The unemployment rate for Negroes is still twice that of whites, and they earn about half as much. The economic *level* of both groups, however, has risen considerably.

Since 1961 (the current expansion started in March of that year), family incomes have risen proportionately as much for Ne-

From the *New York Times Magazine,* May 8, 1966, copyright © 1966 by The New York Times Company.

groes as for whites. The average for Negroes was about $3,800 in 1964 and was probably over the $4,000 mark last year. Unemployment has also dropped proportionately as much for Negroes as for whites. The Negro unemployment rate declined from 12.5 per cent in 1961 to 8.3 per cent last year. During the same period, the rate for whites dropped from 6 per cent to 4.1 per cent. Finally, there has been some upgrading of jobs for those Negroes who are employed. Negro women in particular are breaking into professional, technical and white-collar employment in growing numbers. There has been a marked decrease in the proportion employed as domestics—the most despised of all jobs in the Negro community.

Despite these gains, significant trouble spots remain. They have caused some Negro leaders to deny that any real progress has been made. Adam Clayton Powell, for example, commenting on the announcement of a 12-year low in the unemployment level in March, declared: "I seriously doubt this statistic will gladden the hearts of Appalachian and other rural youngsters trudging hopelessly over the barren soil in search of a job, or Negro teen-agers wandering aimlessly in Harlem or Los Angeles. To date, the war-on-poverty impact on unemployment has been more along the lines of a feather pillow than a machine gun."

This pessimistic view is supported by the results of the recent census in the Watts district of Los Angeles, which showed that the economic status of Negroes in that area has deteriorated in the past five years in sharp contrast to the experience of the nation as a whole. In Watts and similar Negro neighborhoods around Los Angeles, family income has declined, the number of poor people has risen, housing has deteriorated, there has been no improvement in unemployment and no change in the job opportunities available to Negroes. This evidence suggests that, despite the national improvement, places like Watts are losing ground because they are becoming gathering places for persons deeply imbedded in poverty and unlikely to get out of it—unwed mothers, deserted wives, the physically and mentally handicapped and the aged. Successful families tend to move out of such economically and socially depressed areas, leaving behind the incompetent, the uneducated and the unfortunate. As a result, there is a piling up of concentrated and explosive misery in the Negro ghetto which is hidden by the over-all national statistics.

Unemployment is, of course, a sensitive indicator of economic change. As a rule of thumb, the unemployment rate for Negroes is about twice that of whites, regardless of the age or sex of the group that is compared or the general economic climate at the time of the comparison. The 2:1 ratio is particularly stable for adult men and women. Among teen-agers, however, there has been a growing disparity between the rates for whites and Negroes since the recession of 1957-58. Currently, nearly one-fourth of Negro teen-agers are unemployed, as compared with 10 per cent for the whites.

The fact that unemployment rates have dropped sharply—and that they have dropped proportionately as much for Negroes as for whites during the current expansion—is a sign of progress. It must also be noted, however, that the unemployment rate for Negroes at the height of prosperity is greater than the rate for whites during any of the past three recessions. The high rate of youth un-employment is particularly distressing not only because of the immediate frustrations and hardships it causes for the youngsters and their families, but also because it undermines training programs and the attempts to prevent school dropouts. If one-fourth of Negro youths are unable to find jobs after five years of continuous prosperity, they have a right to join the chorus when Bayard Rustin asks: "What is this foolishness about training? You can't train any segment of the population unless there's a demand for their work."

NONWHITE UNEMPLOYMENT RATES
(*Annual averages*)

	20 yrs. old and over		18- and 19-yr.-olds	
	Men	Women	Boys	Girls
1960	10%	8%	25%	25%
1961	12	11	24	28
1962	10	10	22	31
1963	9	9	27	32
1964	8	9	23	29
1965	6	8	20	28

In contrast to the favorable trends in the data for the nation, the census for Watts shows that, in this ghetto, unemployment rates in the peak year of 1965 were nearly as high as they were in the recession year of 1960. About 13 per cent of the men and women are currently unemployed. The situation in several neighboring ghettos, like Avalon, Central and Green Meadows, is not much better.

As significant as the high unemployment rate in Watts is the sharp rise in the proportion of men who have dropped out of the labor force (stopped working or looking for work) during the last five years. In 1960 about 70 per cent of the men in Watts were in the labor force, as compared with only 58 per cent in 1965. (Nationally, about three-fourths of the Negro men are in the labor force.) This change largely reflects a rise in hidden unemployment among men who have simply stopped looking for jobs.

Five years is perhaps too short a period in which to expect changes in occupational distribution. But the past five years are particularly significant because they represent a period of continuous economic expansion combined with new legislation and vigorous efforts to reduce discrimination in employment. Although the results show some improvement, they can hardly be called spectacular. Among Negro men, the most significant change was a drop in the proportion employed as farm workers (from 14 to 10 per cent) and an increase in the proportion employed as professional and technical workers (from 4 to 6 per cent).

The other occupations showed little change. The drop in farm workers is not particularly connected with events of the last few years. It is part of the historic movement from the farm to the city, which must soon come to an end because of the small size of the farm population.

The increase in professional and technical employment among nonwhite men is small proportionately but it translates into about 100,000 additional Negro families that have their feet firmly on the bottom rung of the middle-class ladder. These are the families that can make the break from Harlem to Long Island and from the District of Columbia to Bethesda. These are the new faces that show as TV announcers, government officials and business executives.

It was not so very long ago that Negroes graduating from college could look forward to careers as preachers, teachers or social workers and little more. That situation now seems to have changed. Negroes are now being admitted to the better white colleges in growing numbers and white employers seem to be willing and even anxious to hire qualified Negro professional workers. Many personnel managers claim that the demand for Negro professionals far exceeds the qualified supply. If this is so, the numbers employed in the better-paid professional jobs might be expected to increase more rapidly in the future as more young Negro men complete college.

Despite the small signs of progress, the most striking fact about the occupational distribution of nonwhite men remains their very heavy concentration in low-paid jobs. Despite all the fuss and fury of the past few years, nearly half of the Negro men still work as laborers, janitors, porters, busboys and in similar service jobs.

The progress for women has been much more striking than that for men. Cleaning up white people's homes is still the most common type of job among Negro women. About 30 per cent do this kind of work. The proportion has dropped since 1960, but it is still very high, especially when consideration is given to the fact that an additional 10 per cent or more do the same kind of work as domestics (chambermaids, charwomen, janitors, etc.), but are employed by hotels, restaurants, hospitals and similar service establishments rather than by housewives. Thus, even today, after years of progress, conservatively 40 per cent of the Negro women are doing unskilled and menial housework in one form or another.

Yet there has been a sharp increase in the number of Negro women employed in white-collar jobs. The proportion has risen from 18 to 24 per cent for the three job categories—professional, clerical and managerial-sales. But even this movement by women into better-paying jobs is not an unmixed blessing. It reinforces the dominant role of women in the Negro home and is not conducive to stable family life. So long as most Negro men work at dead-end jobs that provide neither economic security nor regularity of employment, little improvement can be expected in the Negro home. Changes in employment patterns during the last five years provide little cause for optimism in this respect.

Negro family purchasing power has increased at the rate of

about $120 per year since 1960, as compared with a growth rate of $220 per year recorded by white families during the same period. Here again there has been progress, but not enough to make more than a small dent in the reduction of Negro poverty. Since 1960 about one-quarter of a million Negro families have been removed from the poverty category (the equivalent of a $3,000 annual income, or less, for a nonfarm family of four). This is no mean accomplishment, but the fact remains that nearly two million Negro families—39 per cent of the total—are in poverty today, at the height of economic expansion:

| | NONWHITE FAMILIES | | |
	Total Number (millions)	Number of Poor (millions)	Pct. of Total
1964	4.8	1.9	39
1963	4.8	2.0	43
1962	4.6	2.1	47
1961	4.5	2.1	48
1960	4.3	2.1	49

The Negro ghetto goes by different names in different places—Harlem, Watts, Cardozo in Washington, Hough in Cleveland—but it is basically the same everywhere: a decaying part of the central city that has been largely deserted by white residents and those Negroes who can get out. These ghettos have no walls as in medieval European cities and the inhabitants wear no special uniform. Most of them, however, are just as surely locked in as were the Jews in Central and Eastern Europe a century ago. The important point, with respect to poverty, is that nearly half of the poor in the big cities of the United States live in these ghettos. Whereas the white poor in the big cities are dispersed, and a large proportion (25 per cent) are aged, the Negro poor are concentrated and young—nearly 60 per cent are under 21. The heavy concentration of deprived and frustrated Negro youth in urban slums can only spell trouble.

Historically, Negroes in the United States have made their greatest economic gains during periods of wartime. Under these conditions, full employment in industrial centers has simultaneously increased the flow of migrants from the farm to the city and from the South to the North; it has led to an improvement in the occupational structure of Negroes by providing job opportunities that might otherwise be filled by whites, and it has raised the pay of Negroes relative to whites by forcing up wages in the lower-paid occupations. In the light of previous experience, a prolonged war in Vietnam would probably accelerate the rate of improvement in Negro economic status, at least of those Negroes and their families who were not directly involved in the fighting.

We certainly do not want to rely on war to achieve goals that we are now seeking by other means. Such gains are not only undependable but are tainted as well. Although the Negro has been helped by some of the programs now in operation, the progress has been slow and there are many gaps. An acceleration of progress would require far greater commitments of funds and resources than have been made to date, and would increase the inflationary pressures which now threaten economic stability. Yet even if we cannot move boldly forward in our attempt to reduce the economic disparities between Negroes and whites, there are steps that can be taken to strengthen current programs. Although these measures will solve no basic problems, they may help avert the catastrophes of the last two summers.

Perhaps the most urgent need at present is to find work for unemployed youth in the central city. The gutted buildings in Watts still stand as ugly reminders of the damage that can be done by youthful idleness, despair and hate. An expansion and redirection of the Neighborhood Youth Corps could immediately provide several hundred thousand jobs for unemployed young Negroes. Enrollment in this program reached a peak of 278,000 last summer, but has since tapered to about 150,000 per month because of a limitation of funds. About three-fourths of the participants are students; the remainder are dropouts or graduates who can find no other work.

This program has been criticized as unadulterated work relief, and recommendations have been made for its "enrichment" with counseling and other services. The criticism is valid, particularly for the out-of-school youngsters, but the program does provide work for idle hands and money for empty pockets. Sar Levitan of the Upjohn Institute for Employment Research, who is currently making a study of the antipoverty program for the Ford Foundation, has pointed out that "unemployment decreases as youths mature. It may therefore be wiser policy simply to provide as many unemployed youths as possible with jobs to tide them over the critical years when they find it most difficult to secure employment in the market place."

The training and work-experience program for unemployed parents on relief might also be redirected so as to get more people directly into jobs in the private economy where they are needed. The program now attempts to increase the employability of these parents by providing education, training, counseling and other supportive services prior to, or simultaneously with, job placement, which is largely in government and nonprofit institutions. With job shortages in many fields that require relatively little training, there may be advantages in using funds earmarked for rehabilitation and supportive services to place these relief recipients directly into private jobs.

The manpower training program (M.D.T.A.) has now been in existence for four years. Most of those chosen for training have had 12 or more years of schooling. The policy of selecting the best-qualified applicants was followed largely because they are the ones most likely to succeed. In the current tight labor market it should be possible to take greater risks in selecting persons for training and to let the more qualified fend for themselves in the labor market. The social gains that might come from using this program as a vehicle for helping the very needy and uneducated instead of those who are somewhat higher in the social and economic scale might easily offset the inefficiencies that come from "wasting training on poor risks."

The military draft is the last way in which a democratic society should try to solve its social problems. But we are at war and men are being drafted. Many young men are now being rejected for service because of minor physical defects, low scores on intellectual attainment tests and petty criminal records. There has been talk from time to time about changing the draft and enlistment standards so as to make it possible for these men to enter the armed forces, where they might receive special training before being assigned to regular units.

One recent advocate of this kind of change is Selective Service Director Lewis H. Hershey. In recent testimony before a House Merchant Marine subcommittee he stated: "The services can be a rehabilitating force. They can do moral and intellectual as well as physical rehabilitation. . . . I think we are going to have to induct more people and I think we will have to get into correctional procedures the armed services might not like."

These are very modest proposals. Their chief virtue is that they can be made without any appreciable increase in Federal expenditures, but they will solve no basic problems and are at best a holding action. It will take time, money and imagination to bring the Negro into the mainstream of American economic life. Expenditures high in the billions may be required for many years to provide housing, education, medical care, employment and training and a host of other services.

Whether or not we can afford these outlays is a matter of choice, not necessity. The war in Vietnam is expensive, but not so expensive as to preclude a modest expansion in welfare programs. Unless there is an escalation of military activities in Vietnam during the next year, we will spend only 8 per cent of our output on defense. We spent more than that in every year between 1951 and 1963, and did not regard the situation as catastrophic.

The threat of inflation is also serious, but not insurmountable. By recouping some of the tax dollars that were so generously given to middle- and high-income families several years ago, it might be possible to finance the war in Vietnam and to expand welfare programs. As Sar Levitan aptly points out: "Those who oppose expansion of welfare legislation find it convenient at this time to substitute for ideological objections the patriotic grounds of 'helping the boys.' For them, every military cloud has an inflationary lining."

Our progress in helping the Negro during the last five prosperous years has not been outstanding. If we are to do better in the future, we shall have to try harder.

The decision to hold the line in expenditures on most of the Federal programs in aid of the poor during the next fiscal year can only mean that we are again postponing improvements in housing, employment and living conditions of Negroes. Next summer we will probably be working as frantically as we are this summer in trying to find jobs for Negro youth as a form of riot control. This approach to the problem is demoralizing as well as self-defeating. As Bayard Rustin has pointed out, it teaches "impoverished, segregated and ignored Negroes that the only way they can get the ear of America is to rise up in violence."

There are other ways. The President had a noble vision in his concept of the Great Society—perhaps the most noble vision of any President since Lincoln. The vision will become a reality only if we are willing to invest the time, money and effort that are required. A cautious, "prudent" man would never have conceived the Great Society; a cautious, prudent man will never make it work. Bold, new, expensive programs will be required. Some will fail as they inevitably must. In the end, however, it will be a better America for the Negroes and for everyone else.

We Won't End the
Urban Crisis Until
We End "Majority Rule"

by Herbert J. Gans

IN 1962, a group of us, planners and social scientists, assembled a book of essays about the city, and we called it "The Urban Condition." Had the book been published only a couple of years later, it would probably have been entitled "The Urban Problem," and today it would surely come out as "The Urban Crisis." But these catch phrases are misleading, for they divert attention from the real issues. Although American cities are in deep trouble, the real crisis is not urban but national, and stems in large part from shortcomings in American democracy, particularly the dependence on majority rule.

The troubles of the city have been catalogued in long and by now familiar lists, but I would argue that, in reality, they boil down to three: *poverty* and *segregation,* with all their consequences for both their victims and other urban residents; and *municipal decay,* the low quality of public services and the declining tax revenues which are rapidly leading to municipal bankruptcy. Moreover, the first two problems are actually the major

From the *New York Times Magazine,* August 3, 1969, copyright © 1969 by The New York Times Company.

cause of the third, for the inability of the poor to pay their share of keeping up the city as well as the crime and other pathology stimulated by poverty and segregation have brought about much of the municipal decay. In addition, the fear of the ghetto poor has recently accelerated the middle-class exodus, thus depriving cities of an important source of taxes at the very moment their expenditures have been increased by the needs of the poor. Consequently, the elimination of urban poverty and segregation would go far toward relieving the other problems of the city.

Neither poverty and segregation nor municipal decay are unique to the city, however; indeed, they are often more prevalent in rural areas. More important, all three problems are caused by nationwide conditions. Poverty is to a considerable extent a by-product of the American economy, which is today growing only in the industries and services that employ the skilled, semi-professional and professional worker, and, in fact, many of the unskilled now living in urban slums were driven out of rural areas where the demand for their labor had dried up even earlier than in the cities. Municipal decay is similarly national in cause, for small communities can also no longer collect enough in taxes to provide the needed public services, and their populations, too, are becoming increasingly poor and black as the nationwide suburbanization of the middle class proceeds.

In short, the so-called urban crisis is actually an American crisis, brought on largely by our failure to deal with the twin evils of poverty and segregation. This failure has often been ascribed to a lack of national will, as if the country were an individual who could pull himself together if he only wanted to, but even the miraculous emergence of a national consensus would not be sufficient, for the sources of our failure are built into our most important economic and political institutions.

One major source of failure is the corporate economy, which has not realized, or been made to realize, that the rural and urban unskilled workers it has cast aside are part of the same economic process which has created affluence or near-affluence for most Americans. As a result, private enterprise has been able to improve productivity and profit without having to charge against its profit the third of the population which must live in poverty or near-poverty. Instead, government has been left the responsibility for this by-product of the economic process, just as it has often been given the task of removing the waste materials that are a by-product of the production process.

But government has not been able or willing to require private enterprise—and its own public agencies—to incorporate the employable poor into the economy. Not only is there as yet little recognition, among the general public or most of our leaders, of the extent to which urban and rural poverty result from the structure of the economy, but private enterprise is powerful enough to persuade most people that government should take care of the poor or subsidize industry to create jobs for them.

However, government—whether Federal, state or local—has not been able or willing to absorb responsibility for the poor either, and for several important political reasons.

First, most voters—and the politicians that represent them—are not inclined to give the cities the funds and powers to deal with poverty, or segregation. This disinclination is by no means as arbitrary as it may seem, for the plight of the urban poor, the anger of the rebellious, and the bankruptcy of the municipal treasury have not yet hurt or even seriously inconvenienced the vast majority of Americans.

Rural and small-town America makes little use of the city anyway, except for occasional tourist forays, and the city financial institutions which play an influential part in their economies are not impaired in their functioning by the urban condition. Suburbanites may complain about the dirt, crime and traffic congestion when they commute to city jobs, but they can still get downtown without difficulty, and, besides, many of their employers are also moving out to the suburbs.

But even the city-dwellers who are neither poor nor black can pursue their daily routines unchanged, for most of them never need to enter the slum areas and ghettos. Only the urbanites who work in these areas or live near them are directly touched by the urban condition—and they are a small minority of America's voters.

Second, many Americans, regardless of where they live, are opposed to significant governmental activity on behalf of the poor and black—or, for that matter, to further governmental participation in the economy. Not only do they consider taxes an imposition on their ability to spend their earnings, but they view governmental expenditure as economic waste, whereas private enterprise expenditures are proudly counted in the Gross National Product. The average American taxpayer is generous in paying for the defense of the country and for projects that increase American power and prestige in the world, be it a war in Vietnam or a moon shot, but he is often opposed to governmental activities that help anyone other than himself. The very corporations and workers whose incomes depend on government contracts often fight against Federal support of other activities and groups—and without ever becoming aware of the contradiction.

Consequently, many taxpayers and voters refuse to see the extent to which governmental activities create jobs and provide incomes, and how much government subsidizes some sectors of American life but not others. By and large, these subsidies go to people who need them less: there are tax exemptions for home-owners, Federal highway programs and mortgage insurance for suburbanites; direct subsidies to airlines, merchant shipping, large farms, colleges and college students; and, of course, the depletion allowance for oil producers. Grants to the poor are fewer and smaller; the most significant one is public welfare, and it is called a handout, not a subsidy.

Subsidies are generally provided not on the basis of merit but power, and this is a *third* reason for the lack of action in the cities. Even though many Americans live in the city, urban areas and their political representatives have relatively little power, and the poor, of course, yet less. The poor are powerless because they are a minority of the population, are often difficult to organize, and are not even a homogeneous group with similar interests that could be organized into an effective pressure group.

The cities are relatively powerless because of the long-time gerrymandering of American state and Federal governments in favor of rural and small-town areas. As a result, rural-dominated state legislatures can use the tax receipts of the cities to subsidize their own areas, and Congressmen from these areas have been able to outvote the representatives of urban constituencies. The

Supreme Court's requirement of one man–one vote is now bring-ing about reapportionment, but it may be too late for the cities. As more and more Americans leave for the suburbs, it appears that the cities will not be able to increase their power, for voters and politicians from rural and suburban areas who share a com-mon interest in not helping the cities can unite against them.

In effect, then, the cities and the poor and the black are polit-ically outnumbered. This state of affairs suggests the *fourth* and perhaps most important reason for the national failure to act: the structure of American democracy and majority rule.

America, more so than other democratic nations in the world, runs its political structure on the basis of majority rule. A ma-jority vote in our various political institutions determines who will be nominated and elected to office, what legislation will be passed and funded, and who will be appointed to run the administering and administrative agencies. Of course, the candidates, laws and budgets which are subject to the vote of the majority are almost always determined by minorities; the only men who can run for office these days are either affluent or financed by the affluent groups who donate the campaign funds, and the legislation these men vote on is often suggested or even drafted by campaign-fund donors or other small groups with specific interests in government action. Properly speaking, then, American democracy allows affluent minorities to propose, and the majority to dispose.

There is nothing intrinsically conspiratorial about this phe-nomenon, for it follows from the nature of American political participation. Although every citizen is urged to be active in the affairs of his community and nation, in actual practice participa-tion is almost entirely limited to organized interest groups or lobbies who want something from government.

As a result, legislation tends to favor the interests of the organized: of businessmen, not consumers, even though the latter are a vast majority; of landlords, not tenants; doctors, not pa-tients. Unorganized citizens may gripe about the lack of con-sumer legislation or even the defense budget, but only when their interests are similar and immediately threatened so that they can organize or be organized are they able to affect governmental affairs.

This is not to say that governmental decisions often violate the wishes of a majority of Americans, for, by and large, that majority is usually happy—or at least not too unhappy—with the decisions of its governments. The almost $100 billion spent annually for defense and space exploration are appropriated because, until recently, the majority of the voters wanted a victory in Vietnam and a man on the moon before the Russians. There is no Federal mass-transit program because the majority of Americans, even in the cities, prefer to use their cars; and Congress can pay more attention to a small number of tobacco farmers and producers than to the danger of cigarette smoking because the majority is not sufficiently concerned about this danger, and, as a recent study showed, many heavy smokers do not even believe that smoking leads to cancer or heart disease.

But while the American political structure often satisfies the majority, it also creates *outvoted minorities* who can be tyrannized and repressed by majority rule, such as the poor and the black, students, migrant workers and many others. In the past, such minorities have had to rely on the goodwill of the majority, hoping that it would act morally, but it generally offered them only charity, if that much. For example, the majority has granted the poor miserly welfare payments, and then added dehumanizing regulations for obtaining and spending the funds.

Today, many outvoted minorities have tired of waiting for an upturn in public altruism and are exerting political pressure on the majority. Thus, the poor and the black have been organizing their own pressure groups, forming coalitions with more powerful minorities (like the progressive wing of the labor movement) and getting support from liberals, other advocates of social justice and guilty whites. Indeed, such methods enabled the poor and the black to achieve the civil-rights and antipoverty programs of the nineteen-sixties.

Even so, these gains, however much of an improvement they represent over the past, remain fairly small, and have not significantly improved the living conditions of large numbers in the slums and ghettos. Moreover, the activities of ghetto demonstrators and rioters have cooled some of the ardor of white liberals and trade unionists, and it is questionable whether many other groups would derive much benefit from coalition with poor or black organizations. Like all outvoted minorities, they can offer little to a coalition except the moral urgency of their cause.

Consequently, the poor and the black are caught in an almost hopeless political bind, for any programs that would produce significant gains, such as a massive antipoverty effort, an effective assault on segregation or even a workable community-control scheme, are likely to be voted down by the majority, or the coalitions of minorities that make up majorities in American political life. *Moreover, since the poor and the black will probably always be outvoted by the majority, they are thus doomed to be permanently outvoted minorities.*

But if I am correct in arguing that the urban condition cannot be improved until poverty and segregation are eliminated or sharply reduced, it is likely that *under the present structure of American government there cannot be and will not be a real solution to the problem of the cities.*

The only other source of power left to outvoted minorities is *disruption,* upsetting the orderly processes of government and of daily life so as to inconvenience or threaten more powerful groups. This explains why the ghettos have rebelled, why young people sometimes resort to what adults consider to be meaningless delinquency, or students to occupations of school buildings, or working-class people to occasionally violent forms of white backlash.

Although disruption is bitterly attacked as antisocial by defenders of the existing social order, strikes were also once considered antisocial, but are now so legitimate that they are no longer even thought of as a form of disruption. The disrupters of today do not strike, but their methods have not been so unproductive as their opponents would have us believe. The ghetto rebellions have been responsible for stimulating private enterprise to find jobs for the so-called hard-core unemployed; the sit-ins— as well as the organizational activity—of the Welfare Rights movement have won higher grants for welfare recipients in some cities and have helped to arouse the interest of the Nixon Administration in re-examining the Federal welfare program; and the uprisings by college and high school students have been effective in winning them a voice in their schools.

Needless to say, disruption also has disadvantages: the possibility that it will be accompanied by violence and that it will be followed by counter-disruption—for example, police or vigilante violence—and by political efforts of more powerful groups to wipe out the gains achieved through disruption. Thus, the backlash generated by the ghetto rebellions has been partly responsible for the cut-back in antipoverty and civil-rights efforts, and the disruptions by welfare recipients and college students are now producing repressive legislation against both groups. But disruption also creates serious costs for the rest of society, particularly in terms of the polarization of opposing groups, the hardening of attitudes among other citizens, and the hysterical atmosphere which then results in more repressive legislation. Clearly, disruption is not the ideal way for outvoted minorities to achieve their demands.

Nevertheless, disruption has become an accepted political technique, and may be used more widely in the nineteen-seventies, as other groups who feel they are being shortchanged by American democracy begin to voice their demands. Consequently, perhaps the most important domestic issue before the country today is whether outvoted minorities—in the cities and elsewhere—must resort to further disruption, or whether more peaceful and productive ways of meeting their needs can be found.

If the outvoted minorities are to be properly represented in the political structure, two kinds of changes are necessary. First, they must be counted fairly, so that they are actually consulted in the decision-making process, and are not overpowered by other minorities who would be outvoted were they not affluent enough to shape the political agenda. But since even a fairer counting of the voters would still leave the outvoted minorities with little influence, ways of restricting majority rule must be found when that rule is always deaf to their demands.

Majority rule is, of course, one of the unquestioned traditions of American political life, for the first axiom of democracy has always been that the majority should decide. But democracy is not inviolably equivalent to majority rule, for government of the people, by the people and for the people need not mean that a majority is "the people." Indeed, despite its traditional usage in democracies, majority rule is little more than an easily applied quantitative formula for solving the knotty problems of how the wishes of the people are to be determined. Moreover, traditions deserve to be re-examined from time to time, particularly if society has changed since they came into being.

And American society has changed since its government was created. What might be called *majoritarian democracy* was adopted when America was a small and primarily agrarian nation, with a great degree of economic and cultural homogeneity, few conflicting interest groups, and a since-rejected tradition that the propertyless should have fewer rights than the propertied. As a result, there were few serious disputes between majorities and minorities, at least until the Civil War, and majoritarian democracy could be said to have worked. Today, however, America is a highly heterogeneous and pluralistic nation, a society of minority groups, so to speak, and every important political decision requires an intense amount of negotiation and compromise so that enough minorities can be found to create a majority coalition. And even then, America is so pluralistic that not all minorities can be accommodated and must suffer all the consequences of being outvoted.

America has been a pluralistic society for almost a century, but the shortcomings of majority rule have not become a public issue before, mainly because previous generations of outvoted groups had other forms of redress. The outvoted of the past were concentrated among poor ethnic and racial minorities, as they are today, but in earlier years the economy needed their unskilled labor, so that they had less incentive to confront the majority, except to fight for the establishment of labor unions. Moreover, they had little reason even to think about majority rule, for government played a smaller role in the economy and in their lives.

Now all this has changed. When governmental policies and appropriations very nearly decide the fate of the poor, the black, draft-age college students, disadvantaged high school students and not so affluent blue-collar workers, such groups must deal with government; and more often than not, their demands are frustrated by the workings of majority rule.

Thus, it becomes quite pertinent to ask whether majoritarian democracy is still viable, and whether the tradition of majority rule should not be re-examined. If three-fourths of the voters or of a legislative body are agreed on a course of action, it is perhaps hard to argue against majority rule, but what if that rule seriously deprives the other fourth and drives it to disruption? And what if the majority is no more than 55 per cent, and consists only of an uneasy and temporary coalition of minorities? Or if the remaining 45 per cent are unable to obtain compromises from the slender majority?

I believe that the time has come to modernize American democracy and adapt it to the needs of a pluralistic society; in short, to create a *pluralistic democracy*. A pluralistic form of democracy would not do away with majority rule, but would require systems of proposing and disposing which take the needs of minorities into consideration, so that when minority rule has serious negative consequences, outvoted minorities would be able to achieve their most important demands, and not be forced to accept tokenism, or resort to despair or disruption.

Pluralistic democracy would allow the innumerable minorities of which America is made up to live together and share the country's resources more equitably, with full recognition of their various diversities. Legislation and appropriations would be based on the principle of "live and let live," with different programs of action for different groups whenever consensus is impossible. Groups of minorities could still coalesce into a majority, but other minorities would be able to choose their own ways of using public power and funds without being punished for it by a majority.

It would take a book to describe how the American political system might be restructured to create a pluralistic democracy, but I can suggest some specific proposals toward this goal. They fall into two categories: those that incorporate outvoted minorities into the political structure by increasing the responsiveness of governments to the diversity of citizen interests—and to all citizens; and those which restrict majority rule so as to prevent the tyrannization of minorities. Many of my proposals have drawbacks, and some are outright utopian, but I suggest them more to illustrate what has to be done than to provide immediate feasible solutions.

The responsiveness of governments can be increased in several ways.

First, the one man–one vote principle must be extended to all levels of government and the political parties. County and municipal bodies need to be reapportioned to eliminate gerrymandering of the poor and the black; party leaders, high and low, should be elected by party members, and party candidates should be nominated by primaries, rather than by conventions or closed meetings of party leaders.

Second, the seniority system must be abolished in all legislatures, so that politicians can no longer obtain undue power simply because their own districts re-elect them time after time. The power of committee chairmen who may represent only a small number of voters to block legislation wanted by a larger number must also be eliminated.

Third, the administrative agencies and their bureaucracies must become more accountable, perhaps by replacing appointive officers with elective ones, or by requiring such bodies to be run by elected boards of directors.

Fourth, all election campaigns should be funded by government, to discourage the near-monopoly that wealthy individuals now have in becoming candidates, and to prevent affluent interest groups from making demands on candidates as a price for financing their campaigns. If equal amounts—and plenty of free television time—were given to all candidates, even from third, fourth and fifth parties, the diversity of the population would be better represented in the electoral process. This might lead to election by plurality rather than majority, although in a highly diverse community or state such an outcome might not be undesirable, and runoffs can always be required to produce a final majority vote.

Fifth, methods by which the citizenry communicates with its elected representatives ought to be improved. Today, legislators tend to hear only from lobbyists, people in their own social circles, and the writers of letters and newspaper editorialists—a highly biased sample of their constituencies. Indeed, the only way an ordinary citizen can communicate is by organizing or writing letters. Of course, such methods make sure that a legislator hears only from deeply interested citizens, protecting him from being overwhelmed by too much feedback, but they also discriminate against equally interested people who cannot organize or write.

One possible solution is for governments to make postage-free forms available for people who want to write letters to their representatives, to be picked up in banks, post offices, stores and taverns. Another solution is for governments to finance the establishment of regular but independently run public-opinion polls on every major issue, so that government officials can obtain adequate feedback from a random sample of their constituents, and not only on the few issues a handful of private pollsters today decide are worth polling about.

Yet another solution is for governments to encourage people to organize politically, by allowing them to claim as tax deductions the dues and contributions to lobbying organizations (other than political parties). Limits on the size of such deductions would have to be set to prevent affluent minorities from using their funds to gain extra power; and organizations of the poor, whose members cannot afford to pay dues and do not benefit from tax deductions, could be given government grants if they could prove that two-thirds of their members were poor.

Feasible methods for increasing the power of minorities at the expense of majority rule are more difficult to formulate. One approach is to enhance the power of existing institutions that represent minority interests—for example, the courts and Cabinet departments. If constitutional amendments to establish an economic and racial bill of rights could be passed, for instance, a provision giving every American citizen the right to a job or an income above the poverty-line, the power of the poor would be increased somewhat.

Cabinet departments also represent minority interests, particularly at the Federal and state levels, although more often than not they speak for affluent minorities. Nevertheless, if the Office of

Economic Opportunity were raised to full Cabinet status and a Department of Minorities established in Washington, at least some new legislation and higher appropriations for the poor and the black would result. In other Cabinet departments, new bureaus should be set up to represent the interests of outvoted minorities; in Housing and Urban Development (now dominated by builders and mayors), to look after the needs of slum dwellers; in Health, Education and Welfare, to deal with the concerns of patients, students and welfare recipients, respectively. Moreover, the policy-making boards that I suggested earlier to oversee Cabinet departments and other administrative agencies should include their clients. Thus, all school boards should include some students; welfare departments, some welfare recipients; and housing agencies, some residents of public housing and F.H.A.-supported projects.

The financial power of poor minorities could be increased by extending the principles of the progressive income tax and of school-equalization payments to all governmental expenditures. Funding of government programs could be based in part on the incomes of eventual recipients, so that the lower their income, the higher the government grant. Poorer communities would thus obtain more Federal money per capita for all public services, and subsidies for mass transit programs would automatically be higher than for expressways to suburbia.

In addition, changes in the electoral system would be needed. One solution would be election by proportional representation. P.R. has not been popular in America, partly because it wreaks havoc with the two-party system, but it is not at all clear whether a pluralistic society is best served by a two-party system to begin with. Proportional representation by race or income would go against the American grain, but as long as racial and economic integration seems to be unachievable in the near future, this solution might be more desirable than forcing the poor or the black to resort to disruption.

Actually, proportional representation is already practiced informally in many places; in New York City, election slates have always been "balanced" to include candidates from the major ethnic and religious groups. Perhaps we should even think about proportional representation by occupational groups, for job concerns are often uppermost in the voters' choices. After all many pro-Wallace factory workers voted for Humphrey at the last minute, realizing that their job interests were more important than their fear of black militancy.

Another approach would restrict majority rule directly, by making all elections and voting procedures in legislative branches of government go through a two-step process, with majority rule applying only to the final step. This system, somewhat like the runoff used in some state and municipal elections, would require that if any legislative proposal or appropriation obtains at least 25 per cent of the total vote, it must be revised and voted on again until it is either approved by a majority or rejected by 76 per cent of the voting body. In the meantime, compromises would have to be made, either watering down the initial proposal so that a majority could accept it, or satisfying other demands of the minority through the time-honored practice of log-rolling so that they would allow 76 per cent of the voting body to reject the original proposal.

For example, if at least a quarter of a Congressional committee supported a strong negative income tax, it is likely that the second vote would produce at least a weaker version of the tax that the majority could live with. Of course, such a system would work only if outvoted minority groups were able to elect representatives in the first place. (Also, it is always possible that legislators who favored a highly regressive income tax or segregationist policies would be able to obtain legislation for *their* minorities, but if an economic and racial bill of rights were added to the Constitution, such legislation would be thrown out by the courts.)

Outvoted minorities can also achieve greater political power by the alteration of existing political boundaries and powers so that they could even become majorities in their own bailiwicks. Current proposals for decentralization and community control are boundary-altering schemes with just this political consequence, and some of the disadvantages of these schemes today could be alleviated by my previous proposal for progressive methods of government funding to provide more money to poorer communities.

But the concept of redrawing boundaries ought to be applied

more broadly, for many existing political subdivisions are anachronistic. For example, it is difficult to justify the existence of
many of the states as political units today, and it might be useful to think about creating smaller and more homogeneous units
in highly urbanized parts of the country, perhaps of county size,
particularly in order to reduce the number of outvoted minorities.
(Norman Mailer has suggested just that in proposing statehood
for New York City.)

Along the same line, the old idea of replacing geographical political units by groupings along economic and other interests deserves re-examination. For instance, the welfare recipient's lot
would probably be improved if he or she became part of a regional
governmental body of welfare recipients which could determine
how the welfare system ought to be run.

Sometimes, outvoted minorities are tyrannized because their demands are diametrically opposed to the majority's. When this happens within a school or other institution, the minority should have
the right to secede, establishing its own institution without being
financially punished by the majority. If some parents want a Sum-
merhill education for their children, they should be given tax
money to start their own school, just as determined black nationalists should be free to build their own community if and when
public aid for new towns becomes available. In a pluralistic nation,
all impulses for diversity that do not clearly harm the rest of society
should be encouraged.

Finally, changes in the rules of the political system must be
supplemented by changes in the economic system, for ultimately
it is the major obstacle to improving the lot of many outvoted
minorities—and even of the unorganized majority. Some of my
earlier proposals are equally applicable here.

The one man–one vote principle might be extended to stockholders who elect corporate boards of directors; a Cabinet department to represent consumers and other corporate customers
should be set up; feedback from stockholders and customers to the
corporate "legislature" should be improved, and they, as well as
workers, should sit on corporate boards. In an era when many
firms are subsidized by government contracts and tax credits, it

is certainly possible to argue that at least such firms should become more democratic.

Most of the proposals for a pluralistic democracy are purposely intended to enhance the power of poor and black minorities; for, as I noted earlier, this seems to me the only way of solving the problems of the cities. But such a democracy is needed by all minorities who stand in danger of being outvoted by a majority, whatever their income or color. As the current demands of more people for greater equality and more control over their lives accelerate, and the role of government in society continues to mount at the same time, the need for more political pluralism will become increasingly urgent. What we so inaccurately describe as the urban crisis is in reality the beginning of a national political crisis. But it is also an opportunity for Americans to develop new ways of living together.

Part **4**

LEADERS IN
CHANGE: A SET
OF PROFILES

DR. MARTIN LUTHER KING, JR., was perhaps the most outstanding leader in American history in effecting change in the nation's race relations. Certainly he was the dominant figure of the sixties. He was an agent of social change not only in those movements he led directly, such as the Montgomery bus boycott; he served also as a symbol, a rallying point, and an inspiration. His dream became the dream of millions of Americans, black and white.

Social change requires an effort to unlearn old behavior patterns as well as an effort to learn and practice new ones. People therefore naturally resist change unless they can see some advantage in relearning basic behavior patterns. The more any proposed change seems to threaten traditional culture values, the more likely people are to resist it. People are particularly likely to resist changes that they see as forced upon their group by outsiders. As armies of occupation know (and as Americans have seen in the case of Office of Education guidelines for desegregation in the Deep South), changes that seem to be imposed from the outside are likely to be greeted with overt compliance and covert resistance.

When people want change, however, they can absorb massive alterations in the fabric of their society with minimal difficulty. Change requires adjustment and is to some extent necessarily hard on people. But people often accept change with alacrity when it will demonstrably make life more secure (polio vaccine), less costly (nylon instead of silk hose), easier (electric refrigerator), or more fun (television).

The people most likely to push for innovation are those who are in some sense marginal to the society. Race relations leaders are a good example. They act as agents of change not only because they seek to better themselves and their people but because they have less investment in the traditional social structure. The impetus to alter the social structure seldom originates with those in control of it.

A look at leaders in the realm of race relations, then, offers us more than a set of personality portraits. Their behavior and the responses of the social order to their thrusts for change cast in silhouette the present structure of society, the points of resistance to change, and the areas of social life most adaptable to new thoughts and ways.

There Is No Rest for Roy Wilkins

by Martin Arnold

"IN MY YOUTH, godammit, the newspapers did not call a Negro woman a beauty. A Negro man was called a black—a good word now but not then—and a rapist and a clown. There *were* no demonstrations and parades. Who the hell did it? Who got them to allow the demonstrations? What is allowed today is affected by today's climate—the opportunities opened up for the kids by the people taking part in the civil-rights fight 20 years ago and more."

Slender, stoop-shouldered, the slight bulge of his years pushing out from under his neat gray tweed vest, Roy Wilkins, still dedicated, still rebellious, was sitting before a television set, watching Richard Nixon inaugurated as President of the United States.

In his 69th year, when a man should be resting, Wilkins is still enduring what the 19th-century black abolitionist Frederick Douglass called the "awful roar" of struggle. Only now, to his great surprise, the "awful roar" is often sounded by some of his own people, the blacks who are young and militant—and he is the target. So, like a pontiff, a man of great vanity and commanding influence, he takes what he considers the long view of history. He

From the *New York Times Magazine,* September 28, 1969, copyright © 1969 by The New York Times Company.

issues biting encyclicals against those blacks who would exchange his theology of integration for separatism and who, in the process, would tear down his church, the National Association for the Advancement of Colored People. There is no rest for Roy Wilkins.

Wilkins had received two invitations to attend the Nixon inauguration; but in the style and code of black politics, a black leader simply does not go to the inauguration of a Republican President—not if he is to retain any following or any power. And if there is one thing Roy Wilkins understands, it is power.

He watched Nixon being sworn in on television, sizing him up, trying to get a reading of Nixon the President, as opposed to Nixon the Vice President and Nixon the Presidential candidate— all the time letting those watching with him know that he is a man accustomed to sizing up Presidents.

"This inaugural's full of squares, full of lawyers. There are no swingers there like me," he said. He mocked the fact that President-elect Nixon had actually arrived on time for his inaugural concert the previous night: "Kennedy was never on time; Johnson was always comfortably late."

Someone asked him if he could pick up the telephone and get President Nixon on the other end. "I wouldn't say that," he replied. "With a President you don't do that unless he himself has put you in a special category—one known to the White House switchboard and the President's appointments secretary. With Kennedy or Johnson, I had no difficulty getting to them, either in person or on the telephone."

The point was made, and if emphasis were needed, one could look on his desk and see, dated three days previously, a "Dear Roy" letter from Lyndon Johnson thanking Wilkins for "the selfless friendship you gave me throughout my Presidency." (On Inaugural Day, as one of his last official acts, Johnson awarded Wilkins the nation's highest civilian award, the Freedom Medal.)

Wilkins turned back to the television set. An aide noted the sparsity of black faces at the inaugural. "This is an integrated crowd," Wilkins retorted. "What *you* want is a Jim Crow crowd." When "The Star-Spangled Banner" was played, Wilkins sang along—and he tapped his feet in time as the Marine band saluted the new Republican President with "Hail to the Chief."

By April, Wilkins was not so casual about "hailing the Chief." Clifford L. Alexander, Jr., a black, had felt forced to resign as chairman of the Equal Employment Opportunity Commission, citing Nixon's "lack of support." There were indications that the Nixon Administration would allow more flexible school desegregation guidelines—as a sop to Southern Republicans.

By July, Wilkins was speaking in most un-Wilkins-like terms. The new school guidelines were "almost enough to make you vomit." The selection of Warren Burger as Chief Justice of the United States was a disappointment. And the proposed elevation of Clement F. Haynsworth, Jr., to the Supreme Court "was a deadly way of negating completely the legislative victories won through the hardest effort by the nation's minority of black citizens."

Was a new, tougher, more militant Roy Wilkins surfacing? Was the old man trying to recapture some of the youthful militant support he had lost? Most observers thought otherwise. What was emerging was not a new Wilkins, but a new enemy: the Nixon Administration. During the Kennedy-Johnson years, the N.A.-A.C.P. had functioned more or less as an arm of the Democratic party. Neither Kennedy nor Johnson had entirely pleased Wilkins, but they were, he felt, at least on his side, and they were headed in the right direction.

The black youths who were marching in the streets were not old enough to recall that Wilkins had talked tough before—during the Eisenhower years, for example. Now—as then—he suits his tactics to his enemy. For the Democrats he held out the carrot; for Nixon he is brandishing the stick.

He told this year's N.A.A.C.P. convention in Jackson, Miss., that the organization was confronted with "a hostile Administration that doesn't mean us any good." He would attack.

The young militants who had disrupted the 1968 convention in Atlantic City were not among his listeners this year. They had left the organization or, in the words of one N.A.A.C.P. leader, they had been "purged." The remaining Young Turks, as they call themselves, pledged their "respect and allegiance" to the leader —if Wilkins was not all he should be, at least he was in the fight against Nixon.

Had he gone even further on other issues—such as supporting black dormitories for black students—he might have been able to regain some support from the militant black youths. But Wilkins really does not care for such support, and in his perspective on history, that kind of support is not very important. So in June, as if to make that point very clear, he ended his lecture at the C.W. Post College commencement this way: "Knuckling under to raucous demands for blanket amnesty for those detained for acts of trespass, violence and destruction is not a contribution to the development of fiber in white or black youths." Once again, he spoke out against the concept of "non-negotiable" demands by black militants, and against separatist movements. He would fight, but he would fight his way, on his terms.

Wilkins is a politician in the cause of civil rights and, like all successful politicians, like Nixon, he has mastered the mechanics of power. "The Negro has to be a superb diplomat and a great strategist," Wilkins once said. "He has to parlay what actual power he has along with the goodwill of the white majority. He has to devise and pursue those philosophies and activities which will least alienate the white majority opinion. And that doesn't mean that the Negro has to indulge in boot-licking. But he must gain the sympathy of the large majority of the American public. He must also seek to make an identification with the American tradition."

Following this blueprint, Wilkins became the chief advocate of the use of constitutional means to achieve black civil rights. In the American tradition, he involved Presidents, legislatures and the courts in the construction of the logical and legalistic engine that is integration. Wilkins considers himself the architect.

The outstanding monument to the Wilkins method is the 1954 Supreme Court decision that overthrew the doctrine of "separate but equal" facilities in public education. It is, he believes, the greatest American public document since the Emancipation Proclamation. "It is very rare for a person in the civil-rights movement—actually in it—to live to see so many of his goals in sight."

Yet the black revolution is a formless, changing movement. The chief enemy of 1954, the bigoted Southerner, has been replaced by the bigoted Northerner—the landlord, the union leader, the school teacher, the college dean and now, in Wilkins's view, the national Administration. Angry young militants demand black separatism instead of integration; they opt for violent demonstrations in lieu of court proceedings. The establishment, the entire system, has come under attack—and for many young blacks, that includes Wilkins and the N.A.A.C.P.

"Integration as a talking point is dead," a prominent young Negro journalist says. "Black people are trying to work out our own problems. We're putting down white help, not seeking it, like Wilkins does."

Another young Negro writer, his eyes flashing in anger, ostracizes Wilkins as an "Uncle Tom" and adds: "We consider integration not productive at this time, certainly not compared to the concept of black people being totally independent."

The rage against Wilkins reached a new peak last spring with the groundswell of black activism in the nation's colleges. He refused, for example, to tie in the Vietnam war with the civil-rights movement, and he denounced black students for bringing guns onto the Cornell campus. Today, he still threatens to challenge in the courts the concept, espoused by black students, of separate black dormitories and courses of study. "If the country gives racial control to a dormitory or an art center," he says, "finally everything in the country will be racially controlled and we'll be right back at the point where we started."

A young black intellectual shouts, "Betrayal." Wilkins, he says, "has done the worst thing any black man could do. By not supporting the students, he has let the white man use him. The white press, public officials, they point to Wilkins and say, 'See, he agrees with us.' Wilkins has made himself irrelevant to the blacks. Worse, he is helping our enemies."

Roy Innis, national director of the Congress of Racial Equality, insists that the student demands express a legitimate need for "black identity, self-awareness and togetherness." And he calls for Wilkins to "withdraw from the stage" and leave the struggle he helped launch to younger men. Wilkins doesn't even bother to note that CORE, under Innis's direction, has become virtually nonexistent as a national civil-rights group—but such attacks cannot but strike deep.

Wilkins tries to respond to his critics with a cool, understated disdain. He stares ahead, as if at a vision only he can see, and runs his long, slim fingers slowly back and forth across his face. "I am sorry to say I have not had too much contact with the young black militants," he will comment. "I have talked to their groups and such, but I imagine they don't think too much of me. And I'm not too excited about their suggestions for solving problems." Are Detroit and Newark any better for the Negroes now after the rioting? Clearly, he says, the answer is no. He is asked about the new hospital and new garbage collection program in Watts: would they have come without the riots? "Perhaps not so soon. They are good things, but they are small things. Tokenism." Rioting has changed little for the blacks, he feels—except perhaps to harden the white backlash. He adds that the moderate black is strongly against violence and separatism, and that the moderate black is the average black.

The Wilkins way, he insists, is the right way: "The whole point of the N.A.A.C.P. was to establish the Negro as a legal entity, with the rights and privileges of a citizen. Who did that? We did that. We are still doing that. Who goes into court in some small Southern city because a colored woman is earning only $1 an hour doing the same work a white woman gets paid $2.50 an hour for? We do, every week, almost. Judicial rights and legislative approval, that's our continuing fight."

Wilkins believes that the country—even the Nixon Administration—can be moved by negotiation, by litigation, by the black man's increasing voting power and by public pressure, carefully nurtured by Wilkins's pronouncements which increase in decibel count only to keep up with the needs of the moment.

"Of course, there wasn't any real need for Roy to blast off at Johnson," a friend says. "Not that the Johnson Administration was perfect, but it was pretty well committed to eliminating segregation and doing something about the blacks. This Administration, on the other hand, may become more committed as Roy sounds off. Rioting certainly wouldn't get very far with this group in Washington."

Wilkins's response to his critics often exhibits a philosophical schizophrenia of sorts. He bends a bit in the direction of the young militants, snaps back, bends again: "Negro people, particularly the youth, are outraged, angered, frustrated. They do not want to crawl. They want to run, and so do I. But civil rights do not automatically give a man the esteem of his fellows, and the young Negroes must realize that they also need this esteem."

The realization has not come, however, and the attacks have grown ever sharper. Even within his own N.A.A.C.P., criticism of Wilkins's leadership and policies has become the daily fare of the pioneer activist and friend of Presidents.

The career of Roy Wilkins is, in its way, a classic black example of the Horatio Alger syndrome that so enrages his young critics. His father, William, was born and raised on a sharecropper farm in Holly Springs, Miss., where he went to Rust College. For all his better-than-average Negro education, the elder Wilkins "drove mules and plows" before he fled Holly Springs in 1900 "because he was considered a troublemaker, who didn't like the way Negroes were treated." In St. Louis, where Roy was born on Aug. 30, 1901, his father went to work as a foreman in a brick kiln. When Roy was 4, his mother died, and he went with his younger sister and younger brother to live in St. Paul with an aunt and uncle, Mr. and Mrs. Samuel Williams. (His sister died in 1927 and his brother died in 1941.)

For "the great sum of $85 a month," Williams was the private carman on the private railroad car of the president of the Northern Pacific Railroad. He taught Wilkins that if a Negro wanted to get ahead, he had to be educated and neat, have learning and clean fingernails. Wilkins attended the integrated Mechanic Arts High School, a block from the State Capitol; he was editor of the school newspaper. At the University of Minnesota, Wilkins majored in sociology, supporting himself as a Pullman car waiter, redcap and slaughterhouse worker. He was also night editor of the school paper, The Minnesota Daily, and editor of a black weekly, The St. Paul Appeal.

While still a student, Wilkins became secretary of the local N.A.A.C.P. chapter. And the lynching of a black in Duluth prompted him to enter the university's oratorical contest with a strong antilynching speech that won first prize. After receiving his B.A. degree in 1923, he immediately went to work for The Kansas

City (Mo.) Call, a leading black weekly, and soon became its managing editor.

In 1931, Wilkins left The Call and came to New York to work for the N.A.A.C.P. "One of my first jobs was to go South to investigate the conditions among Negroes who were working to build the levees on the Mississippi River. They made 10 cents an hour. Two dollars and fifty cents a day was tops for a Caterpillar driver, and you know how many Negroes had those jobs.

"I lived in the camps and earned 10 cents an hour. We tried to sneak pictures of the work. You didn't say you were from the N.A.A.C.P. It would have meant being lynched.

"It used to be that picketing, except for a labor cause, was against the law. [In 1963, Wilkins was arrested while picketing a Woolworth store in Jackson, Miss., along with the late Medgar Evers, who was shot from ambush just 12 days later.] We went to court over that, and won the right for these kids to march and picket now. I understand their impatience. I share it, but they should have some idea what it has taken to get them their right to raise hell. And before there's a final victory, it will take more than just loud talk."

In his office, which is spare like the man himself, Wilkins leans back in his chair. The walls are beige, the motif early American. It looks as if it had been decorated with little thought, slapped together in a hurry—the office of a man secure in his power with no need for plush-carpet trappings. He points to several automobile models he has made. "I'm a fast-car buff. Maybe if the kids knew that, they'd like me better. I like a car that can handle, that has an easy-steering wheel. I like a car that goes when it's supposed to go. My wife has got a Plymouth Barracuda. I put a four-barrel carburetor on it. I drive a black TR-3. It's 8 years old. It's my only recreation, my only hobby."

Wilkins enjoys words—long words, old words, words not in common usage (he will speak of the "dandelion spread of segregation" or refer to his problems as "nettles"). He slips them into his conversations, his speeches, his news conferences. "If you went to school," he'll tell a puzzled reporter, "you should know what it means." When a book of his writings was published, he sent a copy to a black journalist with this inscription: "Every sentence a gem, Tom." The journalist isn't sure the comment was in jest.

The love of words finds expression, too, in a variety of writing projects: speeches, a weekly newspaper column appearing in 44 papers and frequent editorials for the association magazine, Crisis. Some of the editorials—such as that which denounced demands for segregated black enclaves on campus—are quoted in the national white press, often on the front pages.

A man of aloof charm, Wilkins has few friends, many acquaintances. Of course, the 14-hour day he normally spends on the job allows him little time for purely social matters. But he also has the kind of mind that is more concerned with specific detail and subjects of consequence than with the fuzzy generalizations that make up so much of what passes for social intercourse. He is quickly bored. He is also a man who seems to like his loneliness, his isolated pinnacle.

In 1946, Wilkins underwent stomach surgery for cancer, and he has since refrained from the cigars and occasional cocktail he once enjoyed. He has an inner will, and is generally tougher than his fragile appearance would suggest. Though he is several inches shorter than 6 feet, one has the feeling he is in fact a tall man— he is so slender, except for the small paunch, and his movements are so graceful.

He and his wife, the former Aminda Badeau (a social worker), live in an apartment in Queens. They have no children, and Wilkins's only living blood relative is a nephew, Roger Wilkins, a 36-year-old attorney who works in the field of urban affairs for the Ford Foundation.

"We are good friends," the younger Wilkins says, "but he is not a substitute father to me. Sometimes I know he looks upon me with fatherly pride, but our relationship is not a give-and-take relationship. I don't ask advice and assistance, and he doesn't offer it.

"He is this type of man: Once when Vice President Humphrey wanted to appoint me to a civil-rights committee, he called my uncle and asked him if he should. The answer was prompt: 'No, you should not appoint him.' My uncle didn't want to be compromised. Another time, when I had just gotten out of law school, a member of a very prominent law firm called him and asked him,

'Do you have a nephew named Roger?' He said he did. When the man asked him if I should be hired, he said, 'Well, how do you usually judge people you are going to hire? Judge Roger the same way, hire him or not, as you would anyone else.' And then he hung up. He is a very proud, courageous man, and I love him."

Roger Wilkins, like so many young black leaders, does not always agree with his uncle's actions and attitudes. But he says, "I wouldn't think of trying to change his beliefs. He was in civil rights before I was born."

Wilkins was elected N.A.A.C.P. executive secretary (the title is now executive director) on April 11, 1955, following the death of Walter White. The organization is the oldest (founded in 1909) and the largest (450,673 members as of December, 1968) and richest ($3.2 million income last year) civil-rights organization in the country. It is run, in theory, by a 60-man board of directors. Most of the board members are in their 60's, and they include old-line white liberals, such as Walter Reuther, who were fighting the civil-rights battles 20 and 30 years ago and whose loyalty is to Wilkins. The Young Turks charge (without proof) that the association loads its annual conventions in Wilkins's favor by paying poor blacks "to come up from the South and vote at meetings to keep Roy in control." True or not, board or no, the N.A.A.C.P. is in fact run by Wilkins alone.

The financial strength of the association today is in part the result of a Government ruling four years ago that contributions to its educational and legal programs were tax-exempt charities. That decision started a flow of gifts from philanthropists in general, the Ford, Rockefeller and Carnegie Foundations in particular. Such big-money sources provided somewhat over half of the N.A.-A.C.P.'s income last year. The remainder came from the members —from dues (ranging from $2 a year to a $500 lifetime membership), from the local chapters (which raise money at cake sales and rallies) and from subscriptions (at $1.50 a year) to Crisis, which is published 10 times a year.

The N.A.A.C.P. is the only black organization of national influence that has not suffered financially—or lost other, less tangible support—because of the tensions between blacks and Jews, who in this country make up a large share of the politically liberal community. The association's money—other than the foundation funds—has traditionally come from blacks, who constitute at least 90 per cent of the membership, not from white liberals.

Since N.A.A.C.P. counsel (now Supreme Court Justice) Thurgood Marshall argued the school desegregation case to a successful conclusion in 1954, the association's membership has nearly doubled. But the figures are somewhat misleading. Many of the 1,300 branches of record are wholly inactive. And even among active branches, the percentage of membership participation is sometimes minimal. The Harlem branch, for example, is the largest in the country with 7,000 members—but no more than a few hundred generally show up for the monthly meetings.

As Gloster B. Current, director of the branches, will admit, the association is middle-class oriented. "The typical branch official," Current says, "has a relatively secure income, probably as a minister, doctor or lawyer, is a churchgoer and belongs to at least one fraternal organization."

In the South, members are either professionals and their families or laborers, who are poor by white standards but middle-class by Southern black standards. In the North, Midwest and West, most members are school teachers, sociologists and up-and-coming black politicians.

Wilkins denies it, but the whole structure is held together by the force of his personality and the love that the members have for him. "Roy is in demand every night of the year," says John Morsell, the assistant executive director. "If he let himself, he could be speaking to chapters 365 nights a year. The members want to see him, touch him, hear him. There's nothing else that really holds them. We don't give money to local chapters. We can't really make them do things. It's just Roy Wilkins. They'll do it for him."

The tone of the New York headquarters, where Roy reigns, is brisk, businesslike, quiet. An occasional youth in a cowboy hat or an African dashiki can be seen in the corridors, but the staff consists in the main of neatly dressed black women—not in miniskirts—and black men in three-button suits, button-down shirts and striped ties.

Wilkins is constantly away from the office on his travels in pursuit of the money and influence to fuel his civil-rights machine. Recently he had a two-week schedule that took him to South Carolina, Indiana, Washington, D. C. (twice), New Jersey, Illinois, Texas, Virginia, Pennsylvania and Georgia. Yet his presence hovers over the office whether he's in town or out.

He is not so popular with his staff as with the association's members. "I think of him as a very distant man," says a former N.A.A.C.P. executive. "He is sort of a figure rather than a human being. I had no personal, human contact with him. A lot of the workers were afraid of him. I never heard anyone say they loved him or held him in awe."

Within the last few years, the split between civil-rights traditionalists and the new breed of black militants has brought turmoil to the organization. Many younger N.A.A.C.P. members and staff feel that the Wilkins methods are no longer effective, that the organization has become a *de facto* arm of a go-slow Federal Government. This split has not been a source of pride to Wilkins. And like any strong man faced with a revolution from within, he has moved to squash it, firmly, before it squashes him.

Last summer, at the association's 59th annual convention, 600 youth delegates asked to form an autonomous and more militant organization. The proposal was denied, and the youths staged a walkout.

In the ensuing controversy, Chester Lewis, a 40-year-old Wichita, Kan., attorney, resigned from the association's board. "I was completely fed up. I felt the association no longer was relevant to the needs of the black people. We need viable black power, and the severest critic of black power is Wilkins."

More recently, an article in this magazine produced another crisis between the young and old in the association. The article, written by a young white N.A.A.C.P. staff member, Lewis M. Steel, charged that the Supreme Court was not a libertarian body, that it only attacked the "overtly obnoxious" discrimination patterns in the country and thus helped maintain the status quo. Twenty-five members of the association's board met the following day, while Wilkins was returning home from Europe aboard an ocean liner, and voted unanimously to discharge Steel without a hearing. The entire legal staff including its chief, Robert L. Carter, quit in protest. Wilkins supported the decision.

The future of the N.A.A.C.P. depends in large measure upon who succeeds Wilkins. The matter has apparently been given little thought, and even less has been done to bring a potential successor into the association's power structure (one of the few ways in which the organization is not run exactly like a large corporation). Most speculation centers around Criminal Court Judge William Booth, formerly Human Rights Commissioner under Mayor Lindsay, and Edward McClellan, a bright, articulate former policeman, who is the N.A.A.C.P.'s urban program director for the Chicago area. But as one member says, "Roy doesn't believe he's going to die, so why worry about a successor?"

Wilkins says he is planning to strike out in new directions to develop leadership and economic power in the city slums, where the association is weakest. He admits that the N.A.A.C.P. has a lot of catching up to do. "We were, very frankly, caught off guard. We were geared up for programs of opposition—telling people, 'Don't let the white man do that to you'—and when the barriers started falling, we were not ready to make a shift. Our problem is that we offer the young people nothing spectacular." He admits that other, more militant, leaders do.

The N.A.A.C.P. effort to compete for the young people involves placement of urban program directors in major cities to work in the ghettos. Their assignment: to find new black leadership, to train black urbanists. It has recently approved local branch sponsorship of low-income housing.

The N.A.A.C.P. is also planning a massive legal attack, supported by peaceful demonstrations if necessary, against what Herbert Hill, its labor director, calls "organized labor's racial stranglehold" on hiring practices. The particular target is the building trades unions, which Williams has called "the last bastion against the employment of Negro workers as a policy."

The Federal Model Cities program is the first target. The N.A.A.C.P. will attempt to halt the program unless more minority workers are employed in the building of model cities. Similar efforts will be made to stop all housing built with Federal, state or city funds where such discrimination is practiced.

How successful these efforts to "up-date" the organization will be remains to be seen. The necessity for some action is underlined by Dr. Kenneth Clark, the distinguished black psychologist:

"The problem is, the N.A.A.C.P. and Wilkins are not doing the job now. The work they did in the past brought us to the point where the urban crisis has become uppermost in importance. But the N.A.A.C.P. is not solving that crisis. Neither are the so-called militants. Who is? I don't know the answer, but I think Wilkins and the N.A.A.C.P. will have to find the answer or become irrelevant."

One thing is certain: as long as Roy Wilkins remains in his post, part of the organization's "relevance" will be its connection and, if possible, cooperation with the white power structure.

On that day last winter when President Nixon was inaugurated, after the Chief had been hailed, Wilkins turned away from the television set and spoke briefly of the new man in the White House, a man he looks upon with little favor. Yet Wilkins was somewhat optimistic: "I tend to believe the times will shape him. Nixon knows about the problems of the black people, the oil people, the textile people. He cannot help but know about every element of the American people. He may not speak their precise language, but he knows all about them."

Wilkins is not so sanguine now. He is tightening his belt for the battle. Perhaps with some pushing and speaking out and some new law suits, Nixon can be moved. Maybe 1970 will produce a more liberal Congress, particularly if the war in Vietnam continues. Maybe, if everything works just right, and the old Wilkins machine is running smoothly, it's just possible that in four years Wilkins will be willing to accept a "Dear Roy" letter from Dick Nixon. It doesn't look likely now, but with two men who have mastered the mechanics of power, it is possible.

Meanwhile, the fight for the unsegregated world will go on. "When it's won," Wilkins says, "the youths who are marching now will realize that there's going to be beer, and double-headers with the Yankees, and ice cream, and mortgages and taxes, and all the things that the whites have in their world, and tedium, too. It's not going to be heaven."

Old Con, Black Panther, Brilliant Writer, and Quintessential American

by Harvey Swados

If Jefferson was around today, he'd be wearing love beads, reading Eldridge Cleaver and looking all over for information.—
ISHMAEL REED.

THIS WHIMSY of a young black humorist (black in both senses) asserts a proposition that obviously cannot be proved. But Reed is unarguably on target insofar as his tribute to the Founding Fathers ("America was set up by some very groovy people. Jefferson was a blind racist, but on many other matters he was very correct") points to Eldridge Cleaver as a figure at the very heart of the contemporary scene. For Cleaver, the essayist and agitator now a fugitive from the land in which a year ago he ran for the Presidency, speaks as does almost no one else to the young black

From the *New York Times Magazine,* September 7, 1969, copyright © 1969 by The New York Times Company.

community, to the white student community, and to the community of American writers who came to his defense when the California authorities were trying to throw him back into the prison in which he had already spent half of his adult life.

There are those, however, to whom Eldridge Cleaver does not speak. It is not easy to say whether they are put off because they have read reports of his tediously scabrous speeches or because they have not read his eloquent essays. In any case, there can be little doubt that a portion of the power with which he appeals to the young derives from the very fact that he frightens the old.

In what Pierre Boulez has aptly called "the blotter society," the day that Cleaver makes the cover of Time will mark the beginning of his decline; to be Man of the Yeared or New Yorkerized is to be defanged, tamed, Baldwinized. "Every fury on earth has been absorbed in time, as art, or as religion, or as authority in one form or another. The deadliest blow the enemy of the human soul can strike is to do fury honor," wrote James Agee in "Let Us Now Praise Famous Men." "Swift, Blake, Beethoven, Christ, Joyce, Kafka, name me a one who has not been thus castrated. Official acceptance is the one unmistakable symptom that salvation is beaten again. . . ."

At this point, official acceptance has not yet come to Eldridge Cleaver, nor is it likely that it will in the immediate future. And so salvation remains possible.

Eldridge Cleaver was born in Wabbaseka, Ark., in 1935 to Leroy and Thelma Cleaver, his father a pianist, his mother a grade-school teacher. When Leroy Cleaver became a waiter on the Super Chief, the family moved to Phoenix and then on to Los Angeles. But by the time Eldridge was enrolled in Abraham Lincoln Junior High, his parents had separated and he was picked up for bicycle theft and shipped off to the Fred C. Nelles School for Boys, where he learned about hustling pot. It was for this crime, these days routinely practiced by middle-class college boys for pocket money, that he was sent to the Preston School of Industry in 1953 and then to Soledad. His secondary education, begun at Belmont High School, where he had just made the football team, was completed in prison. There, too, he became an omnivorous reader and evolved a philosophical theory justifying rape as "an insurrectionary act."

During 11 months of freedom, he put outrageous theory into practice, "consciously, deliberately, willfully, methodically" raping white women. When he was apprehended, he was sentenced to 2 to 14 years for assault with intent to kill.

Now Eldridge Cleaver was ready to be processed into that industrial waste which is the human product of our detention system. But he was endowed with exceptional mental equipment.

"After I returned to prison," he later wrote, "I took a long look at myself and for the first time in my life admitted that I was wrong, that I had gone astray—astray not so much from the white man's law as from being human, civilized—for I could not approve the act of rape. Even though I had some insight into my own motivation, I did not feel justified. I lost my self-respect. My pride as a man dissolved and my whole fragile structure seemed to collapse, completely shattered. That is why I started to write. To save myself."

And he discovered the Black Muslims, whose pride, abnegation and discipline appealed to him as to thousands of other convicts across the country. During this period, he began to correspond with sympathetic attorneys on the outside. Charles R. Garry, the veteran West Coast lawyer who was subsequently to become counsel for the Black Panthers, remembers receiving letters from Cleaver in 1960 that were "typically narrow" in their sectarian religious approach to prison problems.

It was only when he came into contact with the civil-rights lawyer Beverly Axelrod that Cleaver, who had followed Malcolm X in his stunning split with Elijah Muhammad, saw another path for himself. His admiration for Miss Axelrod grew into a kind of adoration even as his devotion to Malcolm paralleled the latter's growth from gangsterdom to black mysticism to a maturing racial and political consciousness. With the assassination of Malcolm, Cleaver broke definitively with the Black Muslims and began the search for a new allegiance; at the same time, the impassioned efforts of Beverly Axelrod were introducing him to the basically white literary world.

Edward Keating, the West Coast Catholic layman who was one of the founders of Ramparts, recalls meeting Miss Axelrod at an anti–Vietnam war rally in the summer of 1965. "I've got a client who's a would-be writer," she said, and she handed Keating a pile of manuscript "about an inch and a half high" to read over the weekend. He found the writing flawed but impressive, and suggested that Miss Axelrod bring her client around for an editorial discussion. "That won't be so easy," she replied. "He's in Folsom prison."

Keating, himself a lawyer and the first editor to work with Cleaver, went to Folsom to meet him. "I thought him a very powerful writer, and I was curious as to what he'd be like. This great big, black man walked up, and my very first impression was of how gentle his handshake was. We made small talk about books for a while—I'd brought him some—but he was clearly excited that I cared about his writing."

Keating cared enough to send some of it East, to Maxwell Geismar, Thomas Merton, Norman Mailer and John Howard Griffin. Their enthusiastic response was transmitted to the authorities, but it was not until November, 1966, that Cleaver was paroled. By then he had already written most of the pieces—social commentary, letters, polemics—which were to make him a national figure when gathered together in "Soul on Ice."

He had read widely if superficially, and had discovered the exhilaration that comes from the written expression of utter frankness. Searching his soul and his past, he found that he had the power to commit to paper his reflections on his early life ("Looking back, I see that I was in a frantic, wild and completely abandoned frame of mind"), on his scattered reading (the Zen Buddhism of Alan Watts, for example, reminded him "of a slick advertisement for a labor-saving device, aimed at the American housewife, out of the center page of Life magazine"), on his fascination with Malcolm X ("It was like watching a master do a dance with death on a high-strung tightrope"), on the subculture of prison life ("Negro convicts, basically, rather than see themselves as criminals and perpetrators of misdeeds, look upon themselves as prisoners of war, the victims of a vicious, dog-eat-dog social system that is so heinous as to cancel out their own malefactions").

From these elements evolved a philosophy which was to prove enormously attractive to the young and the disaffected, combining as it did an identification with the first and a commitment to the second. "It is among the white youth of the world that the greatest change is taking place," he wrote. "It is they who are experiencing the great psychic pain of waking into consciousness to find their inherited heroes turned by events into villains. . . . Their revolt is deeper than single-issue protest."

When to this Cleaver added the brew of psychosexuality as essential to an understanding of such varied phenomena as the "national-communal pagan rituals" of spectator sports, the Negro's struggle for identity, rock 'n' roll, the beatniks (derided by "the deep-frozen geeks of the Hot-Dog-and-Malted-Milk Set"), politics and literature, it was inevitable that he himself should become a culture hero, prepared to supplant Ellison and Baldwin. He was a "novelist" who had not yet written a novel, a free spirit who had spent long years in prison liberating himself.

Several of his forays into the tangled symbiosis of sexuality and the American past—"The Allegory of the Black Eunuchs" and "The Primeval Mitosis"—seem to me a mishmash of invaluable insights and half-digested Lawrencian pomposities about such capitalized entities as the Omnipotent Administrator, the Primeval Sphere, the Unitary Sexual Image, the Brute Power Function, the Supermasculine Menial, the Ultrafeminine and the Amazon. But when he focuses, in "Notes on a Native Son," upon a target that is both sharply defined and vulnerable, he draws blood.

Commencing this essay shrewdly with a warm tribute to James Baldwin—as Baldwin in his time had begun a polemic against Richard Wright with a similar tribute—Cleaver goes on to associate himself wholeheartedly with the Norman Mailer of "The White Negro" and to assault Baldwin's "total hatred of the blacks, particularly of himself, and the most shameful, fanatical, fawning, sycophantic love of the whites that one can find in the writings of any black American writer of note in our time." Baldwin's work "is the fruit of a tree with a poison root. Such succulent fruit, such a painful tree, what a malignant root!" At the end, Cleaver locates the poison in homosexuality: "I, for one, do not think homosexuality is the latest advance over heterosexuality on the scale of human evolution. Homosexuality is a sickness, just as are baby rape or wanting to become the head of General Motors."

Years later, in the spring of 1969, a member of a large audience at the University of Illinois put the question directly to James Baldwin: "Mr. Baldwin, would you react to Eldridge Cleaver's attack on you in 'Soul on Ice'?"

Baldwin refrained from observing, as he might have, that in the intervening years Cleaver had produced the wind, but not the works that might have been expected to follow such a brutal attempt to supplant him as a spokesman. Instead, he responded quietly, and with a profound effect upon his audience: "I didn't like the attack. No one likes that sort of attack. But let me say that he was using me to make a point. And if you take me out of it—he was right."

Purged of many conflicts, but obviously afflicted by many others —a hunger for the life of reason coupled with a belief that man was best whipped forward by instinct and unreason, an admiration for the cultural heritage and the ardent rebelliousness of young whites coupled with an intense belief in the political necessity of black pride and black manhood—Cleaver emerged from prison into an America moving fast toward wildness and unreason. Edward Keating asked him what was the single most striking aspect of his being a free man after all those years of confinement. Cleaver hesitated for a moment and replied: "I think it's the ability to make decisions—even small ones, like where I'm going to eat dinner, or what I'll eat." He paused, and then added: "And I like to be able to open a door for a woman."

Seemingly, the door was now open for Eldridge Cleaver's literary career, unimpeded by anything other than the tiresome necessity of reporting periodically to his parole officer. He had a book contract, an editorial job with Ramparts, a wide acquaintanceship. Together with a group of young artists, he founded Black House in San Francisco as a hangout for young people with an interest in avant-garde black culture. A young woman, at that time a college student and now active in the Panthers, remembers Black House (the name was a takeoff on the White House) as a swinging place, where for 25 cents you could hear all kinds of speakers and poetry readings. Then one night in February, 1967, four young men from Oakland turned up, armed, in black berets, black leather jackets, black trousers, black shoes. As their leaders, Huey

P. Newton and Bobby Seale, proceeded to distribute the Black Panther paper, she says: "It blew my mind!"

By his own account, it blew Eldridge's mind too. It was clear at once that Newton, "with a riot pump shotgun in his right hand, barrel pointed down to the floor," was to be Malcolm's successor for him. In his "Introduction to the Biography of Huey P. Newton" (included in the recently published collection "Eldridge Cleaver: Post-Prison Writings and Speeches"), Cleaver says that "you cannot help but be amazed and fascinated by his seriousness, by his willingness and readiness to lay down his life in defense of the rights of his people," and he concludes, "I find myself sharing with Bobby Seale the same attitude toward Huey—the same willingness to place my life in his hands. . . ."

Newton, unquestioned leader of the Black Panther party, is a baby-faced young man possessed of great courage and a will of iron —at this writing he is on strike against working for less than the state minimum wage in the California prison in which he is serving an indeterminate sentence for manslaughter. His lawyer, Charles Garry, whom Cleaver calls "the first White Panther" ("I'm honored by that," says Garry), characterizes Newton as much the less emotional of the two, "soft as they come but hard as nails at the same time."

In the fall of 1967, Newton had been shot and arrested in a confrontation with the Oakland police, blood enemies of the Panthers, in which a policeman died. Nearly everyone was convinced that Newton would be sentenced to the gas chamber, but the jury returned what was apparently a makeshift compromise, a manslaughter verdict, after Newton underwent three days of cross-examination throughout which, his lawyer says, "I sat back relaxed."

Starting early in 1967, Cleaver committed himself to Newton and his growing organization, and came under the scrutiny of a public considerably larger than that represented by the Adult Authority, which controls the penal system of California. In April, he was one of the featured speakers at an anti–Vietnam war rally in San Francisco's Kezar Stadium attended by 65,000 people; in May, he was picked up by the police of Sacramento when Black

Panthers panicked the state legislators by turning up at a hearing on gun control armed to the teeth. The flamboyant gesture achieved the publicity the Panthers had been seeking, but it proved an embarrassment to Cleaver, whom the authorities restricted in his activities thereafter despite the fact that his "weapon" turned out to be a camera, and that he had been with the press as an accredited journalist.

Nevertheless, he, like the Panthers, was gaining increased attention almost daily. His articles were appearing in Ramparts, and he was having an impact on Americans far beyond the borders of the inflamed state of California. One of those Americans was an attractive and clever civil-rights worker named Kathleen Neal, who was working for the Student Nonviolent Coordinating Committee (now the Student National Coordinating Committee) after having been a student briefly at Oberlin and Barnard. Her background was as different from Cleaver's as one could imagine. Her father was a college professor turned diplomat. In the course of his foreign-service tours she had lived in India, the Philippines, Liberia and Sierra Leone. She organized an Easter conference for black students at Fisk University in Nashville at which Eldridge spoke; in December, 1967, they were married.

The first year of Cleaver's marriage was to be even more stunningly eventful for him and his bride than for millions of other Americans. In January, 1968, San Francisco police kicked open the door of their apartment at 3:30 in the morning after Cleaver had refused to admit them; they found nothing and did not trouble to explain the raid. In February, "Soul on Ice" was published and, with the attendant publicity, made of him a national figure. And on April 4, Martin Luther King was assassinated.

The following day, Eldridge Cleaver hurried to an Oakland junior high school threatened with destruction by furious black students. As Gene Marine recounts it in his book, "The Black Panthers," "For a half-hour he pleaded with the youths, arguing the futility of their action, the foolishness of the unorganized blindly striking out. Finally they agreed, as other knots of youth in San Francisco and Richmond, East Palo Alto and Berkeley agreed with Panthers who rushed to every threatening scene."

Nonetheless, a day later Cleaver himself was back in jail, after the Oakland police had surrounded a convoy of Panther cars and Cleaver had ducked into a cellar with Little Bobby Hutton, a teen-age Panther; a series of volleys from both sides was followed by tear gas, and as the two stumbled out to surrender, blinded and wounded, the 17-year-old Hutton was shot fatally in the back.

For Cleaver, however, shocked at finding himself still alive while his young companion lay dead, this remarkable year was only beginning. In June, after he had spent two months in confinement in Vacaville, Charles Garry succeeded to everyone's astonishment in obtaining his release on a writ of habeas corpus. "There is nothing to indicate," wrote Superior Court Judge Raymond J. Sherwin, "why it was deemed necessary to cancel his parole before his trial on the pending of criminal charges of which he is presumed innocent." Judge Sherwin went on to observe: "It has to be stressed that the uncontradicted evidence presented to this court indicated that the petitioner had been a model parolee. The peril of his parole status stemmed from no failure of personal rehabilitation, but from his undue eloquence in pursuing political goals, goals which were offensive to many of his contemporaries."

The Adult Authority, of course, moved—successfully—to have Judge Sherwin's ruling reversed in the Appellate Court, a reversal sustained by the State Supreme Court. But it could not succeed in erasing one of the more luminous moments in American legal history.

Meanwhile, the Black Panther party had reached an understanding with the Peace and Freedom party which, faced with the task of persuading California voters to change their Republican or Democratic registration, had been having little luck except in campus areas. It was Cleaver who, as Minister of Information, played a substantial role in forming the alliance which led to the birth of the California Peace and Freedom party, and it was his youthful black cohorts who wove through the Oakland and Berkeley ghettos with the Peace and Freedom registrars and were instrumental in securing the more than 100,000 voter registrations necessary to place on the ballot a party previously dominated by white anti–Vietnam war radicals of both the Old and the New Left.

"Black people," Cleaver told the founding convention of the California Peace and Freedom party, "now have control of their organizations. White people have developed several organizations in their own community that represent a real power base. . . . We see no reason for continuing this stance of isolation one from the other. . . . Let's get together and move in a common fashion against a common enemy."

Obviously both Cleaver and the Panthers were developing very swiftly. As an old West Coast socialist put it, "They were forced to become political in the full sense of the word. You could actually see it happening. They were saying that any blacks who tried to make it alone were adventurists, that political organization was the only way—and, in fact, the only way that one could find and test whites who could be trusted."

In the summer, the new party designated Eldridge Cleaver as its Presidential candidate, and in September he was invited along with the chief of police of Oakland to lecture in an experimental sociology course at the University of California. When the Board of Regents moved to prevent Cleaver from participating in the Berkeley course, he moved in on Gov. Ronald Reagan with gusto.

"I challenge Ronald Reagan to a duel," he told students at Stanford. "I challenge him to a duel to the death or until he says, 'Uncle, Eldridge.' And I give him his choice of weapons. He can use a gun, a knife, a baseball bat or a marshmallow. And I'll beat him to death with a marshmallow. That's how I feel about him. Here is a man, a demagogue, in the negative sense. I'm a demagogue—in the positive sense. But here, here is a negative demagogue. . . ."

It is not to be wondered at that Cleaver, having captured many intellectuals with the wit and insightfulness of his prison writings, even when they were wrongheaded or overdrawn, should have gone on to captivate the student generation, even when he descended from analysis to the chanting of obscenities. His knack for the simplification of invective, his background as a "street nigger" rather than as a representative of the button-down black *bourgeoisie*, his sense of the political event as theater—all comported with the view of the world held by collegians, particularly by student radicals and those who rallied to them at moments of crisis.

Both Cleaver and the Panther party were being driven, in that violent political year, to become increasingly political. Having committed themselves to an electoral alliance with white radicals, the Panthers came under attack by a whole cluster of nationalist rivals as sellouts and disguised Uncle Toms; in order to explain and defend their actions, they had to turn away from the simplistic formulas of soul-food nationalism. So did their Minister of Information. As his friend Dr. Philip Shapiro, a San Francisco psychoanalyst of the older generation, puts it: "Once Eldridge became deeply involved with the Black Panthers he became increasingly dedicated to politics and less to his own writing." He did manage to finish a long story (sold but not yet published), and his literary agent, Cyrilly Abeles, is aware of his desire to do an autobiographical novel. "But it is his more political stuff that has to come next."

As the fateful year drew to a close and the Adult Authority demonstrated its determination to lock him up as a parole violator even before his pending trial in Oakland (which both he and Garry were confident of winning), Cleaver came to know better than anyone else that his time was running out. After having experienced success, love, accomplishment and political involvement, he faced not just the possibility of years of incarceration, but of physical extinction. Nor was he alone in this belief. Edward Keating remembers clearly a conversation with the warden at the time of his first visit to Cleaver in the penitentiary: "He just looked at me, with the coldest, meanest eyes I've ever seen, and threw it at me: If Cleaver ever got out, he'd throw away the key the day he came back."

Don Cox, known to his fellow Panthers on the West Coast as D.C., puts it another way: "The purpose of prison is to break a man. Eldridge was hated because he couldn't be broken. If a thousand men stood in a chow line, all in order, all meek, Eldridge would cut off his sleeves to demonstrate his determination to remain an individual. He was a true revolutionist."

There were still moments, during his last months as a free man, when Cleaver retained the capacity to view himself with detached amusement. Sandra Levinson, a New York contributing editor of Ramparts, laughs when she remembers offering him a ride to the Peace and Freedom party headquarters late in the election campaign. "He climbed into the back seat," she says, "and I turned around and said, 'What do you think you're doing back there? I'm not your chauffeur!' 'Drive on,' he said, cocking his cigar at an angle like F.D.R.'s cigarette holder. 'You are speaking to the man who may be the next President of the United States.' "

But for the most part he became a frenetically driven man. Time, punctuality, became enormously important to him, according to the girl who served as his secretary at his home; even while he was leaving her notes that were "like little stories," he was delivering two and three speeches a day, writing articles and trying to rid his party of opportunist types. There are those who insist that he kept his cool until the last minute; others feel that he went into a tailspin as the day of his surrender to the Adult Authority approached.

There can be no question, however, that his speechmaking became increasingly erratic, oscillating wildly between the soberly descriptive and the primitive. David McReynolds, the veteran pacifist leader who was his running mate as a New York Congressional candidate on the Peace and Freedom party ticket, met him twice in the late weeks of the campaign. Their first encounter was pleasant, businesslike and characterized by an attitude of mutual respect. "I was very impressed with him as a person. A strong guy, a decent guy, someone I could trust."

But then McReynolds was asked to go out to Long Island to serve as fund raiser at a meeting being addressed by Cleaver. "I was angry at being called away from my own campaign, but that was nothing to what I felt when I had to listen to him leading a chant of four-letter words. It was irresponsible, antipolitical. I was livid, furious. I refused to participate in the session. When I told him how hurt I was, he did not get angry with me personally but shrugged it all off. He seemed to me a driven man, with his rage hardly below the surface. He was caught up in the Panthers' fascination with weapons, but I was convinced of his sincerity when he told a press conference that he disliked guns and feared violence. It's regrettable, but not too surprising, that he is not consistent."

McReynolds was not the only one to be shocked by Cleaver's platform shenanigans. A white Columbia student who had been profoundly impressed by "Soul on Ice" hastened to Ferris Booth Hall to join an overflow crowd listening to a Cleaver campaign speech. "What turned me off and sent me on my way," he said later, "was the feeling that he was pandering to the most mindless of the students, giving the Barnard girls a thrill by shouting dirty words at them."

And an old-line radical who had engaged in serious political discussions with Cleaver felt that he had become somewhat brutalized during the last months of his liberty. "Earlier, in California, when a girl fell out of a tree and hurt herself, he turned up at the hospital next day with flowers. It was the sort of spontaneous thing that endeared him to people. But he wasn't behaving like that toward the end."

Gavin MacFadyen, a film-maker who made a film on Cleaver for the B.B.C. at the Peace and Freedom party's Sixth Avenue loft some six weeks before Cleaver's departure, has a somewhat different recollection. "It's true that he was over his head. But he was playing many roles—disciplinarian to the kids who looked up to him, political infighter, publicist, writer. He gave me the impression of an extremely self-disciplined, fantastically hard man, at the same time amazingly fluid. I felt that he used vulgarity consciously, and the curious thing is that he used none of it in our session. He was cool, almost distant, he spoke of the 'police' rather than of the 'pigs,' and I suspect that was one reason why the B.B.C., which had hoped for a portrait of a wild man, was dissatisfied with the film."

But MacFadyen too, like the radical politician, felt that Cleaver was—if not exactly enchanted—certainly not unmarked by the adulation he had received. "The slavish devotion of the white left impressed him. It may have had something to do with his being able to quote from the thoughts of Chairman Mao with a straight face."

In an affecting account of her life with him, Kathleen Cleaver has written of those last months: "I watched Eldridge daily grow increasingly tense, harassed and paranoid." That last adjective is one frequently resorted to by those attempting to characterize the man and his movement with some degree of precision. But it carries the implication that the persecution which one allegedly suffers is the result of a systematized delusion. Supposing, though, that the delusion itself has some basis in reality? Perhaps the matter has been put best by a radical political analyst who describes the Panthers' view of America as "seen from the bottom of the water looking up, and hence totally distorted." They have, he observes, "a hard-bitten reality orientation coupled with wild abstraction." And in Eldridge Cleaver they have a Minister of Information who is the first auto-didact I've ever met who is interested in abstraction." (He adds that Cleaver is unique in his experience, too, in that he never descended, even in the heat of argument, to the white put-down.)

Five days before he was scheduled to surrender to the authorities, Cleaver made his last public appearance at a San Francisco rally in his behalf. Shortly after he began to talk he declared: "I developed something of a social conscience. I decided to come out here and work with social problems, get involved with the Movement and make whatever contribution I possibly could. When I made that decision, I thought that the parole authorities would be tickled pink with me, because they were always telling me to do exactly that. They would tell me I was selfish. They would ask me why I didn't start relating to other people, and looking beyond the horizons of myself.

"So I did that, you know. And I just want to tell you this: I've had more trouble out of parole officers and the Department of Corrections simply because I've been relating to the Movement than I had when I was committing robberies, rapes and other things that I didn't get caught for."

And as he came to a close, he stated: "I cannot relate to spending the next four years in the penitentiary, not with madmen with supreme power in their hands. Not with Ronald Reagan the head of the Department of Corrections, as he is the head of every other state agency. Not with Dirty Red's being the warden. If they made Dr. Shapiro the warden of San Quentin, I'd go right now."

Dr. Shapiro, seated in the audience, felt everyone looking in his direction. "I was so embarrassed I wanted to hide under the chair," he says. He was uncomfortable at being the object of so much attention, and he was terribly uneasy for Cleaver, who, with "his remarkable gift for writing, qualities of leadership, sense of dedication, sensitivity to people and readiness for any sacrifice, has played a role in developing the Black Panthers against racism and in making them more sophisticated in their dealings with whites."

When Cleaver told the audience that the authorities would have to come and get him, says Dr. Shapiro, "it sent a chill through people who were devoted to him. There were visions of an apocalyptic blood bath. Unquestionably, it was romanticizing on his part. He identified with Che Guevara."

In the event, Cleaver slipped away nonviolently. Outside his house in the Fillmore district, reports his admirer the distinguished writer Kay Boyle, "college professors, college students, men and women of the black community, and C.I.A. men dressed as hippies gathered night and day on the sidewalk. Cleaver's neighbors had hung sheets across the front steps, and across the basement windows of his house, in a sort of barricade of love. They had pinned sprays of flowers to the draped sheets, and printed in bright-colored letters words on them like: 'Eldridge, we love you.'" The authorities made no notable effort to intercept him.

Cleaver was heard of next from Cuba, where, Reuters reported early this summer, he was holed up in an apartment, and sounding not too happy about his first experience of life in a revolutionary regime.

The Cuban interlude could prove to be another stage in the education of Eldridge Cleaver, who had been thoroughly uncritical of foreign revolutionaries on the simplistic principle that the enemy of one's enemy is perforce one's friend.

Meanwhile, his wife had quietly joined him. Then they both turned up in Algiers, where, on July 29, a son, named Antonio Maceo, in honor of a 19th century black Cuban revolutionary, was born.

It was not surprising that Cleaver, who in Folsom prison in 1965 had clipped from The Saturday Evening Post "a beautiful picture of Malcolm X kneeling down in the Mohammed Ali Mosque in Cairo," should have surfaced as an Algerian Government guest at the recent Pan-African Cultural Festival. But perhaps some of those who admire the suppleness and agility of his mind were given pause by his embrace of Moslem terrorism, by his statement that the "Zionist regime" is "a puppet and pawn" of the United States, by his solidarity with the Al Fatah official who asserted that Israeli economic aid to Africa was a false front for American attempts to exert a neocolonialist influence.

Torn between a writer's instinctive awareness of the complexities of the individual human being and the institutions he creates, and an agitator's hunger for easy allegiance and the easy adulation that follows upon such allegiance, Cleaver seemed in Algiers to be opting for the latter. And, as his travels have freed him from the isolated ghettos where Panthers and other half-educated idealists could cling to such myths as that of Negro-Moslem solidarity, he has been willy-nilly divesting himself of the apology of ignorance with which American Negroes have explained their silence on the Nigerian-Biafran horror. It is not only Israel which Egyptian pilots have been bombing, but Biafra as well.

The opening speaker of the Pan-African Cultural Festival at which Cleaver was an honored guest was Chief Anthony Enahoro, Nigerian Information Minister, who the previous year had explained to the world that hunger was a legitimate weapon in the effort to reduce the Biafran uprising. Authentic representatives of Nigerian culture, like the playwright Wole Soyinka and the novelist Chinua Achebe, were unable to join Enahoro and Cleaver in Algiers—Soyinka because he is being held incommunicado in a Nigerian prison for protesting the war, Achebe because he had opted for Biafran identity after charging official Nigerian complicity in what he described as a jihad, a Moslem holy war, being waged against the Ibo people by the Hausa of northern Nigeria.

Perhaps the most valuable single item in the collection of Cleaver's post-prison writings and speeches edited by Robert Scheer is the interview with Cleaver by Nat Hentoff, which originally appeared in Playboy in somewhat lengthier form. It is a wide-ranging give-and-take discussion on a host of issues that go to the heart of the American crisis; in it, Cleaver attempts with evident discomfort to mitigate, without condoning, the antiwhite diatribe of Black Panther Chairman Bobby Seale to an outraged audience of New York whites unwilling to play their assigned roles of guilt-ridden liberal masochists.

But one does not find in either version what Hentoff regards with good reason as one of the most intriguing moments of their discussion. Cleaver had indicated that the review of "Soul on Ice" which impressed him most was Richard Gilman's in The New Republic in the spring of 1968. As a man who saw himself as a novelist, he was gratified to read that "the maneuver he carries out is an effort at grace, complexity and faithfulness." But Gilman made a critical withdrawal:

"It is not my right to compare his thinking with other 'classic' ways of grappling with sexual experience and drama; it isn't my right to draw him into the Western academy and subject his findings to the scrutiny of the tradition. . . .

"I will go on judging and elucidating novels and plays and poetry by Negroes according to what general powers I possess, but this kind of Negro writing I have been talking about, the act of creation of the self in the face of that self's historic denial by our society, seems to me to be at this point beyond my right to intrude on."

A number of readers were disturbed enough by this dichotomy to write to the magazine, and in an article entitled "More on Negro Writing" Gilman returned to the subject some weeks later:

"We can no longer talk to Negroes, or Negroes to us, in the traditional humanistic ways. The old Mediterranean values—belief in the sanctity of the individual soul, the importance of logical clarity, brotherhood, reason as arbiter, political order, community —are dead as *useful* frames of reference or pertinent guides to procedure. . . . I am saying that I don't know what truth for Negroes is . . . that I am willing to stand back and listen, *without comment,* to these new and self-justifying voices."

According to Hentoff, Cleaver saw this as a "stunning misinterpretation," for he looked on his writing as based on precisely what Gilman referred to as "the old Mediterranean values." "I just don't understand that," Cleaver protested. "I do believe in the sanctity of the individual soul, in brotherhood, in community. That's exactly what I was trying to write about."

It is my own feeling, not only that Cleaver was justified in his dismay, but that a refusal to make the attempt to come to terms, not simply with traditional verse and prose, but with less orthodox forms of expression as well is an act of intellectual abdication.

What is more, it demeans those who in attempting to create them-selves (which in a sense is the function of both the artist and the ghetto child) make use of our common language.

If a man "expresses himself" by chanting four-letter words in public, or by verbally assaulting racial or ethnic groups, it is our privilege to walk on by. But once he commits himself to paper with the brilliant and brutal clarity of an Eldridge Cleaver, it be-comes a minimum obligation not to "stand back" but to measure his words, test them—if need be, challenge them. To evade the issues he raises by arbitrarily ruling him out of the Western acad-emy or the Mediterranean value system is no more useful than were earlier attempts to do likewise with Mark Twain because his vulgar frontier humor struck oddly on Bostonian ears, or with Henry Roth because his transliterated ghetto Yiddish was harder to decipher than the genteel ghetto reportage of a Powers Hap-good. These writers were something more than members of an academy: they were Americans. And Eldridge Cleaver, old con and street nigger, is a quintessential American.

Indeed, it was unlikely that he himself realized how much an American he was until he was driven into exile. A reader of his "My Father and Stokely Carmichael" can only be struck by how the following adulatory description of the man who has since broken with Cleaver and the Panthers on the issue of the latter's turn from dogmatic black nationalism to dogmatic élitist Marxism resembles not so much an African or Third World revolutionist as it does Jack Valenti's vision of Lyndon Baines Johnson: "In the days to come I was to be with Carmichael almost constantly and, when he was not moving, making speeches, or eating, he was on the telephone. He simply could not sit down for 10 minutes without being called to the phone or feeling the urge to call someone up himself."

At the trial of Huey Newton, the final defense witness, Gene Marine tells us, was a black sociologist, Prof. Herman Blake, who attempted to explain that "much of the Panther rhetoric was directed at a community that understood it in terms of 'signify-ing' . . . a long-developed black technique of saying one thing to mean another, related thing. Whites in America do not use the word 'signify' in this sense at all, and it is a little different from what whites mean by 'symbolism.' "

But it is more than words, it is their context which must be examined. Vice President Spiro Agnew's outrage at a Black Panther comic book which proclaimed that "the only good pig is a dead pig" was absolutely justified, and it is a matter for some relief that the Oakland Panthers have withdrawn the booklet from circulation among the youngsters whom they have been giving free breakfasts. But surely Mr. Agnew's anger would have been more universally shared had he observed, as did a quiet California priest in a television interview, not only that the Panthers have been feeding more children than any other agency in the state of California, but that they have borrowed their rhetoric not from alien sources but from several very American models: "The only good Injun is a dead Injun," "The only good nigger is a dead nigger." If it is not our chickens but our rhetoric that has come home to roost in the language of Malcolm and Eldridge, we might at least clear the air by conceding as much and going on from there.

The 10-point program of the Black Panther party, which Cleaver helped to formulate and which he pressed until his departure from the country, consists for the most part of aspirations which would be perfectly acceptable to a Whitney Young, a Roy Wilkins or a Spiro Agnew: We want freedom; we want power; we want full employment; we want an end to robbery of the black community; we want decent housing; we want an end to police brutality; we want trial by one's peers. There is a catch-all demand for land, bread, housing, education, clothing, justice and peace.

If we except as a publicity device the demand for a United Nations plebiscite "for the purpose of determining the will of black people as to their national destiny" (a moment's reflection should suffice to persuade its proponents that not only the United States but the Soviet Union would never vote to open that particular can of peas), there remain two planks the espousal of which by Cleaver has rendered many Americans all but speechless with indignation.

The first demands that all black men "be exempt from military service." This special-interest plea parallels those made in the past by university presidents, defense-plant executives and wives. In view of the disproportionate casualties already suffered by black Americans in Vietnam, attempts to redress the balance might be taken in good part.

The second demands "freedom for all black men held in Federal, state, county and city prisons and jails." This raises in many minds the specter of already unsafe streets further infested with criminals and hoodlums, and should perhaps be considered in conjunction with Cleaver's insistence upon black people's arming themselves for self-defense and his tendency to fetishize the gun. Still, let us ponder the following New York Times dispatch from Annapolis, Md., in June of this year. It reports on the address of Dr. Richard R. Korn of the School of Criminology of the University of California to a crime conference attended by magistrates, policemen, parole officers, psychologists and other experts:

"All prisons are 'jungles' rather than correctional institutions, he argued, and those who deny it are 'lying in your face.' Seventy to 80 per cent of all inmates 'should be turned loose right now,' he said, since only about 10 per cent are 'truly dangerous' and these could be cared for in mental institutions."

All of us are frightened. Those who live in the great cities are more frightened than those who do not, and those who live in the ghettos are the most frightened of all, for they are preyed upon more than the rest by the addicted, the alienated, the rootless— and, worst horror of all, by the very police sworn to protect the peace. "While 33 per cent regarded local policemen as harmful to their rights three years ago," reported a Gallup Poll of American Negroes in June, 1969, "46 per cent now hold that view."

In Oakland, Sacramento, Chicago, Cairo and points East, police violence and the police riot are no longer simply the paranoid product of overheated imaginations, but the stuff of our daily papers. The continued weapon obsession of Eldridge Cleaver needs careful examination—and, from my point of view, condemnation—as a contemporary extension of a phenomenon that extends from the Indian fighters down to the embattled membership of the American Rifle Association. But I do not believe that it can be morally challenged unless an alternative is seriously proposed for those who feel themselves threatened and terrorized every moment of their lives.

Until someone in American public life is prepared to place on the political agenda a program for civilizing our penal institutions and disarming, not only our civilian population, but our "overworked, undertrained, underpaid and undereducated" police to the level of the London bobby, I do not see how we can demand that the ghetto militants civilize and disarm unilaterally.

But things move fast in our volatile country. Many police departments are attempting to react rationally to those who have been calling them pigs (an officer at the phenomenal Woodstock festival said: "When our police cars were getting stuck, they even helped us get them out—really amazing. I think a lot of police here are looking at their attitudes"), and "hopeless" ghetto dwellers are organizing themselves and patronizing new black bookshops ("There they are," said one bookseller, "some of them can barely write their name, and they're struggling with something like Cleaver's 'Soul on Ice' ").

In an essay of mine entitled "The Coming Revolution in Literature" that appeared in The Saturday Review in 1965, I quoted myself as having written four years earlier: "In our country the Jew has moved from a marginal position to one of centrality. In the next generation it may very well be the Negro, the 10th American, who will come to be regarded . . . as the most typical American." Then I added, with what strikes me four years later as a certain smugness: "It is my feeling today that this typically will come to be true not just for the Negro as American, but for the Negro writer as American writer."

What I did not foresee was that publishers' eagerness to capitalize on the revolution in racial consciousness would result in the courting and publishing of untalented young men merely because they were black—or that the talented (as had also been the case with the Jews) would find their words distorted by the crazyhouse mirrors of the mass media. Much less did I anticipate that one of the most gifted of the new writers would have to depart for what is regarded as political exile even by many who do not share his politics.

Eldridge Cleaver is as much in flux as his party—or his country.

Thanks to the charm and vigor of his personality, he has gained the friendship and esteem of an impressive collection of his fellow citizens. Thanks to the cutting edge of a diamond-bright prose and an unsparingly honest self-examination, he has won the admiration of black and white readers, and has forced them to confront the questions that James Agee once asked of those who were willing to listen hard enough to Beethoven or Schubert: "Is what you hear pretty? or beautiful? or acceptable in polite or any other society? It is beyond any calculation savage and dangerous and murderous to all equilibrium in human life as human life is; and nothing can equal the rape it does on all that death."

But if he, like the party with which he has thrown in his lot, merely trades in the dogmas of black nationalism for the aridities of Leninism, he will do worse than simply align himself with a set of dubious allies, whether in the Near East or in the Communist countries. He will imperil that which must be most precious to him as a writer and as a thinking and feeling man: that delicate and fine tuning which has enabled him to sense and articulate the revulsions and the revolutionary aspirations of the new generation.

For if anything is clear in a confusing time, it is that the best of our people are sick to death of the killing, everywhere, and of the lies that go with the killing, everywhere; of the conformity, everywhere. Any writer who ignores this, who opts for selective killing, selective lies, selective conformity, selective compulsion dooms himself to what is perhaps an even worse fate than exile: irrelevance.

A Surprising Talk Between a Black Leader and a Top Segregationist

by Julian Bond and R. V. Harris

The idea was to bring together Julian Bond, the articulate, 29-year-old Negro leader, and Roy V. Harris, a veteran Georgia politician and the state's leading segregationist.

If the two, who had never met, would ask the questions each must have for the other—and ask them honestly—it could be a meaningful dialogue. At minimum, it would be dramatic. One imagined that it might be like an elevated train grinding around a steel curve, screeching and throwing sparks every inch of the way.

Who would have thought that the two would spend four amiable hours together—eating, drinking and chatting, and agreeing far more than they disagreed, finding harmony on points ranging from black power to slumlords, from Lester Maddox to Ralph McGill?

Bond has been nationally prominent since 1965, when he was refused a seat in the Georgia Legislature because of his "radical" views on Vietnam and a statement praising the courage of draft-

From the *New York Times Magazine*, April 27, 1969, copyright © 1969 by The New York Times Company.

card burners. Far less militant than an Eldridge Cleaver or a Rap Brown, but far to the left of older civil-rights stalwarts like Roy Wilkins or Whitney Young, he has emerged as a major figure in the black struggle.

Harris, 73, once served as speaker of the Georgia House of Representatives and was an architect of the state's segregationist policies. He sits on the Board of Regents, and, on the day he met with Bond, black students at the University of Georgia were demanding that he be removed.

In 1968, Harris was state campaign manager for George Wallace. He is president of the militantly segregationist Association of Citizens Councils of America, and publishes a right-wing newspaper.

The Bond-Harris meeting was held in Atlanta's plush Commerce Club.* Getting the two men together was the work of Bob Cohn, of Southeastern Newspapers Corporation, and Steve Ball, Jr., of The Atlanta Journal. The following abridgment of the discussion appeared in Atlanta, the magazine of the city's Chamber of Commerce. Questions by Cohn and Ball are italicized.

HARRIS: I think we do have a problem, and I think that one of these days it's got to be worked out—the sooner the better. It's a question of which way we're going and how we're going to solve this problem—whether there will be a fusion of the races, or whether we will work out some pattern by which we can live side by side and work together in a state of peace and harmony.

BOND: It seems likely—over a period of hundreds and hundreds of thousands of years—that there may be a one-race society, but I don't think it's likely to happen any time soon, in either of our lifetimes. . . . I don't think there should be a prohibition against it, either social or legal. It ought not to be a goal to be worked for because it's probably not, from either of our points of view, a desirable goal. You can solve the race problem without that kind of fusion. You can solve it by having an equitable

---

* When it was decided to adjourn for dinner, Bond, Harris and the rest of the group went to the Playboy Club. They settled down at a table and waited for a bunny to take their order. It was only fitting that she would be black and that Harris would, from all surface appearances, fail to notice it.

division of power in this country. As power begins to be divided more equitably, *then* you're going to see a lessening of what you call the racial problem. I don't think it's going to happen quickly, either.

HARRIS: I think you're right. I don't think it can be done quickly. Now, understand this: I believe in black power. I believe in black economy. I believe Negroes are entitled to representation. In Augusta, we used to have the City Council elect two from each ward. Each ward elected its own members. Now you run citywide.

BOND: That's the way they do it here.

HARRIS: And, of course, it was done to keep Negroes out of the City Council.

BOND: You're the only politician who will say that.

HARRIS: How's that?

BOND: You're the only white politician who will say that.

HARRIS: Is that right?

BOND: [Former Mayor William B.] Hartsfield said it was done to keep corruption down.

HARRIS: But, of course, that's the reason. I tell you they're damn hypocrites.

BOND: That's where you're absolutely right. You need to come down and talk to the Fulton County House delegation, Mr. Harris, and get them straightened out. Why don't you write them each a letter?

HARRIS: Nooo. I've got enough troubles of my own. I'll tell you, though, when a majority of Augusta or Atlanta becomes black, they can have it and they're entitled to it.

Does it make any difference who's in the Governor's office as far as Negroes are concerned?

BOND: Before I got put out of the Legislature, I went with all the other Negro legislators to see Governor [Carl] Sanders. We mentioned a lot of problems to him. One thing was that there were no Negroes on any draft boards in the state of Georgia, except in Atlanta. He said, "I'll have to study it." A year later, I finally got in the Legislature and I went to see Lester Maddox. And you know what Governor Maddox said? "Y'all fight in the Army, don't you?" he said. "You ought to be on the draft boards."

He did it just like that. He didn't have to study it or anything. He saw some things are right and some things are wrong. I think that's the difference between the two men. I think Carl Sanders is an equivocator, and he's the kind of man who may talk a good game, but will privately complain about his son having to go to an integrated school.

HARRIS: Yep.

BOND: One thing that strikes me about Lester Maddox is that he comes from a very poor family. He knows what it means to be poor, and he has a lot of sympathy, I think, for poor people. He doesn't care if the poor people are black or white, but, if he thinks he can do something for poor people, I think he'll try to do it. There are some things he's just more decent about than *any* other politician I've seen.

HARRIS: He's like me. He believes in segregation. But, from a practical standpoint, a fellow like Lester Maddox can do more for the Negro people and get by with it than Carl Sanders because Carl is so suspect.

How widespread do you think hypocrisy is among white politicians?

HARRIS: Unfortunately, our leaders amongst the white people have been hypocrites. Like, last Monday morning I went into my office and a very prominent man in Augusta called me to complain that his children had to attend an integrated school. Where's he been the last 15 years? He's been calling *me* a radical and an extremist because he didn't think this thing would ever touch him. I don't know what we are—I'll let somebody else name it—but I think we've at least been honest about it. . . . I was reading in the Atlanta paper one Sunday a write-up of the racial situation in Augusta. The Rev. C. S. Hamilton [a Negro leader] was quoted as saying that the good relations in Augusta were due to eight or ten people, and he named me as one of them, which shocked the hell out of me. I think they all have confidence in me, and I think they know I never have mistreated any of them.

Do you just assume that any white person who favors integration is a hypocrite?

HARRIS: No, no. [The late] Ralph McGill was a fellow that changed, and I think Ralph was sincere. I don't think Ralph was a hypocrite. I knew McGill very closely. . . . He and I used to drink liquor and just argue.

How do you feel about that, Mr. Bond?

BOND: The word "liberal" means two things. It's used in Georgia as a curse word, and, when it's used in another sense, I think it refers to someone like Mr. Sanders, who may say one thing and mean another. He's the bad liberal. Then, I think there is a good liberal. I think [Atlanta Mayor Ivan] Allen—or McGill—are good liberals. McGill—I think you're right about that—said one thing and meant it.

How do you react to liberals, Mr. Harris?

HARRIS: I don't like the idea of using the words "liberal" and "conservative" because I don't know what they mean. I don't know any conservatives, except a few old cranks that belong to the John Birch Society, but there ain't many of them. They're against everything from fluoridation of water up and down. Most of the people I know over the South—from [the late] Judge [Leander] Perez to folks like me, George Wallace and the Citizens Council in Jackson—I don't know where you could find anybody more liberal than we are until you get down to one question, and that's the segregation question.

BOND: He [Wallace] confuses me because he's liberal on a great many questions, except race. He's also conservative on some questions where a great many people who feel as he does about race are very liberal—for instance, labor unions. He's been very bad for labor unions in Alabama. He's been very good for education in Alabama. They got free textbooks for the first time in Alabama under George Wallace.

You've said Negro and white leaders should sit down and devise a plan by which the two races can live harmoniously, Mr. Harris. What do you suggest?

HARRIS: You can't draw an inflexible, exact-to-the-rule line that's as invariable as the law of the Medes and the Persians. See? It's a little bit more delicate. . . . I've eaten with several of them [Negroes]; that's the reason I say you can't draw an exact line. But, I do think, as a general rule, you ought to have separate schools and separate churches.

Separate restaurants?

HARRIS: No, that's a public institution.

BOND: I remember that, many years ago, it used to be possible —before they integrated the University of Georgia—to get the state to pay me to go to Meharry [Medical College, Nashville, Tenn.] if I wanted to go to medical school. That's really wasteful. It increases your taxes and mine—don't you think?

HARRIS: Yeah, well, of course. Understand this, Julian: A lot of things we do are wasteful. But here's the thing. You could not have put it over. You could not have gotten a Negro into the medical college in those days to save your neck. That was better than nothing. That was one of the steps in the transition that had to come, and we're *still* sending some to Meharry.

BOND: Did you know my father used to be president at Fort Valley [State College]?

HARRIS: He was?

BOND: Up until 1945. And Eugene Talmadge, when he was Governor, used to come down once a year, and they used to have a big celebration.

HARRIS: That was Ham Day, wasn't it?

BOND: A ham-and-egg supper. You remember that? They used to have guys come in from the railroad and lay ties and sing those songs. Anyway, they took a lot of pictures of Talmadge eating with Negroes. My father kept these pictures and, when the appropriation came up in the Legislature, he sent them to Governor Talmadge. He said, "Governor Talmadge, here are the pictures. Do you want me to send them to the Journal and Constitution?" It was Herman [Eugene Talmadge's father]. It must have been Herman.

HARRIS: It wasn't Gene.

BOND: It was Herman, and he wrote back and said, "No, Dr. Bond, you'll get your appropriation this year." The next year my father left and went up to Pennsylvania to another school.

Getting back to solutions, Mr. Harris.

HARRIS: I don't say that Atlanta is ideal, but you've got more Negro wealth in Atlanta than in Chicago and New York put together.

BOND: That's true.

HARRIS: You've got more Negro colleges and universities in

Atlanta than any other city in the world. The Negro has made greater progress in Atlanta than any place that I've known in this country.

BOND: I would agree with that, but I also would temper it by saying there's a tremendous amount of poverty existing right next to this educational . . .

HARRIS: I agree with you there. You know, the thing we've overlooked in all the agitation over the Negro question is that we've got more poor white folks in Georgia than we've got poor Negroes.

BOND: That's true all over the country.

HARRIS: I don't think you can find anywhere in the country where over the years—of course, it hasn't been ideal—where you've had the relationship that you've had here in Atlanta. And I think it's come nearer to being a model than anything you can find anywhere.

BOND: Atlanta has been unique. What bothers me is that other cities haven't had these advantages. They haven't had an educated class of Negroes. They haven't had the kind of Negroes that went into commerce, into banking, into insurance. But, even with all those advantages, as you say, there are an awful lot of poor white people here, and there are tremendous numbers of poor Negroes here. What is to become of those people? No one, I think, cares much about either group—the poor whites or the poor Negroes. Those are the ones, it seems to me, who are completely cut off in this city and in most American cities.

HARRIS: I learned a long time ago that the average fellow is having such a hard time scratching for himself that he doesn't worry too damn much about the other fellow. This inflationary spiral is going to wreck and ruin poor folks everywhere. The cost of living has gone up so much that they can't make it.

BOND: That's right. I was just reading a Negro newspaper editor in Georgia almost one hundred years ago who said that, in the end, the rich will be found on one side, whether they are black or white, and the poor will be found on the other, whether they are black or white. I think that's something that's likely to happen in this country—that you're going to see that kind of division.

HARRIS: There's no difference between the Negro people and

the average white man. If you don't work for a big corporation or a big chain, and you are out here in independent business, you've got to compete with them and you've got a helluva job.

BOND: When you were speaking earlier of the kind of progress that's been made in Atlanta, I thought you were going to say what a lot of people have said: that because there's so much black capital here, it ought to be turned toward developing other black business that would provide more jobs—sort of spreading around the black money that's been earned here. It just struck me that it would be an unusual thing for a rich black person to do because rich white people don't do it either. It's unusual for rich people to help poor people. It's usual for rich people to help themselves get richer and richer.

HARRIS: The Jewish people are the only ones I know who do help one another. That was the old-type Jew.

Getting back to the solutions, Mr. Harris.

HARRIS: I think we've got to acknowledge this: Instead of having a fusion of the races, we ought to have two races. Then, you've got to figure out how these two races are going to work together, live together. They've [Negroes] got a lot more power now.

BOND: It's slipping away. You've got this man in Washington now. . . .

HARRIS: 'Course, I'm cussing him out because he's going the other way.

BOND: He's a bad man.

HARRIS: Between him and Hubert Humphrey, I would have taken Humphrey—although I managed George Wallace's campaign in Georgia.

BOND: Why do you say that?

HARRIS: Well, of all the things I don't like about Hubert Humphrey, I do think the S.O.B. is honest. I don't mean that "S.O.B." exactly like it sounds. A man on the other side is *always* an S.O.B. I don't think Nixon's got any convictions.

BOND: I think you're right about that. I think if you look over the next four years—if you measure progress in terms of the numbers integrated or not—you'll see a lessening of that kind of progress.

HARRIS: This week's U.S. News and World Report has an interview with [Secretary of Health, Education and Welfare Robert] Finch, and the way I interpret that is that they're not going to let up in the South.

BOND: I got it just the other way. Maybe Nixon's figured he can't get the South again.

HARRIS: He can't today.

BOND: I guess he figures he can't get it in '72, so he might as well ignore it.

HARRIS: He may. That's the way I interpret this [article]. Now, Finch wiggles around on the court decisions, but when he gets through, if you read it, he's going to push it in the South and not in the North.

Some people, like Wallace, see a race war as the final solution. How do you feel about it?

BOND: I think that's possible, but I don't think it's probable. I just don't think it will happen for a couple of reasons. First, I think most black people realize we're on the losing end of something like that. We're outnumbered nine-to-one. Secondly, I don't think that the white people who want to preserve the status quo have to go to war in order to do so. All they need is a guy like Finch. I don't think Finch is going to push as hard in the South as he says he is. Apparently, [Sen. Strom] Thurmond is overseeing every move Finch makes in the South.

HARRIS: If it was left to the ghettos of New York, Chicago and Philadelphia, you would probably have a black-and-white race war. But you've got a different condition when you get to Atlanta and Augusta. You've got enough wealthy and educated Negro people. They've got a vested interest, just the same as the rest of the people have. You take the week after Martin Luther King's death. You had riots in 125 cities, but there wasn't one in Georgia. Negro people in Georgia, like white people, have got roots. They've been here a long time. But, you take Harlem. You've got those people who come in there from all over the world. They've got no deep roots, and they never had a decent way of making a living. It's been tough here, but, the thing is, it hasn't required as much money. As long as we were rural people, we raised a lot of our food. We're living in a period of time that is a little different

than it was at the turn of the century when you could open up—
these boys here don't know anything about it. Julian, you know
what a potato hill is?

BOND: Oh, yes. It's a big hill with all the potatoes inside. These
[pointing to the reporters in the room] are all big-city boys.

HARRIS: All year 'round you could go to the potato hill and get
a potato, or you could pull up a turnip right out of the garden.
Now, when those folks get in there [a ghetto], they can't get along
on a maid or cook's salary, and there isn't a potato hill. When
you create a ghetto like that, you create an artificial situation that
requires a helluva lot more than money and . . .

BOND: I'm going to agree with Mr. Harris, and disagree at the
same time. I think there *is* a difference in the South, and the
difference, I think, is this: If you're black and you live *anyplace*
in this whole region of the Southeast . . . you can see a change
over the past 10 years of your life—no matter how old you are,
who you are, or what your job is. If I lived in Atlanta—you can
say five years ago, or ten years ago, rather—I couldn't eat at
Rich's, except in the basement, and now, today, I can, so my life
has improved X points. If you live in Harlem, on the other hand,
you can say to yourself, "I've lived in Harlem 25 or 30 years.
When I came here, I could eat at Woolworth's; ten years ago, I
could eat at Woolworth's; five years ago, I could eat at Woolworth's; and I ate at Woolworth's this morning. But my life is
exactly the same now as it was. I still have the same sorry job; I
still work in the garment district pushing a truck. Things have not
changed for me. Things are just like they were when I first came
up here from South Carolina or Georgia."

I think the difference is . . . the first thing here in the South
. . . is hopefulness. Southern black people have a lot of hopefulness because they have *seen* some measurable change. In my opinion, it's not been very important. But I think in the average guy's
opinion it has been important. He can do things today he couldn't
do several years ago. The second thing is, Southern black people
are still very close to the church—and I'm not sure exactly what
role the church plays in this hopefulness—but it does play some
role: that things will get better by and by. That still is very important to a lot of people. Something I want to go back to, Mr.

Harris, talking about riots, is the real difference between the kind of riots you see in the 1960's—in Watts, or New York, or Detroit —and the kind of riots you used to have years ago. I imagine you remember the Atlanta riot?

HARRIS: I've heard about it. I'm acquainted with it.

BOND: The difference between that riot and the others that took place during the same period, and those that took place recently, is that the first were *really* confrontations between black and white. And, in the Atlanta riot, for instance, there were over 100 black people killed—I mean murdered. They were taken off street-cars, their throats cut. They were stomped to death. They were lynched in downtown Atlanta. And nothing like that, except for isolated incidents, has ever happened in any of these current riots. What you have now is a conflict between black people and white institutions. You have black people burning down a store. You have black people burning out a loan shark. You have black people attacking the physical image of white power. But, in those riots, you had white people physically murdering, person against person. And now it's person against institutions, or race against institutions. I think it's a very important difference.

HARRIS: I think he's right about that. The Atlanta riot . . . was a very personal thing. I think he's right. They are fighting the order now.

How do you account for the disillusionment of the Negro in the North?

HARRIS: You take Harlem. They never got out of Harlem. They live there all the time. Negroes in the South aren't tied in. They're tied up there. Some of those people have never been a mile or two from where they were born. The easiest way of life for them is prostitution, peddling dope, or selling numbers tickets.

BOND: If you're black and you come from Mississippi to Chicago by Greyhound bus, you get off at that bus terminal—I forget where it is—and somebody from the local Democratic party meets you. He tells you he works for Congressman Dawson. He tells you where there's an apartment to be found. He gives you a phone number. It's the phone number of the local [Democratic] precinct captain, and your whole life is laid out before you. If you're white, you have to live in a certain section of Chicago, where all white people from Appalachia come to live, but the same kind of machinery doesn't meet you. A lot of whites come up there, spend five years, and go back. But the black people who come up there are really sucked into a kind of machinery.

HARRIS: That's right.

BOND: It just pulls them in.

HARRIS: That's right.

BOND: Chicago is the worst example. It's worse than New York. They're put on welfare. The precinct captain says, "You've got three kids, your husband's not here, you're on welfare. Just remember to pull the Democratic lever at election time." And they're just pulled into machinery they cannot escape from. That's why nobody can beat Dawson. . . . The only escape from it is the gangs. But the older people are just in it, and can't get out. I've got an uncle who used to work for the city of Chicago, and his job was to see what the water level was in Lake Michigan every day. He'd go down and look at a pile with the numbers on it, and, if it was 10 feet, he'd write down 10 feet, and he'd go turn it in. He's retired now on a pension. Why should he fight against anything? . . . Chicago strikes me as the most hostile city of any I've ever been in. I always get the feeling, as I'm walking down the street in Chicago, that anybody, white or black, at any moment, is going to hit me for no reason whatsoever. . . . I felt that same way when I moved to Atlanta. . . . The only thing I knew about the South was what I read about in The Pittsburgh Courier. My mother wanted me to go to Rich's to buy a new suit so I could go to college in the fall. I wouldn't go because I thought that white people in Rich's would beat me up. That's funny now, but I believed that. I let her go instead. I let my mother go.

What is the answer to the plight of these trapped people, Mr. Bond?

BOND: You have to find some mechanism to raise people's income, whether simply by dole, which I think would be least desirable, or by guaranteed job—some kind of WPA project. I don't know. We've got to find some way to put money in people's hands. The easiest would be the dole. Just increase welfare benefits and say that, if you make under a certain amount of money, you qualify for it. This is probably the least expensive in the short run. The best thing to do is to find some way to get people jobs.

Look at all the things that need to be done in a state like this—highway construction or beautification. People could be put to work at those kinds of things at government expense.

HARRIS: He's right. The easy way always is the dole. It's simpler, and you just get rid of it [the problem], just kind of brush it under the rug. Now, the old WPA served a good purpose back in its day, and it did a lot of good all over the state. Of course, they talked about seeing them hanging on their shovels—standing up resting on the handles of the shovels. But look what they've done with these damn poverty funds, like in Chicago. I think the most flagrant example occurred with one of those gangs. They just hired them to be good. They didn't burn up any houses, and they didn't riot. Now, I guess that's better than nothing, but it doesn't solve anything. It would have been a lot better if they had gone in there and organized those folks into a work force. During the old Depression, England had a corps similar to ours for middle-aged people. They took them and the first thing they did was give them a set of teeth. Then they fixed their hernias up. Then they started training them on something they could make a living on. When you do that you put a man into shape where he can get out and earn three meals a day.

Mr. Bond, you introduced your first piece of legislation this year. What is it about?

BOND: It's a local bill just applying to the city of Atlanta. If you have a home that's declared unfit for human habitation, you don't pay rent to the landlord, but for six months you pay rent to an escrow account in the bank. At the end of six months, if the landlord hasn't brought it up to code standard, then you can withdraw the money from the bank account. . . .

HARRIS: Well, let me tell you something: That's one I would have joined you in.

That's what?

HARRIS: That's one I would have joined you in. Among my pet peeves in life are these damn loan sharks, and the next thing is these folks who take these houses out there and don't ever do a thing to them—just keep renting them year in and year out. They don't give a damn what shape they're in, and that's the kind of property that won't get in an urban renewal project.

BOND: That's right.

HARRIS: Now, of course, what these damn landlords say is that they've got tenants that won't take care of them. But, I'll tell you what: You know that Hornsby subdivision [Negro homes] we started in Augusta? You go down there and you don't find any nicer neighborhood or houses any better kept. They're still that way today. Who in the hell gives a damn about an old broken-down shack? Who *wants* to take care of it?

BOND: Especially if you don't own it.

HARRIS: Yeah, and the other fellow is making you pay twice what it's worth.

Mr. Bond, how would you differentiate yourself from Eldridge Cleaver?

BOND: I wouldn't call *him* a pig. That's the difference between the two of us.

HARRIS: You don't think that Cleaver is representing any substantial element of the Negro people, do you?

BOND: No, not a substantial number.

HARRIS: A minority that's very active.

BOND: It is very active, but I think it has to be listened to.

HARRIS: That's right.

BOND: I have a feeling that he's losing his popularity. When Malcolm X was killed, his [Malcolm X's] popularity mushroomed. When Cleaver disappeared, his popularity diminished. It mushroomed for a while, and now it's diminished because people are saying that, if you're the leader of a revolution, you cannot absent yourself from it.

Cleaver advocates violence, if needed, to gain black power. How does that strike you, Mr. Harris?

HARRIS: I think this. We [whites] probably needed some jarring, but I do believe the thing has got in position now. In other words, I don't think you're going to have to resort to violence. If you pretty well leave people to their own now, they'll solve it.

BOND: I think leaving it to their own usually means the minority group comes out on the short end of the stick. It means you're the last guy to get a job, the last guy to get a good school, the last guy to get a good house, and so on.

HARRIS: Well, Julian, I don't agree with you.

Have you followed Mr. Bond's career, Mr. Harris?

HARRIS: Well, as far as the newspapers are concerned.

BOND: You know you can't believe all that, Mr. Harris.

HARRIS: I think that statement he made back there about the draft-card burning was right unfortunate.

BOND: Well, I'll tell you something I feel about that draft-card burning thing, and that is that people didn't really understand what had been said. And I think part of the fault is due to the Atlanta papers, which ran these scare headlines and never printed the original statement until three days after the statement, on Sunday. I thought it was a legitimate statement. What I said was that I wouldn't burn my card, but I understood why people did burn theirs, and I admired their courage because I thought they did it with full knowledge of what the penalty was. And any reasonable man can agree with that, can't he?

HARRIS: Yeah, I don't think I would object to that, as big an extremist as I am.

BOND: I wish you'd been in the Legislature.

(After their meeting, Julian Bond and Roy Harris wrote impressions of each other. Here is Bond's appraisal of Harris.)

Bond on Harris

A meeting with a man like Roy Harris is approached with trepidation. Will he rant and rave? Will he scream and shout? Will he attempt to gather a lynch mob from among the members of the Commerce Club, where we were scheduled to meet?

In such surroundings—paneled walls, cut-glass dishes on oak sideboards, humble servants—is it proper for one gentleman to call another a racist?

Is he a gentleman?

Roy Harris, of Augusta, Ga., at 73, is either unable or unwilling to mount a defense of his positions on race. He smiles, jokes, laughs, remembers.

Can this be the same man who said that the issue of the 1968 Presidential campaign would be "Niggers"? (He was right.)

Confrontation is the order of the day, so Bond and Harris try to confront. But there is no clash of will or wit. He recalls the good old days gone by; remarks that he once worked with "Negroes" (and pronounces it correctly); scores liberals as hypocrites; lauds Atlanta as a center of black development; says Negroes, in all fairness, ought to "take over" Augusta if population figures dictate it; and refuses—softly, not evasively—to give a straight answer to most questions.

Can this be the same man? It is. Roy Harris ("Mr. Roy" to the others gathered, "Mr. Harris" to me; I am "Julian" to him. Is that age speaking to youth, or white to black? Let it pass), member of the Board of Regents, former speaker of the Georgia House, former campaign manager for George Wallace, bus line owner (integrated buses) and newspaper (of sorts) publisher, Citizens Council organizer, former farm boy—he is the same.

But what a contradiction. There is no open meanness in him, no vitriol like that in those who read his sheet, none of the open, quick hatred that causes children at prayer to face bombs and makes big, brave men use baseball bats to keep children from their ABC's.

His children are the beaters and bombers. One thinks he believes they are children, and treats them so. He tells them stories that are not true, promises dreams that cannot be, explains their condition by blaming others, raises egos by suggesting subjugation, supports law and order by defying laws. Treat them like children, as he has, and they react in kind—childlike: muttered anger, blind acts committed in secret, and denial of the truth. In these plush surroundings we talk, 15 stories and as many miles above the streets below, where the evil results abound—broken lives, hopeless futures, stunted growths, black and white.

Can he bear alone the responsibility for their condition? Not he alone. But certainly Roy Harris, acting in concert with others, must be blamed for today.

—*Julian Bond.*

Harris on Bond

The fight today is not between segregationists and Negroes, but between hypocritical whites who favor integration until it affects them, and people like me.

Therefore, it came as no surprise to me that Julian Bond and I would agree on many things, although the basic difference between us is that he believes in integration and I am a strong believer in the segregation of the races.

I did not find the experience with Bond to be dissimilar to those experiences I've had in talking with Negro college presidents, Negro college students, Negro teachers, Negro businessmen and just ordinary Negroes. They all treat me with respect, and I treat them the same way.

In his conversation, he didn't appear to be militant. In fact, he leaned over backwards to be polite to me, and I did the same for him. He did surprise me by disclaiming any militancy because his speeches have been to the contrary. He has left the impression in these speeches that the Negroes' only hope for making any progress was by the use of violent methods.

I have no objections to black power. I think the Negroes are entitled to be represented in government; however, until crime among the Negro people has been curbed and some of their leaders are pointed in a different direction, black rule is dangerous. It has proved to be so in the nation's capital.

They are entitled to economic power as well as political power, and I believe that experience has shown that they have been able to develop their own banks, insurance companies and businesses only where they have lived under a pattern of segregation.

Certainly they have done much better in Atlanta than they have in New York, Chicago or Philadelphia.

One of the great troubles now is that we have practically lost communication. When they try to ram integration down the throats of white people, it creates a state of ill feeling. I've always said the race problem can't be settled without a mutual agreement between the races, and you can't ever get together without more dialogues like the one Bond and I had. You just can't let the hypocritical whites and militant Negroes settle it.

—Roy Harris.

"We Can't Cuss White People Any More. It's in Our Hands Now"

by Walter Rugaber

JACKSON, MISS.

THE CROWD gathered in Charles H. Griffin's campaign headquarters in Jackson on the night of March 12 exuded satisfaction and relief. Griffin had just won a Congressional seat in a special election, and Mississippi's white Democracy had thus turned back the first serious challenge by a major Negro candidate in 88 years. Then something unheard of occurred. Charles Evers, the Great Nigra Peril himself, walked in the door, calmly signed the guest book and strode up to his victorious opponent. Griffin had sufficient presence of mind to flash a cordial smile as he shook hands. "Congratulations," said the loser. "I'll do anything I can to help you. Just remember, we're all Mississippians." The startled whites applauded.

Charles Evers had lost to Griffin by a 2-to-1 margin. Still, he didn't *feel* like a loser. "Do you realize," he asked later, "that 43,000 Negroes voted who never would have before, and that we

From the *New York Times Magazine,* August 4, 1968, copyright © 1968 by The New York Times Company.

came out and challenged the entire political system of Mississippi? You watch us next time. We're going to take every sheriff we run. The local school boards are up, and we're going to take some of them, too."

Yes, this is Mississippi. No, Evers was not just dream-talking. A decade after virtually being run out of the state, five years after his younger brother Medgar was slain from ambush, Charles Evers has made a fair start—though only a start—on turning Mississippi around. He has launched Negro registration drives and follow-up election campaigns that provided the first breaks in Mississippi's lily-white government. He has organized tight, tough economic boycotts in some of the South's most hard-bitten areas, winning Negro advances in employment and the desegregation of public facilities. And he has made of himself, as politician and business-man, a symbol of what the Negro can aspire to, even in rural Mississippi.

Just how far Evers has come was indicated in the special election to fill the 10-month unexpired Congressional term of newly elected Governor John Bell Williams. It took place in the Third District of southwestern Mississippi, which includes the capital city of Jackson; an estimated 64 per cent of the voters are white. In the Feb. 27 primary, the white vote was split among six white candidates, and Evers—on leave from his post as state field secretary for the National Association for the Advancement of Colored People—led the field. In the runoff, the white vote united against him.

But Griffin will have to run for the office again in the fall, and for a time Evers considered opposing him. The state House of Representatives rushed through a change in the election law—aimed directly at Evers—calling for a runoff if no candidate achieved a majority in the general election. The bill died in the Senate, and Evers does not plan to make the race, but the wide-spread support the measure had gained underlined the impact of the Evers threat.

The events of the last few months have done nothing to diminish his position. On May 21, Evers was one of some 40 Negroes named to participate in the state Democratic convention—the first of their race since 1876. He was also elected chairman of the

Jefferson County Democratic executive committee. The next day, he announced that he would serve as state co-chairman of Senator Robert F. Kennedy's Presidential campaign. (He was with the Senator in Los Angeles when Kennedy was shot June 5.)

One morning early this month Evers was elected a delegate to the Democratic National Convention—and resigned the same afternoon, arguing that he could not be "used as a pawn" by a state party leadership fundamentally unreconciled to change. Only four Negroes had been named to the state's 68-member delegation to Chicago.

But Evers will be in Chicago this month, a much more visible figure than he would have been as a member of the state delegation. He is expected to provide the cutting edge for a challenge to that delegation by a coalition of Negroes and white liberals. And the Mississippi challenge is expected to serve in turn as the cutting edge for similar challenges from several other Southern states. Those who recall the emotional confrontation over the seating of the Mississippi Freedom Democratic party at the 1964 convention will recognize the potential dramatic impact of a more broadly based and determined challenge this year. It will be all of that and more, if Evers has his way.

Charles Evers is a big, husky man whose voice and manner can slip suddenly and easily from gentle humor to stinging condemnation. He was born 45 years ago in Decatur, a country town in east-central Mississippi which he remembers as "a very small, quiet place" with relatively few Negroes and hence "not too much violence." The Evers family, which ran a funeral home and a lumber contracting business, was successful and well established in the Negro community there. Charles and Medgar grew up with distinctly different personalities.

"They were brothers," an acquaintance recalls, "but that's about as far as it went." Medgar was gentle and easygoing and usually took pains not to offend others. His brother is blunt and direct, and there is hardly a toe—black or white—that he has left unstomped. But for all the disparity, the two shared a fierce antagonism toward white supremacy. It was an essential bond.

Each day they walked two miles to the Decatur Consolidated School. "We never understood," Charles says, "why the white kids could ride by in their big, yellow, shiny bus while we sloshed through the mud. That disturbed us. Although we were a little more fortunate than many, we never did feel any different than other Negroes, and Medgar and I always said, when we got grown, we'd change it."

They went off to high school in nearby Newton and roomed there with a white woman who ran a small restaurant where Charles worked. "She taught us a lot that we learned about white people. She was always kind to us—she was like a mother to me. I remember they had separate entrances to the restaurant, and every chance I'd get I'd go in the white side. Since I worked there, I wouldn't be questioned too much about it. I wanted to see how it was so different."

Mrs. Payne tried to explain things:

"Charles, that's just the way Mississippi is. The colored have their side, and the whites have theirs."

"But ours is so dirty."

"Well, you just have to keep it clean."

The brothers remained entirely unconvinced. There were many such incidents, all part of the dreary business of growing up black in the rural South. Most young Negroes learned their "place," but Charles and Medgar resisted the process with a particular intensity.

"We weren't going to let anything or anybody stop us," Charles says. "I think it really dawned on us the time they killed a friend of my father's. They drug him out and hung him to a tree. Our parents rushed us back in the house, but we could hear everybody yelling and hollering. We were just kids, but I remember it just as good as if it was the day it happened."

In 1941, after completing the 11th grade, Charles volunteered for the Army serving in the Pacific. He then finished high school in Newton and in 1950 received a degree in social science from Alcorn A. & M. College, a Negro institution in Lorman. After a year in Korea with his reserve unit, he moved to Philadelphia, a small town 23 miles north of Decatur, where he took over his family's funeral parlor and started a hotel, a restaurant, a taxicab service and a gas station.

Philadelphia was about as tough then as the world found it a decade or so later when three young civil-rights workers were murdered there. But Evers and his brother, who had graduated from Alcorn to work for an insurance company in which the family had an interest, began their civil-rights agitation. They would assemble four or five Negroes in a deserted pasture or an out-of-the-way barn and enroll them in the N.A.A.C.P. The membership cards came back from New York in unmarked envelopes, and one of the brothers would secretly deliver them.

In 1954, the N.A.A.C.P. decided to hire a full-time staff worker for the state. The brothers easily agreed that Medgar was the more diplomatic, and he moved to Jackson for $3,000 a year. Charles stayed and even gained brief popularity over radio station WHOC as Mississippi's first Negro disk jockey. But he found himself more and more isolated in Philadelphia.

The town's segregationists began to apply various pressures: his Negro employees were threatened, lawsuits were filed, credit was more or less impossible to obtain. And in 1957, Charles left the state. He arrived in Chicago with a new Ford, $2 in cash and a driving ambition which even today feeds an active set of ulcers.

During the day he carried sides of beef at Swift & Co. At night he worked as a washroom attendant at hotels in the Loop. On weekends he tended bar at a little tavern on California Avenue. In just two years he had the money to start his own cocktail lounge, and later he opened a second.

Evers owned the jukeboxes at both places, an impertinence that greatly offended the Chicago syndicate. Medgar telephoned one day early in June, 1963, and cautioned his brother that big-city hoodlums could be quite as unpleasant as Southern sheriffs.

"I thought I got you out of trouble down here," Medgar laughed.

"Don't worry about me," Charles replied. "You just take care of those rednecks down there."

Medgar was shot a few nights later.

"We made an agreement when we were boys," Evers says. "If anything happened to either one of us, the other would carry on [with the civil-rights effort]." Evers confronted the N.A.A.C.P.'s national leadership and more or less demanded his brother's job. "I wasn't going to let anybody mess up what he had done. I knew nobody else could do [the work] like I could." In the tense, emotional aftermath of Medgar's assassination, there was no particular resistance; he took over two days before Medgar's burial at Arlington National Cemetery.

It is practically impossible to compare the performance of the two brothers. Mrs. Ruby Hurley, Southeastern regional director of the N.A.A.C.P. and an associate of both men, recently mused: "The times were so different; the personalities were so different."

Medgar's tenure coincided with the South's most militant resistance to desegregation—the days of Emmett Till and Mack Charles Parker, of the white Citizens Councils and the State Sovereignty Commission. Medgar did some work on voter registration and employment opportunities for Negroes, mainly in Jackson and the Delta region; but as Charles observes, "His work was much harder than mine. He spent a lot of time just trying to keep Negroes alive." Within a few years of his appointment, Charles had the advantage of a more relaxed climate and a series of important Federal laws and court decisions. But the actual implementation of advances in such areas as education and employment posed a major challenge.

Charles Evers built his organization in southwestern Mississippi almost entirely on an N.A.A.C.P. base. He established local branches in each county, attended most meetings and played a major role in choosing officers and setting policy. Today, the branch presidents serve as his leading deputies and the members make up his main field force. There is little significant opposition evident among Negroes in the area.

They had been battered for decades by an unusually rigid pattern of oppression, and Evers found almost no indigenous civil-rights movement in the area. "This was the worst section of Mississippi as far as violence was concerned," he said, "and maybe that gave them the feeling that I wasn't pretending, I wasn't joking, I wasn't doing it for publicity." Evers is proud of the organizing he did and regularly insists upon his status as an insider, a neighbor more than a civil-rights leader.

"Everybody likes to know what's going to benefit him," he said. "I'd always go to the ministers first and try to get their support. We'd more or less show them what it would do in their behalf in uniting their church: the more progressive you are and the more leadership you show, the more people will cater to you. We'd show them it's their duty, it's their God-given duty, because they had been chosen to be leaders.

"Then I'd go to the common Negroes, the laborers, the maids, the unemployed. You start, for instance, with the welfare. Everybody wants to know about the welfare. The conditions, really, are what we work on. In any community, a man can go in and start cussing the welfare or cussing the school system, and he's going to get some support."

One of Evers's key weapons was the boycott, and he proved himself a superb tactician—organizing local Negroes to stay away from white stores until the black community's demands were met. The white merchants fought him bitterly, but sooner or later they capitulated and extended major gains. In Natchez, for example, he not only got a signed agreement but also insisted that the Board of Aldermen formally ratify it. The boycott led to such steps as the desegregation of a hospital and the employment of Negroes as clerks, cashiers, policemen, deputy sheriffs and salesmen. Similar advances were won after boycotts in Fayette, Port Gibson and other towns.

The campaigns were strict and unyielding, but Evers rarely missed a chance to show off a better side. Once he sat back and allowed an "outsider," young and sharply militant, to lash the white leadership. Then Evers quietly led the Mayor aside and offered the town a choice: "Work with me—or that wild youngster over there."

But after a bomb injured a local N.A.A.C.P. leader in Natchez, Evers himself blew up: "We're not going to take it any longer. We're not going to start any riots, but we've got guns and we're going to fight back. I may be fired [from the N.A.A.C.P.] for saying this, but that's what we're going to do."

Despite such angry talk, the Evers view of Mississippi's whites is uncommonly optimistic, as in the following exchange:

"You've often said you think Mississippi will be way ahead of the country some day [in race relations]."

"I know so."

"A lot of people would think that means you think the white people are basically your friends."

"They are. They really are. They just don't know any better

now. They don't hate us for any reason other than because we're black."

"That's enough, isn't it?"

"Well, once you convince this rascal that black is nothing dirty and there's nothing disgraceful about it, he's going to change. Once we stand up to them and let them know that we can do whatever they can do, they're going to start accepting us. And once we get them to accept us, we're going to be on our way."

For Evers, the transition from civil rights to politics was natural and inevitable. The way to solve the Negro's problems was to get rid of the people responsible—"the board of supervisors that's responsible for welfare, the mayor who allows police brutality, the sheriff who administers it, the constable and justice of the peace who arrest you falsely and judge you falsely." The way to get rid of them, he preached, was to register and to vote.

Registration, of course, must be the first step. There are a variety of techniques an organizer can use, and Evers has used most of them—staging marches and rallies, sending workers out on door-to-door canvasses of Negro neighborhoods. Essential to the effort are his records for each area listing the names of those Negroes who have registered and those who require more encouragement.

An Evers election campaign begins with the selection of qualified candidates, for he has found that Negroes will not vote for just anyone with a black face. Then a coordinator is appointed for each district, and workers are selected to drive people to the polls. As Negro voters appear there on election day, their names are checked off. At noon and again at 4 P.M. each district makes up a list of those who have failed to vote, and workers make special visits in an effort to coax them out.

This now goes on, to a greater or lesser extent, in six south-western counties. In three—Jefferson, Claiborne and Wilkinson—Negroes have a majority of the registered vote. In three others—Adams (Natchez), Copiah and Franklin—whites still hold the edge. Soon Evers hopes to move effectively into Yazoo, Warren (Vicksburg) and other counties to the north.

The political program requires tireless pump-priming by Evers himself. His speeches are an awesome blend of reprimand and forgiveness, mockery and cajolery; he threatens and he pleads. "You've got to do it yourselves," he tells audiences. "We can't march anymore. We can't picket. We can't cuss white people anymore. It's in our hands now."

One night during last summer's campaign, Evers spoke at the Mt. Zion Baptist Church in Rodney, a village deep in the Mississippi backwoods. The church is a simple structure with unadorned windows, crude wooden benches and a picture of Jesus on the wall. At the back there is an inadequate window fan and a jug of drinking water with a porcelain dipper hanging on the wall above it. A clock gave up at 1:45 one day, and the light bulbs flicker in their dangling sockets. More than 100 Negroes, most of them in work clothes, were waiting when Evers walked in.

"On Aug. 8," he said sternly, "you all voted for the white man." A murmur of protest went up from his audience. "Yes, you did," Evers insisted, "We read the returns. You, the Negroes in Rodney, didn't care enough. Or maybe you didn't know. But we can't make that mistake again. You are the ones who can keep denying yourselves decent homes, decent jobs, decent schools. It ain't never going to change until you send some of our own people down there to represent us at the courthouse."

At a planning session in Lafayette Evers told his drivers: "I don't want you to haul a single Negro who gets in your car and starts talking about how he 'ain't gonna vote for no niggers.' Put him out right there." Then he turned to lash more formidable enemies. "If we find out that one of these preachers is up in his pulpit campaigning for a white against a Negro, he can't preach in this county anymore. We want our ministers to do right. If we find out they're doing wrong, they're going to go."

Criticism of his sometimes heavy-handed methods tends to center on his team of about 65 Negro youths, variously described as "a goon squad," "The Black Hats" and "The Defenders." The group's sole purpose, Evers insists, is protection. Whites often harass Negro rallies in the South, and the Federal Bureau of Investigation has warned Evers repeatedly of assassination plots cooked up against him by hot-eyed haters in the Ku Klux Klan. (He owns a small arsenal of weapons and almost never ventures out without a gun.) In this year's Congressional campaign, an Evers bodyguard exchanged shots in Jackson with a white youth in a passing car.

But many have seen the Evers "army" jostle Negroes entering stores under boycott, and some shoppers have had their packages knocked to the streets. Evers points out that the boycotts all had the ardent support of the Negro community at large, and he solemnly denies any knowledge of strong-arm tactics in enforcing them. Yet such dismaying incidents have occurred—though they had little to do with the decisions of thousands of Negroes to boycott white stores for months at a time.

A man who has worked with both Evers and his critics says of such tactics, "Philosophically, of course, I disapprove of it. But I think he's getting results, and maybe you need a little benevolent dictatorship."

Evers is no less a success as a small-town entrepreneur. Few civil-rights leaders are as openly and happily in pursuit of the dollar. In Fayette, Evers built a modern grocery store, a lounge, a radio repair shop, a ballroom and a liquor store, all contained in an attractive complex which he named the Medgar Evers Shopping Center. (He has also helped organize "cooperative" groceries, shares of which are held by Negroes, at Natchez, Port Gibson and Hazlehurst.) He maintains a home in Jackson for his second wife (an early marriage ended in divorce) and three daughters; a fourth daughter is married. He commutes the 77 miles to his home when he can, but he is found most often at his Fayette shopping center, which includes a small apartment at one end.

"Good day, ladies," he chirps to customers. "Come right in, come right in." He sweeps to the front of his Fayette grocery to peck both women on the cheek. "We've got a lot of wonderful buys around here today." He waves his arm at the brightly lit shelves. "Come on back here and let me show you some pork chops." It goes on like that for hours.

But some of the most bitter criticism of Evers has stemmed from his performance as a businessman. His affluence is in strong contrast to the economic status of so many well-known civil-rights leaders who are poorly paid ministers or professionals. Even more to the point, there is the fact that he profits from the civil-rights movement: his customers are often the same people he has organized, and it seems to some observers that he opened his stores in unseemly proximity to the time when white competitors were being hit by the boycotts he had initiated.

"The trouble with Charles," one critic contends bluntly, "is that he's something of a hustler. He's not putting everything out on the table any of the time, and he always has an eye out for things that will help Charles as much as the movement." Even friendly observers have their doubts. "He didn't call those boycotts to make a buck for his stores," said one. "The cause-and-effect relationship just isn't there. But he sure didn't hesitate to utilize them. I think he would have been better advised not to have done it."

"I don't have to boycott the white man to get business," Evers retorts. And it is true that, though boycotts in the area have been over for years, his Fayette shopping center is as jammed with customers as it ever was. "People have to look at my background and see I've been a businessman all my life. That's why I've been able to go out and confront and fight discrimination and segregation. I was independent, and I lived off what the Negroes did for me and not what some racist, some bigot, handed out. If we had more Negro leaders as independent businessmen, they could fight harder and it would be less likely for them to be bought off by the power structure."

The Evers approach to life has sometimes alienated civil-rights leaders; he has little appreciation for the niceties of corporate association activity. For example, when the nation's most prominent rights leaders hurried to Mississippi for the 1966 James Meredith march, Evers said that he hoped the demonstration wouldn't "turn into another Selma, where everyone goes home with the cameramen and leaves us holding the bag." A militant-minded critic recalled this broadside some months later and noted dryly that "the only Negro I've seen on television in Mississippi lately has been Charles Evers." Evers used to delight in dismissing groups such as the Student Nonviolent Coordinating Committee as "those boys running all over the country looking for glamour and glory."

Of late, though, Evers has been less abrasive. In a recent interview, for instance, he remarked that "if America would straighten up and do what she's supposed to do" there would be no need for S.N.C.C. or its black power philosophy. Until then, presumably, the need remains. "Everybody's not as patient as Medgar and I happen to have been." And though he sometimes implies that the

N.A.A.C.P.'s national leadership doesn't understand the hard realities of Mississippi, he avoids any direct criticism.

Local Negroes seem overwhelmingly loyal to Evers. They refer to him as "the big boss," and some recall times before 1963 as "B.C.—before Charles." A wry, middle-aged workman in Port Gibson says, "We're going to take good care of him; he's done more around here than any of us ever thought of." A local clergyman says, "There are a lot of problems with Charles, but the people want him."

One of the problems, some critics feel, is Evers's great popularity itself. They say that the N.A.A.C.P. local structure is built almost entirely around Evers and that other Negroes have little chance to share the responsibility. The loss of Evers, they warn, would mean disaster. One astute Negro, commenting on the still slow political progress, put it this way:

"I think some of the Negroes just *want* to vote for the white man. He puts some gravel in somebody's driveway, and—you know—who can argue with gravel? . . . Evers didn't do his homework. They didn't do the kind of citizenship education that ought to be done. Evers tried to do it all by himself. That's one of his shortcomings. I like Charles—you just can't tell him a goddam thing. And you know, maybe if I was in Mississippi under them circumstances you couldn't tell me anything either."

"I may suggest certain things, and usually my suggestions are carried out," Evers says with an easy laugh, "but I certainly don't tell people what to do. We have adult education classes, poverty programs, we try to get people jobs, we talk about the issue at meetings and everybody is supposed to get up and say what they think—I don't know what else you can do. When you lose the spoke out of a wheel, you weaken it; but I don't think it would stop the wheel from turning." That, of course, depends on the number of spokes there are.

Though he has at least his share of critics, Evers has begun to forge a unity among Negro groups that seems unmatched anywhere in the South. The Freedom Democratic party, for example, a militant Negro organization that has often been opposed to the Evers approach, lent its support in the Congressional race.

Evers is convinced that growing political unity and sophistication will lead not only to local victories in counties where the Negro is in a majority but also to effective alliances with progressive whites on a statewide basis. Four years from now, he says, there will be a Negro running for Lieutenant Governor to test the liberal strength. He acknowledges that it will prove a difficult course even if Mississippi's Negro registration climbs above the one-quarter level at which it now stands.

"Negroes haven't learned to trust each other yet. Many of them think Negroes can't do the job. They say to me, 'Mr. Evers, Negroes have never done this before. We have been taught all our lives to be servants, and that this is the white man's world, and that he's supposed to make all the laws and all the rules. The Negro mind has to be freed, too, and it will be. Too many have died for this, too many have suffered for this, we have worked for this too long."

For years, the civil-rights movement in general has been turned outward—toward Congress, the white liberal and national opinion in general. Now there are signs in the North of an inward turn, a separatist movement. Evers, too, has an inward direction—but of a very different kind, one that includes not only the individual problems and needs of the Mississippi Negroes but of their segregationist neighbors as well.

"We in Mississippi," he says, "white and Negro, are going to have to work out our own problems." For those who believe that only the outside world can hold the state's racial terror in check, it must be disconcerting and more than a bit offensive to hear Evers suggest, as he often does, that even an archfoe such as Senator James O. Eastland will eventually come around.

"I believe in proving a point and letting it go," Evers says. "Once you get what you ask for, then there's no point in hanging on and hanging on and just wearing it out. I definitely believe in working with white people if they want to work on a man-to-man basis. There's no point in anybody fooling themselves. I don't care how much the black power boys scream, I don't care how much the Ku Klux Klan screams, we can't get along without each other. They may as well realize that unless we do these things together we're all going to be in a continuous turmoil."

Part 5

OPTIONS FACING AMERICANS: PATHS TO SEPARATISM OR INTEGRATION

THE BURDEN of desegregating American society has so far been that of black Americans, not whites. Open occupancy, even when it is token, means black people moving into white neighborhoods, not whites into black ones. When busing is proposed as a means of desegregating schools, we know which kids are likely to be bused out of their neighborhood into a strange one—blacks. With all the achievements of the direct-action, nonviolent protest movement—desegregation of lunch counters, golf courses, buses, theaters—it is still true that in desegregating these public accommodations we achieved change only in highly visible facilities and not in central institutions. We have not yet basically altered the inequality of access to opportunity in those institutions central to the American economic and social order, institutions which are so critical to the everyday lives of everyday black Americans—housing, jobs, and income.

Some say that the civil rights protest movement has failed. Has it? How different are things today from what they were at the time of the Supreme Court decision of 1954? How different are the patterns of segregation in American life from what they were when Dr. Martin Luther King led a bus boycott in the capital of the Old Confederacy and fired our imaginations about a new desegregated America? Most important, how far has America come in its political, religious, economic, and educational life and leadership from our once unthinking acceptance of segregated institutions as normal and normative? During the decade spanned by the 1954 Supreme Court decision on school desegregation and the Civil Rights Act of 1964, we destroyed the legal foundations of racism in America. The movement has not failed; it has succeeded in upsetting a three-centuries-old way of life and in challenging us as a society to chart the next steps toward its ultimate goals.

"Integration is no longer the main goal," announces a recent headline in the *New York Times*. The story quotes Roy Innis, Associate National Director of CORE. "People today talk about control of their community schools. Integration is counter to the mood of the black people." Just when social scientists are tackling the problem of ethnocentrism and the chauvinistic tunnel vision of too many textbooks, we hear demands that black students should be taught black economics and black history by black teachers in black neighborhood schools. American schools have taught white history for more than three centuries; that such discrimination is standard in American society is not at issue here. The question is whether most Negro Americans want to replace white discrimination with black segregation, or whether they still have some hope for the integration of American society.

Those who preach hatred and separatism bring nothing new to America. Those who would separate and hate and "get whitey" see themselves as radicals. But in the light of sociological analysis they are not radicals; they are conservative preservers of the American tradition of racial separatism and social segregation. In his own language, H. Rap Brown—like violence—is "as American as cherry pie." Cries of "Burn, baby, burn," Stokely Carmichael's talk of "Get your guns"—these are the statements of men totally assimilated into the American way of life. As the President's Commission on Civil Disorders says: "The Black Power advocates of today consciously feel that they are the most militant group in the Negro protest movement. Yet they have retreated from a direct confrontation with American society on the issue of integration and, by preaching separatism, unconsciously function as an accommodation to white racism. Much of their economic program, as well as their interest in Negro history, self-help, racial solidarity, and separation, is reminiscent of Booker T. Washington. The rhetoric is different, but the programs are remarkably similar."

Pleas for separatism are disquieting because integration has been a liberal article of faith for both white and black Americans. Most Americans now alive have grown up with the assumption that citizens opposed to desegregation are anti-Negro. Now we find black militant spokesmen addressing us from diverse platforms with insistent pleas that black Americans must build their own separate political and economic base on black pride and within the black community. Do most American Negroes agree? How do Negro Americans (not "spokesmen," but most Negro Americans) feel about the desegregation of American institutions as opposed to the new separatism?

In 1967, William Brink and Louis Harris published a study of racial attitudes. They reported that only 11 per cent of 1,059 Negroes favored separatism. In January 1968, *Fortune* magazine published Daniel Yankelovich's interviews with three hundred Negroes in thirteen American cities. When asked their feelings about needs, the largest proportion of his interviewees (97 per cent) cited "more education for my children." The next largest response (93 per cent) was "more desegregation in schools, neighborhoods, and jobs." Only 5 per cent expressed the opinion that desegregation of any kind was undesirable.

Most American Negroes still have faith in their pursuit of equality through desegregation. Only one circumstance, they feel, could persuade them to follow those extremists who hold that promises of equality within the traditional American structure are hollow, and that the best chance for the Negro is to "go it alone." That circumstance would be a white community failure to continue the process of desegregation, not only in the schools but in all other institutions. Most black Americans are not interested in a separatism that will fragment the group. They would simply like to see evidence of equality of opportunity in other areas: quality of public schools, housing, access to union membership, and even congressional censure. If white America will respect the decisions of the Supreme Court and live up to the implications of the Constitution, the current talk of black separatism will become an odd and interesting item in a history of our attempt to achieve America.

The Mill: A Giant Step for the Southern Negro

by Reese Cleghorn

ERWIN, N. C.

IN THE dusty yard between buildings of Erwin Mills, 54-year-old James McDougald skillfully wheels a forklift from a warehouse to a waiting tractor-trailer to load blue denim cloth similar to the denim first made in this plant more than half a century ago. Inside, the process of manufacturing cloth is essentially the same, too: from the picking machines, cleaning the cotton, to the carding, drawing, roving and spinning machines, and finally to looms still attended by men called weavers. One building of the mill, in fact, is the original. It is red brick with sawtooth corners and exposed iron braces, built when the virgin forest was cleared here in 1903, soon after the South's first "bring-the-mills-to-the-cotton" campaign.

Until the early nineteen-fifties a visitor to Erwin would have seen very much the same kind of mill town that had been here from the start. But change has come steadily since then. One of the changes is in the life of James McDougald.

He is a hefty man who has worked for the mills for 22 years. Five years ago, because he is black, he would not have been opera-

From the *New York Times Magazine,* November 9, 1969, copyright © 1969 by The New York Times Company.

ting a forklift, a small machine which hoists and moves heavy weights. This is a relatively skilled job, and such positions were reserved for whites. The few Negroes who were in the plant (under 4 per cent in 1965) did only menial work. Now blacks are moving into more skilled jobs, and they constitute 17 per cent of the mill's work force of 1,774 men and women. McDougald can earn about $85 a week, and his life is better.

The number of Negroes in the plant at Erwin is rising steadily. In one recent month more than half those hired were black. The trend is the same throughout the textile industry, almost nine-tenths of which is now in the South. A recent Federal estimate was that 11.6 per cent of the industry's production workers were Negro, compared with 3.3 per cent in 1960. The percentage is higher in the South. Dr. Richard Rowan of the University of Pennsylvania estimates, on the basis of a study of 46 companies, that Negroes during the latter half of 1968 constituted 12.7 per cent of the production workers industrywide and 13.4 per cent in the South. The percentage has risen since then. It is clear that for many black Southerners textile mills are becoming what they traditionally have been for many low-income whites: the first industrial step away from the farm or marginal small-town subsistence, and a vehicle for economic mobility upward. The new black employment already seems to be slowing migration from parts of the South to other areas of the country.

Much of what has happened in the textile industry is exemplified in Erwin, a town of 30,000 on the edge of the Piedmont, 40 miles southeast of Raleigh. C. W. Howell is manager of Erwin Mills, a division of Burlington Industries, the nation's largest textile firm. He says the plant's experience with Negro employees has been good. "On turnover, absenteeism and job performance, we can't tell the difference, really," he says. "Their work record and performance are comparable with those of any other group." He sees no difference in the amounts of premium pay earned by Negroes and whites for superior production. And a spokesman for Burlington concludes: "Our experience in recent years dispels the myths in some Southern communities that there's a difference in performance. As for the attitudes of white employees, I think the greatest surprise some of our managers had at first was the acceptance by whites of the Negroes."

The discriminatory pattern had been fixed from the start in most Southern textile mills. The first major campaigns to establish cotton mills in the South were in the eighteen-eighties. As the region was beating civic drums for industry, it simultaneously was moving toward a system of rigid, legalized white supremacy. This development barred Negroes from all but the lowliest industrial jobs. Southern states enacted laws making white supremacy absolute. One example: until 1968, South Carolina had a statute (already made meaningless by Federal action but still on the books) prohibiting textile manufacturers from allowing whites and Negroes to work in the same rooms, or even to use the same doors and stairways.

The Civil Rights Act of 1964 and Presidential Executive orders concerning Government contracts have been the principal battering rams against white supremacy in the textile industry. Some industry spokesmen say, however, that from now on a bigger factor will be a shortage of white workers. Textiles are the largest industrial employer in North and South Carolina and Georgia (about 470,000 workers). Increasing industrialization in these states has opened new opportunities for workers. As higher-wage industries compete for the labor force, textile mills are finding their readiest source of labor among Negroes. Some shifting of plant locations already has resulted. In the Carolinas, textiles have been concentrated in the Piedmont areas, where there are relatively few Negroes; now the industry is moving toward the more southerly Black Belt areas of these states, where the Negro population is large. One Burlington plant in the coastal area of North Carolina already is about fifty-fifty racially.

Erwin is between the Piedmont and the Black Belt, which is the old plantation country. A red-and-white billboard on an interstate highway near the town depicts a hooded figure on horseback and tells travelers: "Welcome to North Carolina. You are in the heart of Klan country." But there is little evidence of Klan activity, and both blacks and whites say the Klan is largely an illusion. Its violent spirit has not been evidenced in the attitudes of Erwin's mill workers as integration has proceeded. What is found among the "hands" is a perhaps surprising amount of tolerance, with some genuine friendships across racial lines, but also a large measure of unsophisticated prejudice.

David Griffin, a chunky, 39-year-old weaver who is president of Local 250 of the Textile Workers Union of America in Erwin, says he does not believe there is great resentment among white workers about the hiring of Negroes. Nor, he says, have any Negro members of the union filed grievances against the management on grounds of racial discrimination.

Griffin himself sees the increase in black employment as a hopeful development for the union, whose membership in Erwin hovers around half the work force or less. He thinks Negroes are being attracted to the union in somewhat higher proportion than whites. "I think within the next few years we'll have many more Negroes," he says. "Whites hate to organize. They want to 'get along' with management. But Negroes *know* it's not on *their* side. They've known that kind of thing all the way back to slavery times." For the Erwin local, success in attracting Negroes may be a life-or-death matter. For the T.W.U.A. in general, as for management, success in dealing with Negroes will be increasingly important.

Two members of the union probably speak for many others who take the changes in stride. One is Mrs. Ann Johnson, 32, a tall, blue-eyed woman with a sensitive face who has worked for Erwin Mills for six years and is a union shop steward in the spooling department. The other is Mrs. Mamie Chance, 40, a sturdy, animated Negro woman, who works in the same department. They are in many ways representative of the white and black employees in the mill, though they seem to have strengths considerably beyond the average. Both grew up on farms nearby, and both are glad not to be doing heavy farm labor for a living.

Mrs. Johnson's grandmother owned a substantial amount of cotton and tobacco land, but that was gone by the time she was a child. She grew up working on the farm, chopping cotton and doing other hard labor. Now she earns an average of about $90 a week, and she likes the work. "I'd rather be in the mill," she says emphatically. Even so, she and her husband, who also works in the mill, "just barely make out." They are paying for a house and a car, and they have two children.

She says she sees no reason why Negroes should not hold equal positions in the mill. "I feel they're entitled to work as much as I am," she says. "They have families to raise and feed just like I have. In our department everybody seems to be working together without any problem." What if she had a Negro supervisor? "I know I'd just as soon work for colored as work for *one* white supervisor I know." She is an outspoken union advocate, and she is hoping Negroes will strengthen the union.

Mrs. Chance, whose blue print dress and tennis shoes are a common form of attire among the women workers, has been at the mill since 1967. She was hired during a strike. "They said the union didn't hire me, so don't get in here and join the union," she recalls. But she later did, and the union's grievance committee came to her aid when she received a warning about missing a day during bad weather. She can earn $70 or $80 a week, depending upon the amount of premium pay for high production. Before, she was sometimes paid 75 cents an hour for chopping cotton or as much as $12 a day as a "hander," passing along the leaves in a tobacco farm.

Around Erwin, the number of farm jobs has been drastically reduced by mechanization. "First, the cotton pickers took all the cotton work," Mrs. Chance says, "and now tobacco harvesters are taking the tobacco work." As with many others in the mill, Mrs. Chance still lives on a farm. She and her husband are separated, and she has six children at home. She raises hogs, chickens and vegetables to reduce living costs.

"I can get along with everybody," she says when asked about the whites. "We'd go clean up their houses, wash their clothes, cook for their husbands. Why can't we work with them? One family here, we played together when we were kids, out in the field." Then she looks aside with mock seriousness and says, "I can get along with *everybody* but Ann." It is a small joke between them, and it is the kind of interplay that is beginning to produce genuine friendships of equality across racial lines.

There are many other opinions of what the changes mean. Paul Carroll, a lean, shaggy weaver who has the appearance of a mountain man, and who was until he married an Erwin girl, says: "I get along with 'em just fine. Some of 'em are lazy. They're just not gonna work like us white people. But I never hear nothing about it. They're just another working man."

Alfred L. Ferguson, a small, alert Negro in shirt sleeves and tie who graduated last year from Fayetteville State College and who is in the plant's production and planning department: "I had anticipated trouble, and there's been none at all. I'm surprised to a degree. I see it as a challenge."

Bradley Caudle, a weaver, veteran of 22 years at the mill and a part-time farmer, commenting on his reaction if the Negro employment should become 50 per cent: "It won't bother me. If they tend to their business, I will, too. As far as I know, they do."

Mrs. Betty Long, white, a spinner and a veteran of 26 years in the mill: "The good Lord made us all alike. We'll get along and it's better than the farm. I've plowed, sawed, pulled fodder. I'll take the mill. I've heard people say the mill is the hardest work, but they just never worked the way I did on the farm."

The industry that Mamie Chance has moved into is an improvement on her job as a tobacco hander, but it nevertheless is a low-wage, largely nonunion industry (only about 10 per cent organized). The T.W.U.A. contends that the industry is "dedicated to maintaining substandard wages and working conditions." But recent improvements are evident. A Bureau of Labor Statistics study shows that last September average "straight-line" earnings (without premium pay for production) of production-related workers in the textile industry was $2.06 an hour, 18 per cent better than three years ago. The study also showed that regional wage differentials have virtually disappeared in textiles, which once paid Southern workers substantially less than those in New England.

Although there still is enough hiring discrimination in the industry to concern civil-rights organizations, the movement of Negroes into upper levels within the plants probably is now of greater concern. Among Erwin Mills' 80 supervisors, not one is a Negro. Among the 107 upper-level employees who are salaried rather than on an hourly wage, a recent count showed only four Negroes. Burlington, considered one of the more forward of the big textile companies on matters of equal employment and union-management relations, has initiated a program called BEST (Burlington Education Skills Training) as a means of increasing Negro employment. Through BEST, a number of school dropouts and unskilled ghetto dwellers have been able to combine classwork and job training. But this is an attack on segregation patterns at the lowest level. Without similar industry initiatives at the supervisory level, antidiscrimination critics of the industry say, old patterns will not soon be broken there.

TEAM (Textiles Employment and Advancement for Minorities) is an organization that addresses itself to these problems, as well as to the effectiveness of Federal efforts to end discrimination in the industry. TEAM combines the antidiscrimination efforts of six agencies concerned with civil rights. Its principal weapons have been Presidential Executive orders, threatening withdrawal of Federal contracts from businesses guilty of racial discrimination, and Title VII of the Civil Rights Act of 1964, which prohibits discrimination by employers of 25 or more people.

Not every mill has accepted the changes as easily as Erwin; but those watching the scene know of few serious incidents. "You will hear of individual unpleasant experiences and perhaps even of a whole plant whose integration attempt was plagued with difficulty," says Dr. Emory Via, who works closely with TEAM in his capacity as director of the Labor Program of the Southern Regional Council. "But the important report is that there are few exceptions to this general rule: Wherever management has taken a firm stand that it will hire and promote without discrimination, the employees accept the situation, sometimes in a surprisingly cooperative way."

One of the biggest changes in the industry is not directly related to the influx of Negroes, but it will affect their lives as textile workers. It is the evolution of the "mill village." Negroes will not be entering the system of paternalism and industrial serfdom which generations of poor white Southerners experienced. Erwin, a town once entirely owned by the mill, typifies this change, too.

A North Carolina newspaper told its readers about Erwin not long after the mill was built. The headline said: "William A. Erwin, the Splendid Controlling Spirit, Has Done a Great Work."

The owners were seen as great benefactors, and the workers were humbly grateful recipients of new opportunities. The newspaper reported that at Erwin "all who labor to turn cotton into manufactured goods have more than usual encouragement to work with ready mind and willing hands, not only for their own support, but for the interest of the company which has done so much for them over and above giving them employment."

In the mill-controlled churches in towns like Erwin, as well as in state legislatures, the workers could hear this same refrain. But the conditions were raw by any standard. Mr. Erwin was praised as a man "of great heart" for being one of the first North Carolina mill owners to reduce working hours from 12 to 11 a day and for refusing to employ children under 12 years of age.

Today, the Erwin mill is not representative of Burlington's best plants. But it is very much like scores of others in the Carolinas, Georgia and other parts of the South. The plant occupies four major manufacturing buildings. Although the industry as a whole now uses more synthetic fiber than cotton, Erwin still uses more cotton: 2,000 bales a week, more than the entire annual cotton production in Erwin's country of Harnett. The principal products are traditional denim, stretch and sports fabrics.

In the early nineteen-fifties the mill sold its houses, wooden and usually L-shaped with porches, to employees. (Later it also sold the buildings in Erwin's small business district, which formerly had been leased to the occupants.) Many of the old mill houses are occupied by retired employees, who have given them more individual appearance with the addition of siding, roofing and other improvements of various styles and colors. "People have taken a lot more pride in their houses since the mill sold them," says Manager Howell. "It has changed the whole environment. The housing was really a burden to the company."

The sale of mill housing in most Southern mill towns has several explanations: the availability of other houses, new concepts of employee relations, a desire to change the mill-town "image," and, more recently, the impending desegregation of housing. In Erwin the housing remains completely segregated, and the mill can conveniently say this is not its business. The inferiority of the houses which the mill formerly provided for Negroes is clear: they are smaller, of poorer construction, and more distant from the mill. Only about 50 such houses exist, and few of the new Negro employees will ever live in them.

Erwin has become a place of Jaycees and garden-club members. Though the mill is still dominant, the standard trappings of small-town life are everywhere. Erwin's evolution was formalized two years ago when the residents voted to incorporate and elect city officials. Some employee animosity emerged when at least one voter in the mayoralty race wrote in the name of the mill manager, embellished as "Sir Clifton W. Howell." But a turnout of almost 90 per cent of the voters suggested that most people in Erwin took the change seriously.

For Negro employees, all this may mean little more than that they will not be living in company housing, with company schools and a company store in a company town. Their children as of this year attend a completely integrated school system in Erwin. But downtown business is still a white man's world. It moves much as it did before the mill became fully integrated, and with standard Southern small-town prejudices. Despite what the mill management and the union say, for instance, most of the town's business people are convinced that Negroes will be undesirable employees.

"I think it's lowered the standard some," says Charles N. Crawford, the postmaster. "Some employees who were good, they see somebody else getting by with a lot, and they get lax." Erwin's Mayor, Leonidas Jackson, a 69-year-old druggist, is pleased that the town has taken school integration in stride but he, too, thinks the new black employment means trouble for the mill management. "There's been a big turnover," he says. "Lots of them go in and work two or three weeks and then quit, from all reports."

The same view about plant turnover is volunteered by the town banker, W. H. Harrington, manager of the local branch of the Central Carolina Bank and Trust Company. "You've got so many colored people who'd just rather be on relief than work," he says. "Burlington is just like everybody else, bending over backwards for the Negro . . . it's the Government contracts, pure and simple."

Erwin's businessmen, it appears, have more difficulty than the mill's white workers in accepting the idea that Negroes can be integrated-and-equal production workers. This contrast seems singular. Through the years, mill workers have provided more than their share of Ku Klux Klansmen and white supremacist votes. Certainly mill managements feared the reactions of their white employees more than those of the general public when they began to hire Negroes. Will the South's lowest-level industrial workers accept integration more readily than the white-collar people downtown?

Rufus Cross is the kind of man who often is called a "cracker" and presumed to be living evidence that another generation must pass before Southern poor whites accept poor Negroes as equals. He is a slight man, 39 years old, with knobby, sinewy arms and troubled gray eyes. His ill-painted house, one of those formerly owned by the mill, overlooks the plant's parking lot. In overalls and a short-sleeved shirt, he greets a stranger at his door: "Come in and set down." He sprawls on a red leatherette sofa. His tattered shoes are off, and feet clad in green socks rest on torn linoleum covering the floor. A stovepipe from a wood-burning heater leads upward into a wall, as it probably always has; a television set is the room's only trace of luxury or even modernity.

"I just thumbed my way out of Georgia," Cross says in explaining how he came to Erwin. From childhood he had worked as a farm laborer and sawmill hand around Bainbridge, Ga. Two decades ago, making a peanut crop in Georgia, he was given room and board and only $20 for a season's work. That was when he decided to leave. In Erwin, he can earn $75 when he has a full week's work as a doffer, removing filled bobbins from carding machines and replacing them with empty ones. "It's good pay," he says.

Negroes now work alongside him in the doffing department. He gets along well with them, he says, and he voices no objections. "The ones they hired, they act like niggers," he says. What does he mean? "They stay on their own jobs. They're good doffers. Yes, sir, they're good doffers, all right. Say yessuh, nossuh. They're real nice. Act like they're friends. We try to get along. As fur as I know, they ain't had a bit of trouble, all through the mill." What if the number of Negroes grows? "People just as well make their mind up," he says. "They'll be here. I believe if you treat a nigger good, he'll act nice."

Cross clings to the special status that always attached to being a white man, however poor and uneducated, in the South. He likes to think black workers in the mill will accord him at least some of the courtesies he associates with that status, and perhaps in some compassion they do. What seems most arresting, however, is his almost casual acceptance of the change.

His son, Mack, a seventh-grader, enters the room and listens to the conversation. Shy and shirtless, he sits close to his father on the sofa for a moment and then silently leaves. "My boy has a nigger teacher this year," Cross says slowly, hunching over and looking at the floor. There is a waiting now for an eruption of the kind expected of a poor white Southerner who finished only the eighth grade and who works in a cotton mill. He finally goes on: "He says he likes her all right." Another silence. But what about *that,* he is asked. "It's all right with me," he says. "I went back to Bainbridge a while back, and every nigger I saw down there would speak to me. Some of 'em knowed me after 23 years. Some I knew when I was a kid and we played together. Everybody acted like there wasn't a bit of trouble."

It may be that Rufus Cross is the kind of man who, ultimately, must "get along" if whites and blacks are to work things out together at the bottom of the industrial ladder. They have been deprived together. They will work together on the same looms and carding machines. Their children will go to school together.

Cross and James McDougald, the forklift operator, have much in common, just as Ann Johnson and Mamie Chance do. McDougald, like Cross, finished only the eighth grade before he had to go to work. He, like Cross, dislikes the cities, preferring a semirural life. The big difference is that formerly the sons of the Rufus Crosses sometimes could move out beyond the lives of their parents, finding higher economic status within the region they grew up in, but the sons of the James McDougalds most often could not.

McDougald can see that pattern breaking in his own family. His choice as a young man was to leave for other parts of the country or to stay at home with little hope of getting much beyond subsistence status. His oldest son, James Jr., faced the same choice, and he left for California, "too far from home" to suit his father. But a third choice, staying near home and moving ahead there, is open to the family's second son. Lenard McDougald has returned from Vietnam, and after working in the mill briefly as a clerk he has enrolled at nearby Fayetteville State College. The mill offered him training for a supervisory job, and when he decided on college instead, Burlington extended an educational loan. Both his father and the mill hope he will return to Erwin.

McDougald's daughter, Erata, has had three years of college and now works in the mill's shipping department, with chances of promotion which her father never had. Another son, Ronald, is a senior in an integrated local high school, and McDougald expects him to become the fourth member of the family to go to college.

The three McDougald children who are still at home eventually may decide to move elsewhere, as thousands of young Negroes in Harnett County have done in recent years. But they, at least, will have a local choice worth thinking about. "I'd much rather they would stay around here," McDougald says. "I never did like the city. I stayed in one for a week right after I got married, and I've been in the country ever since then. I'd rather step outdoors instead of onto somebody else's property." His shrewd eyes look away, he smiles, and he expresses the deep bias of a rural man who never would have felt at home in the city. Clearly it is a part of his thinking about his children. "Where I live it's real unusual to hear anybody cuss," he says. "The air's fresher, too."

The Negro's Stake in America's Future

by Nathan Glazer

SOMETHING VERY strange is happening in the American racial crisis. On the one hand, the concrete situation of Negro Americans is rapidly improving. This is not only true when we look at economics—for we all know this is an inadequate measure of group progress, and that a people that feels oppressed will not be satisfied with the argument, "you never had it so good." But it is also true that things are improving when we look at political participation and power, and even when we look at the critical area of police behavior. Despite recent instances of police violence against black militants, there is no question that the police in city after city are becoming more careful in how they address Negro Americans and in the use of force and firearms. The history of police response to the riots alone demonstrates that.

On the other hand, as the Negro's situation improves, his political attitudes are becoming more extreme. The riots are called rebellions, and hardly any Negro leader bothers to deplore them these days. Militant groups become larger and their language and demands more shocking, even to a demand for political separation. This is sobering, for we know what may happen when a country begins to break up; look at Nigeria.

From the *New York Times Magazine,* September 22, 1968, copyright © 1968 by The New York Times Company.

Social policy faces a dilemma; most of us—black and white, liberals and conservatives—believe that political and social attitudes reflect concrete conditions (when things get better people become more satisfied and less violent) and that we can change attitudes by changing conditions. When political attitudes become more extreme as conditions are improving, we resort to two explanations: the well-known revolution of rising expectations and the theory of Alexis de Tocqueville that the improvement of conditions increases the desire for change because people begin to feel stronger and more potent.

Both of these theories undoubtedly have some validity, but one's attitude toward them must depend upon one's attitude toward society. One who looks upon American society as the French looked upon their Old Regime—as conservative, sclerotic, repressive, irrational and selfish—will look favorably upon the rise of extreme opinion and the crash of the American Old Regime. But one who sees American society as fundamentally democratic and responsive to people's wishes will be deeply concerned about its fate. That expectations rise is good; that they rise so fast that no policy of any type carried out by anybody can satisfy them is bad. That people feel powerful and free to express their resentments is good; that their resentment may overthrow a system capable of satisfying their needs and hopes is bad. There must be a point at which improvement will moderate extremism despite the revolution of rising expectations and the Tocquevillian hypothesis. But if such a point exists, we are getting further away from it rather than closer to it.

There is, of course, another possible explanation for what is happening: that the Negro is no longer interested in advancing within the American social system. The theory here is that Negroes have begun to see themselves as a subject people, and—like all such people—will be satisfied only by independent political existence. This is the direction that militant Negro demands have now begun to take, and if Negroes follow them this nation will have to use all its political ingenuity and creativity to avoid being torn apart. It is this rise of Negro separatism, and how we might respond to it, that I wish to explore here.

First, let us show briefly that things *are* getting better. Many liberal shapers of opinion insist that the situation of the Negro has not changed or has grown worse. Sadly, social scientists, who should know better, are often among the worst offenders. Elliot Liebow, the writer of "Tally's Corner," a fine study of unemployed Negro men, states casually, for example, that "the number of the poor and their problems have grown steadily since World War II." Some who insist that the Negro's economic situation is getting worse point to the rising *absolute* gap between Negro and white incomes and ignore the fact that the *percentage* gap is diminishing. According to their logic, if at some fortunate time median white incomes are $10,000 and median nonwhite incomes are $8,000, one might conclude that Negroes are worse off than they were when whites made $5,000 and they made $3,250.

In October, 1967, the Bureau of Labor Statistics and the Bureau of the Census published a compendium of statistics on the social and economic conditions of the Negro. Here are some of the major findings:

Income: In 1966, 23 per cent of the nonwhite families had incomes of more than $7,000, and 53 per cent of white families made that much or more. Ten years earlier, using dollars of the same value, the figures were only 9 per cent for nonwhite families and 31 per cent for white families. Outside the South, Negroes did better: 38 per cent of nonwhite families had incomes above $7,000, against 59 per cent of white families.

Occupation: Between 1960 and 1966, the number of nonwhites in the better-paying and more secure job categories rose faster than the number of whites. There was a 50 per cent increase for nonwhites in professional, technical and managerial work, and a 13 per cent increase for whites; in clerical jobs the increases were 48 per cent for nonwhites and 19 per cent for whites; in sales, the changes were 32 per cent and 7 per cent, and among foremen and craftsmen they were 45 per cent and 10 per cent. During the same period, the proportion of nonwhites employed as laborers and in private households dropped.

Education: In 1960 there was gap of 1.9 years between non-white and white males over 25 in median years of schooling; by 1966, there was a gap of only 0.5 years. In 1960, 36 per cent of nonwhite males and 63 per cent of white males over 25 had completed high school; by 1966, the figures were 53 per cent for nonwhite males and 73 per cent for white males. In 1960, 3.9 per cent of Negro males and 15.7 per cent of white males had completed college; in 1966, college graduates included 7.4 per cent of Negro males and 17.9 per cent of white males. This represents a 90 per cent increase in nonwhite college graduates and an increase of only 14 per cent among whites.

Housing: Between 1960 and 1966, there was a 25 per cent drop in the number of substandard housing units occupied by nonwhites (from 2.26 million to 1.69 million) and a 44 per cent increase in the number of standard units (from 2.88 million to 4.13 million).

Political participation: Negro voter registration in the South increased from 2.16 million in March, 1964, to 3.07 million in May, 1968, while Negro population remained stable. And the National Advisory Commission on Civil Disorders reported after a survey of 20 cities that they averaged 16 per cent in Negro population while Negroes accounted for 10 per cent of the elected political representatives. This figure must be interpreted in light of the fact that Negroes of voting age are generally a smaller fraction in the total Negro population than whites of voting age are in the white population; Negroes in cities have a higher proportion of young families and children, whites a higher proportion of the aged.

The police: Even on this sorest point of black-white relations, the Kerner Commission reports progress in one significant respect: there are now substantial numbers of Negroes on many city police forces. In Washington, 21 per cent of the force is Negro; in Philadelphia, 20 per cent; in Chicago, 17; St. Louis, 11; Hartford, 11; Newark, 10; and Atlanta, 10.

These are simply over-all measures. When one considers the number of programs devoted to getting Negroes into colleges, graduate schools and corporations, to raising their grades in the civil service and to moderating police attitudes, one must conclude that the situation of the Negro is improving.

Of course all these figures can be argued with. For instance, we have recently become aware that 14 per cent of Negro males and only 2 per cent of white males were not counted in the 1960 census, and if they were counted they would probably lower the average figures for Negro earnings, education, employment, housing. On the other hand, we probably have not been counting similar proportions of white and Negro males in earlier censuses, so any improvement indicated by change from one census or sample census survey to another is real.

It can also be argued that the quality of jobs held by Negroes, even if they are in white-collar and skilled-labor categories, is lower than that of the whites' jobs, and this is true. But the quality of jobs held by Negroes certainly has not decreased on the average. Fewer Negro professionals today are preachers, more are engineers.

Some people argue that the improvement in economic, educational and housing conditions is largely a result of the Negro's migration from the South to the North and West and from small towns and rural areas to big cities; if we were to study Negroes in the North and West alone, we would not find such marked changes over the last few years. But the statistics show improvement in every section.

Another argument is that these over-all measures of improvement apply only to the Negro middle class and stable working class, that the lower working class has shown no progress. But an unpublished analysis by Albert Wohlstetter of the University of Chicago indicates that the Negro lower-income group has recently made greater progress relative to the white lower-income group than have upper-income Negroes relative to the corresponding white group. It is true, however, that such other measures of social condition as the proportion of broken homes and illegitimacy continue to show worsening conditions among low-income Negroes.

Finally, one may argue that much of the advance to which I have pointed has taken place since the Vietnam war expanded in 1965, just as the previous economic advance of the Negro took place during the Korean War and ended with it. Though there was a relative decline or stagnation between the wars, the advances were not fully wiped out; it was rather that the rate of advance was not maintained. By now the build-up of Negro political power and national programs is so great, and the scale of recent achievements is so massive, that I cannot believe they will not continue after the war—provided there is not a radical change in the political situation.

More striking, however, than the advance itself is that on the basis of our present statistics we cannot single out the Negro as a group which suffers unique deprivation as compared to other ethnic and racial groups which suffer from the effects of poor education, depressed rural background and recent migration to urban areas. Social scientists disagree on how to view Negroes in the context of the ethnic and racial history of the United States. One tendency is to emphasize the many unique things: the manner of their arrival (by force and in chains); the condition in which they lived for 200 years (slavery); the condition in which they have lived for the last 100 years (legal inferiority in much of the country); and the special role of the Negro in helping shape American culture and imagination.

But one can also view Negroes in the American context as part of a series of ethnic and racial groups that have moved into society and become a part of it. There is a new illusion which asserts that all white ethnic groups moving into American society have quickly achieved respectable levels of income, good living conditions and political power; that all racially distinct groups have been held back; and that the Negro, because of the unique character of slavery, is furthest back. The truth is nothing like this. Some white ethnic groups—the Jews, for instance—have shown a rapid economic rise; others have been much slower to achieve in this area. One of the economically backward white ethnic groups, the Irish, has been politically gifted, and its members are among elected officials at all levels in almost every part of the country. Other ethnic groups, such as Italians and Poles, have done poorly both economically and politically. Some racially distinct groups—the Japanese, for example—have done remarkably well in education and occupation; most others have done badly.

The Negro's situation is more complex than the gross simplification of having started at the bottom and having stayed there. By some measures, Puerto Ricans do worse in New York and

Mexican Americans do worse in the Southwest. One can argue that the Negro is worse off than other groups in this country, but the difference is not great enough to explain by itself the special quality of despair and hysteria that dominates much Negro political discourse. Of course we must realize that our national obligation to improve the Negro's position is much greater than our obligation to those who came here voluntarily. The Negro is aware of this, and the inferiority of his position is thus more grating than it would be to other groups.

Regardless of how we view their social position, a growing number of the 22 million United States Negroes believe that Americans are racists and that the only solution is some form of separate political existence. One indication of how far this trend has gone is in the use of words—"genocide," for example. In February, Stokely Carmichael, speaking to a Negro audience in Oakland, Calif., felt the need to justify his use of "genocide" in describing the dangers facing Negroes: ". . . we are not talking about politics tonight, we're not talking about economics tonight, we're talking about the survival of a race of people. . . . Many of us feel— many of our generation feel—that they are getting ready to commit genocide against us. Now many people say that's a horrible thing to say about anybody. But if it's a horrible thing to say, then we should do as Brother Malcolm said—we should examine history."

We have moved far since February. An official of the Southern Christian Leadership Conference warns that genocide is a danger. James Baldwin, in The New York Times Book Review, asserts: "White America appears to be seriously considering the possibilities of mass extermination." By now even moderate leaders use the term "genocide," perhaps feeling they have to show they are not Toms. And by now, of course, white men who want to demonstrate their sympathy for Negroes also use the term—thus, Eliot Fremont-Smith, reviewing John Hersey's "The Algiers Motel Incident" in The New York Times, says that the book "shows America to be deeply—and unknowingly to most of its citizens —genocidal."

The public-opinion polls report rapid changes of attitude among Negroes. A Harris poll conducted *before* Martin Luther King's assassination concluded that the number of Negroes alienated rose from 34 per cent in 1966 to 56 per cent in 1968. The proportion of respondents who agreed with the statement "Few people really understand how it is to live like I live" rose from 32 per cent to 66 per cent; those who agreed that "People running the country don't really care what happens to people like ourselves" rose from 32 per cent to 52 per cent. Yet in the same poll, 73 per cent of the respondents agreed that there had been more racial progress in recent years than previously.

More impressive than attitudes and the use of words, however, is action—the rioting, the expectation of guerrilla warfare, the rise of such groups as the Black Panthers, who call for armed resistance to the police, the freeing of black prisoners and—ultimately—a separate national political existence.

There are three points of view on what to do about rising extremism in the face of social improvement. One group contends that we must strengthen the police, create riot-control forces and put down extremism. A second holds that we must increase the rate of social improvement in the hope of creating a harmonious nation. The third position is that social improvement is no longer the issue, that separate political power for Negroes is the only thing that will satisfy them.

The majority of white Americans, I think, reject the first point of view, though most of them believe that the maintenance of civil order must be part of the national response to the crisis. The second position is the one for which the Kerner Commission has written a brief and to which, undoubtedly, most liberals subscribe. It is almost the only position open to one who believes, as I do, that our society is on the whole a success and that it can handle the complex and frightening problems of an advanced technology better than such alternatives as the varied assortment of Communist authoritarian states or the unexplicated utopia that is the vague hope of the New Left. The liberal position does, however, have at least one basic difficulty.

It is that we have already carried out social programs on an ever-expanding scale without any movement toward the reward of a united and peaceful nation that is the Kerner Commission's hope. Take the commission's own figures: "Federal expenditures for manpower development and training have increased from less than $60-million in 1963 to $1.6-billion in 1968. The President has proposed a further increase, to $2.1-billion, in 1969. . . . Federal expenditures for education, training and related services have increased from $4.7-billion in fiscal 1964 to $12.3-billion in fiscal 1969. . . . Direct Federal expenditures for housing and community development have increased from $600-million in fiscal 1964 to nearly $3-billion in fiscal 1969." There have been similar increases in health and welfare expenditures.

I am left with the uneasy feeling that if these increases have taken place at the same time as the spread of urban riots and political extremism, it is questionable whether a further expansion will stem them. I am for expanding and improving the programs because they are our major means for achieving equality in education, housing and the like, but I do not think we can count on them to moderate attitudes; political attitudes have a life of their own and are not simply reflections of economic and social conditions. The demand for separatism will not easily be moderated by social programs. We must face up to it on its own terms.

White America must recognize that separatism means a host of things, many of them—positive identification with the group, greater political representation and economic power for the black man, the teaching of black history and arts in the schools—valuable and healthy for Negroes and American society. The major problem is the demand for territorial autonomy—a group of states set aside as a black nation or black enclaves in the cities with certain rights and powers. Certainly most white Americans will resist these demands for territorial autonomy and extraterritoriality.* One war has been fought to keep the nation united, and the sense of what all Americans gain from a united nation and what they might lose from a divided one is strong enough to insure that these demands will continue to be resisted. Nor is it clear that any substantial number of Negroes want autonomy. The leaders who demand it are powerfully supported, I think, not by the realities of

* Greater local community control—over schools, police, urban renewal —is a definite possibility and even a likelihood. It is territorial autonomy for black areas as such which raises the major issue.

the Negro condition and the hope they offer of improving it, but by powerful ideologies, in particular by the belief that American Negroes are a colonial people who must be freed from their colonial status even if they enjoy all the rights of every other American.

If the demand for territorial independence captures the minds of Negroes, it will be because Americans—black and white— have failed to understand the relationship between their society and the groups that make it up. Many people see society as far more monolithic and homogeneous than it has ever been. I am afraid that whites will fight to retain something that has never existed and blacks will fight because they do not realize the enormous scope the society grants for group diversity and self-fulfillment.

Almost every group that has settled in this country has been nationalistic and separatist, and the laws have permitted for most of them a degree of separatism not yet reached by Negroes. Many groups have supported—sometimes with armed volunteers— nationalist leaders intent upon freeing or revolutionizing their homelands, even when this was a matter of great embarrassment to the United States. Most groups have maintained schools in their own languages and have tried to foster their religious and ethnic customs and beliefs among their children. The major outer limits set on the development of racial and ethnic groups in this country have been an insistence on political loyalty to the United States and a denial of territorial autonomy.

All Americans are aware of the prejudice almost all immigrant and racial groups have faced, but we tend to be less aware of the adjustments our society has eventually made to accommodate them. We have, for instance, developed a political system in which groups of any substantial number are represented among appointed or elected officials; the system has worked well without any laws specifying how much or what kind of recognition should be given. The general freedom this country grants to business enterprises has aided the economic integration of minority groups. (Unfortunately, the ability to create independent economic bases is now considerably limited by—among other things—state and local licensing requirements, union regulations and Federal tax and accounting procedures. This, of course, makes it more difficult for the less sophisticated and literate to become successful in business.) We have granted full freedom to religious organization, and under its protection a wide range of educational, cultural, political and social activities is carried on.

Compared with most countries that have tried to create themselves out of a mixed population, there has been a certain genius in the American style of handling this problem. The principle has been that there is no formal recognition of an ethnic or racial group, but there is every informal recognition of the right to self-development and integration at the group's own rate and to independence in social, religious and political matters. The principle has often been ignored; we have enacted laws that discriminate against some groups—most notably Negroes, but also American Indians and Orientals—and we have often restricted the development of certain groups through "Americanization" movements. But most breaks with these principles—from slavery to immigration quotas by race—have in the end been recognized as un-American and overturned by the courts and legislatures and, in the most important case, war.

To say that Negroes have been a part of this pattern may seem to be no more than a refusal to face the evil in American society. Prof. Robert Blauner of the University of California at Berkeley has argued forcefully that there are "colonized" peoples in the United States who do not fit the ethnic pattern I have described; among them, he says, are Negroes, American Indians and, to some extent, Mexican Americans. According to this argument, the self-regulated rate of integration prevailed only for European immigrants and, to a much more modest degree, prevails now for the Chinese and Japanese. Blauner contends that there has been a different pattern for peoples we have conquered or brought here as slaves: this is a pattern of internal colonization, whereby these groups have been made inferior to the "settlers" politically, economically, socially and culturally; for them the only meaningful course is the colonial one: rebellion, resistance and, conceivably, forceful overthrow of the "settler." If Professor Blauner is right, we settlers must figure out how to grant to the colonized the independence that will make them whole or how to resist their effort to take it and perhaps destroy the society in doing so.

For one basic reason, I think the Blauner argument is wrong. Whatever relevance the colonization theory may have had in the past—when Negroes lived as agricultural workers in the South, Mexican Americans in villages in the Southwest and Indians on their reservations—it is scarcely relevant today, when three-quarters of American Negroes have moved to cities to become not only workers and servants but skilled workers, foremen, civil servants, professionals and white-collar workers of all types; when at a slower rate the same thing is happening to Mexican Americans, and when even Indians can free themselves from any politically inferior status by giving up the reservation and moving to the city, as more and more are doing. These moves are voluntary—or if involuntary to some extent, no more so than the migration of many other groups escaping political persecution and economic misery. They lead to the creation of a voluntary community of self-help institutions. They lead to a largely self-regulated rate at which group cultural patterns are given up and new ones adopted. It is all quite comparable to what happened to the European immigrant.

The existence of prejudice and discrimination does not make the colonial analogy fit. They occur wherever different groups interact socially. Are the Algerian workers in the slum settlements around Paris and the Spanish and Turkish immigrant workers in Europe "colonized"? Or are they simply immigrants facing the discrimination that is so often the lot of immigrants? Nor are prejudice and discrimination insuperable obstacles to political and economic advancement. The important questions, rather, are the *level* of discrimination, how it is reflected in *harmful policies,* what *state assistance* it gets and to what extent the *state acts against it.* Tested this way, the colonial analogy becomes meaningless. There has been a steady decline in all forms of expressed prejudice against Negroes; it is indicated by opinion polls and by everyday behavior. There is ever-stronger state action against prejudice and discrimination, even in parts of the South.

The colonial pattern makes sense if there is a *legal* inferiority of the colonized, or if, even in the case of *formal* equality, in fact only tiny proportions of the colonized can reach high statuses.

But this is not true of the Negro Americans—nor will it be true, shortly, of the Mexican Americans and, if they so choose, of American Indians. The fact is that instead of keeping these groups out of privileged statuses, most public policy and the policy of most large private institutions is to bring them in larger and larger numbers into privileged statuses—what else is the meaning of the work of the Federal Civil Service in upgrading minority employees, of the colleges in recruiting minority students in greater numbers than could normally qualify, of the various corporation programs for increasing numbers of minority-group executives and franchise holders? The scale of most of this effort is still much too small, but its aim is to speed up the incorporation of the minority groups into the mixed American society rather than to slow it down.

The question of whether American Negroes are "colonized" is ultimately to be answered only by the Negroes. If they see themselves as being prevented by the American pattern from achieving the independence they want, they will do everything in their power to break the pattern. Then all Americans may have to choose between the suffering of another war of national unity and the dangers of separatism.

Three factors still argue against the eventual victory of the colonial theory. The first is the large number of Negroes who *are* integrated—civil servants, white-collar workers, union members, party members and elected officials. Second, there is the possibility that moderate social change may still pacify the militants. While they demand independence, they might be satisfied with more and better jobs, more political power, better schools and housing and as much institutional identity and control as the American society can allow. Finally, there is the enormous practical difficulty of satisfying the demand of a scattered people for territorial separation or of finding acceptable alternatives.

Among the factors working toward the success of the colonial analogy among Negroes is the importance to them of their experience in the South, where they were indeed colonized and where there remains in large sections the most unrelenting resistance to black equality. The colonial imagery of the South has been transported to the cities of East and West, which are largely free of colonialism. There it struggles against the immigrant analogy, and on the whole it is losing.

The second factor working for the colonial analogy is our failure to adopt rapidly enough new approaches to achieving effective equality for the Negro. Negro businesses must be created, subsidized, sustained and advised; job programs must become more meaningful: colleges must learn how to incorporate large numbers of minority students and urban schools must undergo a transformation (though which one it is hard to say). All this is so demanding we may not succeed. Mayor Lindsay of New York, perhaps the dominant liberal member of the Kerner Commission, told businessmen what they must do to make the hard-core unemployed effective:

"You've got to literally adopt this kind of employee, be responsible for his total condition, 24 hours a day, 7 days a week. . . . Adopt their families, a piece of the block where they live, a chunk of the city and its future. Know where they live, their economic condition, how their children are, whether there's a police problem, what the neighborhood pressures are. . . .

"The businessman who does hire the hard-core unemployed is going to be confronted with absenteeism, poor working habits, deficiencies in reading and writing, negative attitudes. . . ."

If this is what businessmen—and perhaps teachers—must do to employ and educate a substantial part of our minority population, we may not have the compassion, commitment and capacity to succeed.

The third reason that the colonial analogy may win out is the inability of both blacks and whites to understand the American pattern of group incorporation. On the white side, there is a fear of Negro separatism and Negro power that is based on a failure to understand that every group has gone through—and some have maintained—a substantial degree of separatism; all have demanded, and many won, political representation in appointive and elected office and control over pieces of the political action.

As long as we do not succumb to the temptation to become a society of fixed quotas and compartments, we can go some distance in meeting separatist demands. If suburban towns can have their own school systems and police forces, then I can see no reason why parts of a larger city cannot have them. In any case, when the authority of teachers and policemen has been destroyed —and it has in large measure been destroyed in ghetto areas— there is no alternative to some pragmatic adjustment to the creation of new social forms.

Among the blacks, too—and here they are joined by many whites—there is a failure to understand the relationship of the group to society, to understand that, even while prejudice and discrimination exist, those discriminated against can achieve their goals and a respected place in society. There is a failure to understand that different groups vary in their cultural characteristics and in the area and character of their achievements and that an owlish insistence on equality in every area and every characteristic denies the significance of special characteristics and achievements. There may come a time when the special gifts of the American Negro will mean a massive representation in politics or the arts, even if today they mean only an overrepresentation in such fields as professional sports. The special character of American group life—its acceptance of individual merit and its flexible arrangements for group character and pride—should not be destroyed by a demand for fixed quotas and their incorporation into legal and semilegal arrangements.

Above all, I think, black militants and their too-complaisant white allies fail to understand that there *is* an American society with tremendous power to incorporate new groups—to their advantage and its own—and that this is not a *white* society. There is nothing so sad as to hear the Government, the universities and the corporations denounced as white racist institutions. A hundred years ago the same reasoning would have branded them English institutions, but the Germans and Irish became a part of them; 50 years ago they might have been called Christian institutions, but Jews became a part of them. They are not essentially white institutions today any more than they were essentially Christian 50 years ago or English a century ago. They will become white institutions only if Negro Americans insist on full political separation and decide for themselves that the American pattern of group life cannot include them.

The Road to the Top Is Through Higher Education— Not Black Studies

by W. Arthur Lewis

WHEN A FRIEND suggested that, since I had spent all my adult life in black-power movements and in universities, I might make some comments on the highly topical subject of black power in the American university, it did not at first seem to be a good idea. Now that I have come to grips with it I am even more conscious of my folly in tackling so difficult and controversial a subject.

I am also very conscious that my credentials are inadequate, since the black-power movements in the countries with which I am familiar differ fundamentally from black power in the United States. My stamping grounds are the West Indies, where I was born, and Africa, where I have worked, and which I shall be visiting for the 14th time next month. But in both those places blacks are the great majority of the people—97 per cent in Jamaica, 99 per cent in Nigeria. The objective of the political movements was therefore to capture the central legislature, and the executive and judicial powers. In the United States, in contrast, blacks are only 11 per cent of the population, and have neither claim to nor pros-

From the *New York Times Magazine,* May 11, 1969, copyright © 1969 by The New York Times Company.

pect of capturing the Congress, the executive branch or the Supreme Court for themselves alone. The objectives have to be different, and the strategy must also be different. Comparison between the colonial situation and the position of blacks in America is bound to mislead if it is suggested as a basis for deciding political strategy.

The fact of the matter is that the struggle of the blacks in America is a unique experience, with no parallel in Africa. And since it is unique, the appropriate strategies are likely to be forged only by trial and error. We are all finding the process a great trial, and since our leaders are going off in all directions at once, a great deal of error is also inevitable. I myself, in venturing onto this ground, claim the protection of the First Amendment, but do not aspire to wear the cloak of papal infallibility.

The goals and tactics of black power in America have to be adjusted to the reality of America. Take the issue of segregation. Everywhere in the black world, except among a small minority of American blacks, the fight against segregation has been in the foreground of black-power movements. This goes without saying in countries where blacks are the great majority; yet there are situations where a minority may strengthen itself by temporary self-segregation of a limited kind.

All American minorities have passed through a stage of temporary self-segregation, not just the Afro-Americans. Foreigners speak of the United States as a "melting pot" and it may one day be that; but for the present America is really not a melting pot but a welding shop. It is a country in which many different groups of people live and work together side by side, without coalescing. There are Poles, and Irish, and Chinese, and Jews, and Germans and many other ethnic groups.

But their way of living together is set by the clock; there is integration between 7 o'clock in the morning and 5 o'clock at night, when all mingle and work together in the center of the city, in the banks and factories, department stores and universities. But after 5 o'clock each ethnic group returns to its own neighborhood. There it has its own separate social life. There Poles do not marry Italians, even though they are both white Catholics. The neighborhood has its own schools, its own little shops, its own doctors, and its own celebrations. Integration by day is accompanied by segregation by night.

It is important to note that this self-segregation is voluntary and not imposed by law. An Italian *can* buy a house in an Irish neighborhood if he wishes to do so, *can* marry an Irish girl, and *can* go to an Irish Catholic Church. Many people also insist that this voluntary segregation is only a temporary phase in the acculturation of ethnic groups. They live together until they have found their feet on the American way of life, after which they disperse. The immigrants from Germany and Scandinavia have for the most part already moved out of segregated neighborhoods. The Irish and the Jews are just in the process, and sooner or later the Poles, the Chinese and even the Afro-Americans may disperse. But in the meantime this voluntary self-segregation shelters those who are not yet ready to lose themselves completely in the American mainstream. Other people believe that there will always be cultural pluralism in America, and that this may even be a source of strength. Whether or not they are right about the long run, there is no disputing that voluntary social self-segregation is the current norm.

The black-power movement is therefore fully in the American tradition in recognizing that certain neighborhoods are essentially black neighborhoods, where the black politician, the black doctor, the black teacher, the black grocer and the black clergyman are going to be able to play roles which are not open to them, *de facto,* in other neighborhoods. Many Southern Negroes claim vigorously that blacks are better off in the South than in the North precisely because the Southern white philosophy has reserved a place for a black middle class in the black neighborhoods—for the black preacher or doctor or grocer.

Essentially, what black power is now saying in the North is that the North, too, should recognize that the middle-class occupations in the black neighborhoods belong to blacks, who are not permitted to hold such jobs in Italian, Polish or other ethnic neighborhoods. The issue is phrased in terms of community power —that is to say, of giving to each neighborhood control over its own institutions—but this is tied inextricably to the distribution of middle-class jobs inside the neighborhood. It is unquestionably part of the American tradition that members of each ethnic group should be trained for the middle-class occupations in their neighborhoods, and that, given the training, they should have preference in employment in their own neighborhoods.

This kind of voluntary self-segregation has nothing in common with the compulsory segregation of other countries. An American neighborhood is not a ghetto. A ghetto is an area where members of an ethnic group are forced by law to live, and from which it is a criminal offense to emerge without the license of the oppressing power. This is what apartheid means in the Union of South Africa. An American neighborhood is not a place where members of an ethnic group are required by law to live; they may in the first instance have been forced to live there by circumstances, but it is soon transmuted, ideally, into a place where members of the group *choose* to live, and from which, ideally, anybody can emerge at any time that he wishes to do so. To confuse this neighborhood concept with apartheid is an egregious error.

The fundamental difference between apartheid and the American neighborhood comes out most clearly when one turns from what happens after 5 P.M. to what happens during the daytime. A neighborhood is a work place for less than half the community. The teachers, the doctors, the police, the grocers—these work where they live. But these people are supported by the labors of those who work in the factories and in other basic occupations outside the neighborhood. Some 50 to 60 per cent of the labor force moves out of the neighborhood every morning to work in the country's basic industries.

So a black strategy which concentrated exclusively on building up the black neighborhoods would be dealing with less than half the black man's economic problems. The neighborhood itself will not flourish unless the man who goes out of it in the morning brings back into it from the outside world an income adequate to support its institutions.

I wrote earlier that the American pattern is segregation in *social* life after 5 P.M. but integration in the *economic* life of the country during the day. American economic life is dominated by a few large corporations which do the greater part of the country's business; indeed, in manufacturing, half the assets of the entire country are owned by just 100 corporations. The world of these big corporations is an integrated world. There will be black grocery shops in black neighborhoods, but in your lifetime and mine there isn't going to be a black General Motors, a black Union Carbide, a black Penn-Central Railroad, or a black Standard Oil Company. These great corporations serve all ethnic groups and employ all ethnic groups. American economic life is inconceivable except on an integrated basis.

The majority of Afro-Americans work not in their neighborhoods but for one of the non-neighborhood corporations or employers, and so it shall be for as far ahead as we can see. The black problem is that while we are 11 per cent of the population, we have only 2 per cent of the jobs at the top, 4 per cent of the jobs in the middle, and are forced into 16 per cent of the jobs at the bottom—indeed into as much as 40 per cent of some of the jobs at the very bottom. Clearly, our minimum objective must be to capture 11 per cent of the jobs in the middle, and 11 per cent of the jobs at the top. Or, for those of us who have a pride in ourselves, it could even be an objective to have 15 per cent of the jobs at the top and in the middle, and only 8 per cent of those at the bottom, leaving the very bottom to less ambitious ethnic groups.

Not all our leaders understand that our central economic problem is not in the neighborhoods, but is in the fact that outside the neighborhoods, where most of us have to work, we are concentrated in the bottom jobs. For if they understood this they could not be as hostile as they are toward the black middle and upper classes. The measure of whether we are winning our battle is in how many of us rise to the middle and the top.

When a so-called militant abuses a successful Afro-American for having, by virtue of extreme hard work and immense self-discipline, managed to get to the top in the outside world, instead of devoting his energies to being—in the neighborhood—a social worker, or a night-school teacher, or a semi-politician, such a critic is merely being absurd. Rising from the bottom to the middle or the top, in the face of stiff white competition, prejudice and arbitrary barriers, takes everything that a man can give to it. It is our militants who should month by month chalk up the score of those who have broken through the barriers, should glory in their achievement, and should hold it up before our young to show them what black men can achieve.

Now, at last, I reach my central topic, which is the black man and the university. The road to the top in the great American corporations and other institutions is through higher education. Scientists, research workers, engineers, accountants, lawyers, financial administrators, Presidential advisers—all these people are recruited from the university. And indeed nearly all of the top people are taken from a very small number of colleges—from not more than some 50 or 60 of the 2,000 degree-granting institutions in the United States. The Afro-American could not make it to the top so long as he was effectively excluded from this small number of select institutions. The breakthrough of the Afro-American into these colleges is therefore absolutely fundamental to the larger economic strategy of black power.

I do not mean to suggest that the most important black strategy is to get more blacks into the best colleges. Probably the greatest contribution to black advancement would be to break the trade-union barriers which keep our people out of apprenticeships in the building and printing trades, and prevent our upgrading or promotion in other industries. The trade unions are the black man's greatest enemy in the United States.

The number of people who would be at the top, if we had our numerical share of the top, would be small. Our greatest task, in terms of numbers, is to conquer the middle—getting into skilled posts, foremen's posts, supervisory and white-collar jobs—through better use of apprenticeships, of the high schools and of technical colleges. I am going to discuss the universities not because this is numerically important, but partly because it has become so controversial, and partly because if we did conquer the top it would make much easier the conquering of the middle—both in our own minds, and in other people's minds, by altering our young people's image of themselves and of what they can achieve.

What can the good white college do for its black students that Howard or Lincoln or Fisk cannot do? It can open the road into the top jobs. To put it in unpopular language, it can train them tc become top members of the establishment.

If it is wrong for young blacks to be trained for the top jobs in the big corporations, for top jobs in the government service, for ambassadorships, for the editorial staff of The New York Times and so on—then there is little point in sending them to the best white colleges. On the contrary, if what one wants is people trained to live and work in black neighborhoods, they will do much better to go to the black colleges, of which there are, after all, more than 100, which know much better than Yale or Princeton or Dartmouth what the problems of black neighborhoods are, and how people should be trained to handle them. The point about the best white colleges is that they are a part, not of the neighborhood side of American life, but of the integrated part of American life, training people to run the economy and the administration in the integrated part of the day before 5 P.M.

But how can it be wrong for young Afro-Americans to be trained to hold superior positions in the integrated working world outside the neighborhood when in fact the neighborhood cannot provide work for even half of its people? Whether we like it or not, most Afro-Americans *have* to work in the integrated world, and if we do not train for superior positions there, all that will happen is what happens now—that we shall be crowded into the worst-paid jobs.

If one grasps this point, that these 50 colleges are the gateway to the superior jobs, then the current attitude of some of our black leaders to these colleges is not a little bewildering. In its most extreme form, what is asked is that the college should set aside a special part of itself which is to be the black part. There will be a separate building for black studies, and separate dormitories and living accommodations for blacks. There will be separate teachers, all black, teaching classes open only to blacks. The teachers are to be chosen by the students, and will for the most part be men whom no African or Indian or Chinese university would recognize as scholars, or be willing to hire as teachers.

Doubtless some colleges under militant pressure will give in to this, but I do not see what Afro-Americans will gain thereby. Employers will not hire the students who emerge from this process, and their usefulness even in black neighborhoods will be minimal.

I yield to none in thinking that every respectable university should give courses on African life and on Afro-American life, which are of course two entirely different subjects, and I am very anxious to see such courses developed. It is, however, my hope that they will be attended mostly by white students, and that the majority of black students will find more important uses for their time; that they may attend one or two such courses, but will reject any suggestion that black studies must be the major focus of their programs.

The principal argument for forcing black students to spend a great deal of their time in college studying African and Afro-American anthropology, history, languages and literature is that they need such studies to overcome their racial inferiority complex. I am not impressed by this argument. The youngster discovers that he is black around the age of 6 or 7; from then on, the whites he meets, the books he reads, and the situation of the Negro in America all combine to persuade him that he is an inferior species of *Homo sapiens.*

By the time he is 14 or 15 he has made up his mind on this one way or the other. Nothing that the college can do, after he reaches 18 or 19, is going to have much effect on his basic personality. To expect the colleges to eradicate the inferiority complexes of young black adults is to ask the impossible. And to expect this to come about by segregating black students in black studies under inferior teachers suggests some deficiency of thought.

Perhaps I am wrong about this. The proposition is essentially that the young black has been brainwashed into thinking himself inferior, so now he must spend four years in some place where he will be re-brainwashed into thinking himself equal. But the prospect that the 50 best colleges in the United States can be forced to take on this re-brainwashing operation is an idle dream. Those who are now putting all their energies into working for this are doomed to disappointment.

We are knocking our heads against the wrong wall. Every black student should learn some Afro-American history, and study various aspects of his people's culture, but the place for him to do this compulsorily is in the high school, and the best age to start this seriously is even earlier, perhaps around the age of 10. By the time the student gets to a first-rate college he should be ready for business—for the business of acquiring the skills which he is going to be able to use, whether in his neighborhood, or in the integrated economy. Let the clever young black go to a university to study engineering, medicine, chemistry, economics, law, agriculture and other subjects which are going to be of value to him and his people. And let the clever white go to college to read black novels, to learn Swahili, and to record the exploits of Negro heroes of the past. He is the one to whom this will come as an eye-opener.

This, incidentally, is very much what happens in African universities. Most of these have well-equipped departments of African studies, which are popular with visiting whites, but very few African students waste their time (as they see it) on such studies, when there is so much to be learned for the jobs they will have to do. The attitude of Africans to their past conforms to the historian's observation that only decadent peoples, on the way down, feel an urgent need to mythologize and live in their past. A vigorous people, on the way up, has visions of its future, and cares next to nothing about its past.

My attitude toward the role of black studies in the education of college blacks derives not only from an unconventional view of what is to be gained therefrom, but also from an unconventional view of the purpose of going to college. The United States is the only country in the world which thinks that the purpose of going to colleges is to be educated. Everywhere else one goes to high school to be educated, but goes to college to be trained for one's lifework. In the United States serious training does not begin until one reaches graduate school at the age of 22. Before that, one spends four years in college being educated—that is to say, spending 12 weeks getting some tidbits on religion, 12 weeks learning French, 12 weeks seeing whether the history professor is stimulating, 12 weeks seeking entertainment from the economics professor, 12 weeks confirming that one is not going to be able to master calculus, and so on.

If the purpose of going to college is to be educated, and serious study will not begin until one is 22, one might just as well, perhaps, spend the four years reading black novels, studying black history and learning to speak Fanti. But I do not think that American blacks can afford this luxury. I think our young people ought to get down to the business of serious preparation for their lifework as soon after 18 as they can.

And I also note, incidentally, that many of the more intelligent white students are now in revolt against the way so many colleges fritter away their precious years in meaningless peregrination from subject to subject between the ages of 18 and 22.

Any Afro-American who wishes to become a specialist in black studies, or to spend some of his time on such work, should be absolutely free to do so. But I hope that, of those students who get the opportunity to attend the 50 best colleges, the proportion who want to specialize in black studies may, in their interest and that of the black community, turn out to be rather small, in comparison with our scientists, or engineers, accountants, economists or doctors.

Another attitude which puzzles me is that which requires black students in the better white colleges to mix only with each other; to have a domitory to themselves; to eat at separate tables in the refectory; and so on. I have pointed out that these colleges are the gateway to leadership positions in the integrated part of the economy, and that what they can best do for young blacks is to prepare them to capture our 11 per cent share of the best jobs at the top—one of every nine ambassadorships, one of every nine vice presidencies of General Motors, one of every nine senior directors of engineering laboratories, and so on.

Now I am told that the reason black students stick together is that they are uncomfortable in white company. But how is one to be Ambassador to Finland or Luxembourg—jobs which American Negroes have already held with distinction—if one is uncomfortable in white company? Anybody who occupies a supervisory post, from foreman upwards, is going to have white people working under him, who will expect him to be friendly and fair. Is this going to be possible, after four years spent in boycotting white company?

Nowadays in business and in government most decisions are made in committees. Top Afro-Americans cannot hope to be more than one in nine; they will always be greatly outnumbered by white people at their level. But how can one survive as the only black vice president sitting on the executive committee of a large corporation if one is not so familiar with the ways and thoughts of other vice presidents that one can even anticipate how they are going to think?

Blacks in America are inevitably and perpetually a minority. This means that in all administrative and leadership positions we are going to be outnumbered by white folks, and will have to compete with them not on our terms but on theirs. The only way to win this game is to know them so thoroughly that we can outpace them. For us to turn our backs on this opportunity, by insisting on mingling only with other black students in college, is folly of the highest order.

This kind of social self-segregation is encouraged by two myths about the possibilities for black economic progress in the United States which need to be nailed. One is the Nixon myth, and the other, its opposite, is the revolutionary myth.

The first postulates that the solution is black capitalism—to help as many blacks as possible to become big businessmen. To be sure, it is feasible to have more successful small businesses operating inside the protection of the neighborhood—more groceries and drugstores and lunch counters; but I have emphasized that the members of every ethnic group mostly work outside their neighborhood in the integrated economy, buying from and selling to all ethnic groups. In this part of the economy the prospects for small business are bleak.

No doubt a few Negroes, born with the special talents which success in a highly competitive business world demands, will succeed in establishing sizable and highly competitive concerns. But the great majority who start on this road, whether white or black, go bankrupt in a short time. Indeed, about half of the new white businesses go bankrupt within the first three years. To tell the blacks that this is the direction in which they must move is almost a form of cruelty. To pretend that black America is going to be saved by the emergence of black capitalism, competing in the integrated economy with white capitalism, is little more than a hoax.

Neither is black America going to be saved by a Marxist revolution. Revolution takes power from one set of persons and gives it to another, but it does not change the hierarchical structure of the economy. Any kind of America that you can visualize, whether capitalist, Communist, Fascist, or any other kind of ist, is going to consist of large institutions like General Motors under one name or another. It will have people at the top, people in the middle and people at the bottom. Its leading engineers, doctors, scientists and administrators—leaving out a few top professional politicians—are going to be recruited from a small number of highly select colleges.

The problem of the black will essentially be the same—that problem being whether he is going to be mostly in the bottom jobs, or whether he will also get his 11 per cent share of the top and the middle. And his chance at the top is going to depend on his getting into those select schools and getting the same kind of technical training that the whites are getting—not some segregated schooling specially adapted for him, but the same kind that the whites get as their gateway to the top. Those black leaders who wish us to concentrate our efforts on working for revolution in America are living on a myth, for our problems and needed strategies are going to be exactly the same whether there is a revolution or not. In the integrated part of the American economy our essential strategy has to be to use all the normal channels of advancement—the high schools, the colleges, apprenticeships, night schools: It is only by climbing this ladder that the black man is going to escape from his concentration in the bottom jobs of the economy.

This is not, of course, simply a matter of schooling. The barriers of prejudice which keep us off the ladder still have to be broken down: the task of the civil-rights movement is still not completed, and we need all the liberal help, black and white, that we can get to help to keep the ladder clear. We need also to raise our own sights, to recognize that there are now more opportunities than there were, and to take every opportunity that offers. Here our record is good. For as the barriers came down in sports and entertainment, our young people moved swiftly to the top in baseball, football, the theater, or wherever else the road was cleared. We will do exactly the same in other spheres, given the opportunity.

The secret is to inspire our young people with confidence in their potential achievement. And psychologists tell us that the background to this is a warm and secure family life. The most successful minorities in America, the Chinese, the Japanese and the Jews, are distinguished by their close and highly disciplined family, which is the exact opposite of what has now become the stereotype of the white American family, with its undisciplined and uncontrollable children reared on what are alleged to be the principles of Dr. Spock. African families are warm, highly disciplined structures, just like Jewish or Chinese families. If black Americans are looking to Africa for aspects of culture which will distinguish them from white Americans, let them turn their backs on Spockism, and rear their children on African principles, for this is the way to the middle and the top. Given a disciplined family life and open doors to opportunity, I have no doubt that American blacks will capture one field after another, as fast as barriers come down.

The point which I have been trying to make is that the choice some of our leaders offer us between segregation and integration is false in the American context. America is integrated in the day and segregates itself at night. Some of our leaders who have just discovered the potential strength of neighborhood self-segregation have got drunk on it to the point of advocating segregation for all spheres of Afro-American life. But the struggle for community power in the neighborhood is not an alternative to the struggle for a better share of the integrated world outside the neighborhood, in which inevitably most of our people must earn their living. The way to a better share of this integrated economy is through the integrated colleges; but they can help us only if we take from them the same things that they give to our white competitors.

If we enter them merely to segregate ourselves in blackness, we shall lose the opportunity of our lives. Render homage unto segregated community power in the neighborhoods where it belongs, but do not let it mess up our chance of capturing our share of the economic world outside the neighborhood, where segregation weakens our power to compete.

A Way Out of
the Exploding Ghetto

by Bayard Rustin

THERE IS no longer any denying that this country is in the throes of a historic national crisis. Its ramifications are so vast and frightening that even now, shocked into numbness and disbelief, the American people have not yet fully grasped what is happening to them.

The grim data are clear enough and still coming in. Since this summer began, 30 of our cities, big and small, have been wracked by racial disorder; scores of citizens, almost all of them black, have been killed, thousands injured and even more arrested. Property damage has exceeded a billion dollars; total income loss is incalculable.

As a people, we are not unaccustomed to violence. Frontier lawlessness, Southern vigilante-ism, Chicago gangsterism: these are images and themes embedded in the American tradition. We have only just lost a President to an assassin's bullet. But, having escaped the bombs of two world wars, we are not familiar with the horror of burned-out buildings, smoking rubble, tanks in our streets, the blasts of Molotov cocktails, the ring of snipers' bullets from rooftops. Today we look at sections of Detroit and think of

From the *New York Times Magazine,* August 13, 1967, copyright © 1967 by The New York Times Company.

war-torn Berlin. We see rampaging, looting mobs and think of the unstable politics of underdeveloped countries. A nation's identity has been overturned.

In our own history we can find no precedent in this century for the massive destruction the past three years have brought to our cities—no precedent since the Civil War. But the greatest toll is not in property damage or even in lives lost. Nor is the greatest danger that the violence will go on indefinitely, any more than the Civil War did. It is that the aftermath of that war will be repeated, that as in the Compromise of 1877 the country will turn its back on the Negro, on the root causes of his discontent, on its own democratic future.

Not since the Great Depression have social policy, our national institutions, our political order been more severely tested than at present. The coming months will shape the character of America in the remainder of the 20th century—and I am trying to speak with the utmost sobriety, precision and restraint.

Why does the Republic find itself at a crossroads? What has actually happened?

The term "race riot" is unilluminating and anachronistic. It describes the Detroit disorders of 1943, when the Negro and white communities were locked in combat. White mobs invaded the ghetto. Negroes forayed downtown. Men were beaten and murdered for the color of their skins. In the upheavals of the last four summers, destruction has been confined to the ghetto; nor, discounting the police, were black and white citizens fighting. In fact, in Detroit whites joined in the looting and sniping. And I am told that whites were free to walk through the embattled ghetto without fear of violence from Negroes.

This is not to deny the importance of antiwhite hostility. One has only to hear the sick racial epithets "honkey" and "whitey" to recognize the deep and bitter hatred that is loose on the streets of the ghettos. But if white blood was what the rioters thirsted for, they didn't go very far to get it. What they assaulted were the symbols of white power—police and property, the latter embracing the entire ghetto. These are traditional targets of rebellions and in that sense the riots can be called rebellions.

That sense, however, must be sharply qualified. Is it correct to speak of "race rebellion," or "Negro rebellion"? Are America's Negroes on the verge of revolution? More than one newspaper and television commentator has already begun to draw comparisons between the ghetto uprisings and the French, Russian, Algerian, Irish and Black African independence revolutions. Some Black Power advocates have proclaimed the beginnings of guerrilla warfare and see the urban Negro as a counterpart to the Vietcong. And in Paris it has become fashionable to speak of the *"révolution des noires"* in the U.S.

The reality is that the revolutionary rhetoric now employed by some young Negro militants cannot create the preconditions for successful, or even authentic, revolution. The independence movements in colonial territories provide no model for the simple reason that American Negroes can have no geographical focus for nationalist sentiment.

Moreover, American Negroes do not constitute a popular majority struggling against a relatively small white colonial ruling group—the ideal condition for guerrilla warfare. Whatever separatist impulses exist among American Negroes cannot find appropriate models in the colonial world.

If independence revolutions are no model, what of social revolutions? This is a more interesting subject because the phrase "social revolution" has been widely used by the civil-rights and liberal movements generally. But in this sense—and the sense in which I have been using it for 30 years—the phrase designates fundamental changes in social and economic class relations resulting from mass political action. Such action would be democratic. That is, it would aim to create a new majority coalition capable of exercising political power in the interest of new social policies. By definition the coalition has to be interracial.

As a minority, Negroes by themselves cannot bring about such a social revolution. They can participate in it as a powerful and stimulating force; or they can provoke a counterrevolution. In either case the decisive factor will be the political direction in which the majority will move.

Numbers are not the only issue. Also important is the class content of revolt. At least in the French and Russian revolutions, revolutionary leaders and parties sought to mobilize fairly definable and cohesive socio-economic classes—workers, peasants, the middle class—which, though oppressed or aggrieved, were part of the society they sought to transform. Upon what classes do the advocates of rioting, the voices of the apocalypse, base their revolutionary perspective? This is another way of posing the question I left hanging earlier: Who is rioting?

Daniel Patrick Moynihan is correct in locating the riots in the "lower class" or, in the words of another controversial man, Karl Marx, in the *"lumpenproletariat"* or "slum proletariat." Lower class does not mean working class; the distinction is often overlooked in a middle-class culture that tends to lump the two together.

The distinction is important. The working class is employed. It has a relation to the production of goods and services; much of it is organized in unions. It enjoys a measure of cohesion, discipline and stability lacking in the lower class. The latter is unemployed or marginally employed. It is relatively unorganized, incohesive, unstable. It contains the petty criminal and antisocial elements. Above all, unlike the working class, it lacks the sense of a stake in society. When the slum proletariat is black, its alienation is even greater.

From the revolutionist point of view, the question is not whether steps could be taken to strengthen organization among the *lumpenproletariat* but whether that group could be a central agent of social transformation. Generally, the answer has been no.

The black slum proletariat has been growing in numbers and density. As agricultural mechanization and other factors continue pushing Negroes out of the South, the urban ghettos expand each year by half a million; only 40,000 Negroes annually find their way into the suburbs. This trend has not been affected at all by any antipoverty or Great Society programs.

When the migration of Negroes to Northern and Western cities was at its height during World War II, factory jobs were available at decent wages. With the advent of advanced technology eliminating many semiskilled and unskilled jobs, and with the movement of plants from the central cities to the suburbs (New York lost 200,000 factory jobs in a decade), urban Negroes suffered rising joblessness or employment in low-paying service jobs.

The depth of the unemployment problem in the slum ghettos is indicated in a recent U.S. Department of Labor report on "subemployment" in cities and slums. While the traditional unemployment rate counts only those "actively looking" but unable to find work, the subemployment index reflects in addition: (1) those who have dropped out of the labor market in despair, (2) those who are working part-time but want full-time jobs, (3) heads of households under 65 working full time but earning poverty wages (less than $60 a week), (4) individuals under 65 who are not heads of households and earn less than $56 a week in full-time jobs and (5) a conservatively estimated portion of males known to be living in the slums but who somehow do not show up in employment or unemployment counts.

The report states: "If the traditional statistical concept of 'unemployment' (which produced the nationwide average of 3.7 per cent unemployment rate for January, 1967) is applied to the urban slum situation, the *'unemployment rate' in these areas is about 10 per cent . . . three times the average for the rest of the country."* [Original italics.] The figure for Detroit's Central Woodward area, incidentally, is 10.1 per cent.

The subemployment rate in the 10 cities surveyed yields an average figure of almost 35 per cent. Though possibly in need of further refining, the subemployment rate is the more meaningful figure. Not only does it include the categories listed above, but it also tends to reflect the number of people who experience unemployment over a period of time. By contrast, the official rate counts those unemployed at a point in time (i.e., the time the survey is taken).

High unemployment and low income are not the only problems afflicting the black slum proletariat, but they are the crucial ones. Without adequate income, there is no access to the decent housing market, educational opportunity, even proper health care. (In 1964, East and Central Harlem, comprising 24 per cent of Manhattan's population, accounted for 40 per cent of its TB deaths,

33 per cent of its infant deaths; in Bedford-Stuyvesant, which contains 9 per cent of Brooklyn's population, the respective figures were 24 and 22 per cent.)

The tendency of much current antipoverty rhetoric to create a multitude of disparate problems out of a central multifaceted one is a mistake. It is precisely in the expansion of public facilities and social services that new employment opportunities can be generated, at varying skill levels. High subemployment rates and the lack of decent housing in the slums are two sides of the same coin.

Meanwhile, within the slum proletariat, youth constitutes a subdivision of increasing economic and political importance. While according to the official unemployment rates the joblessness gap between Negro and white men over 20 has been narrowing since 1961, even this official rate records a widening of the gap between Negro and white teen-agers since 1957. Right now the national Negro unemployment rate is 25 per cent nationally but for 16-to-19-year-olds in the 10 slum areas surveyed, it is over 38 per cent! Moreover, this rate was unaffected by the downward trend of the nation's over-all unemployment rate late last year. For white teen-agers, on the other hand, unemployment since 1957 never went beyond 15 per cent and is now at 10 per cent.

Nor is there any evidence that Negro teen-agers do not want to work. Whenever job programs have been announced, they have turned out in large numbers, only to find that the jobs weren't there. In Oakland, a "Job Fair" attracted 15,000 people; only 250 were placed. In Philadelphia, 6,000 were on a waiting list for a training program.

What Negro teen-agers are not inclined to accept are dead-end jobs that pay little and promise no advancement or training. Many would prefer to live by their wits as hustlers or petty racketeers, their version of the self-employed businessman or salesman. That their pursuit of this distorted entrepreneurial ideal only mires them deeper in the slum proletariat is not the point. They want to be part of the white-collar organization man's world that is America's future, not trapped behind brooms and pushcarts.

Nor can they fairly be blamed by a society which has itself produced these yearnings, reveled in its affluence, encouraged the consumption of trivia and proclaimed the coming of computerized utopias. The middle classes may nostalgically extol their immigrant parents' fortitude and perseverance in manual labor, but they do not steer their own children toward the construction gang or the garment district. They show them the push buttons, not the pushcart. Might they not then show some compassionate understanding of black youngsters who dream of better things, even when crippled by poor education, broken families, and the disabilities bred by slum life? If it is true that a Negro boy is nobody unless he owns alligator shoes and an alpaca sweater, who created these symbols? Who whetted this appetite? Who profited from the sale of these commodities, and who advertised them? And who is victimized?

The ghetto youth who is out of school, unemployed and rejected even by the draft (as 52 per cent are in Harlem) is the extreme embodiment of the bitter frustration in the slum proletariat. He is utterly propertyless, devoid of experience in the productive process and without a stake in existing social arrangements. At the same time, because he is young and not beaten down, he is irreverent, filled with bravado, hostile to the alien authority of the police and determined to "make it" in any way that he can. He is at the core of the rioting.

In Detroit, the riot begins when pimps and prostitutes taunt police who are raiding a "blind pig" at 5 A.M. In Minneapolis, two women fight over a wig, the police try to break it up and a riot erupts in an atmosphere already charged by delays in the mailing of Federal Youth Opportunity Program paychecks to youths in the ghetto area. In Cairo, Ill., a Negro soldier dies in the city jail; police say it was suicide but order the body embalmed without an autopsy, and fire bombing and shooting follow.

In these cases, the police figure prominently in the incidents that triggered the rioting. Sometimes they are not directly involved, but rumors of police brutality flood through the ghetto. Although it may be of some interest to search for a pattern, no very profound purpose is served by concentrating on who struck the match. There are always matches lying around. We must ask why there was also a fuse and why the fuse was connected to a powder keg.

To pursue this analogy: Whether the match is struck by police misconduct or by an "extremist" exhorting his listeners to violence, the fuse is the condition of life among the black slum proletariat —hostile, frustrated and with nothing to lose. The powder keg is the social background against which the riots break out and which extends their scope. They become more than riots pure and simple, yet less than politically coherent rebellions. They are *riotous manifestations of rebellion*.

The social background is defined by the fact that the black slum proletariat is part of a larger community of oppressed and segregated citizens—the overwhelming majority of the Negro population. Were it not for this the riots could be dismissed merely as wild, inchoate sprees of looting and violence, the expressions of criminal greed, a carnival of destruction to be suppressed by police force. Such actions, detached from political policies, programs and goals—and, make no mistake about it, the riots were not on behalf of the black power ideology; the latter is an after-the-fact justification employed by people in search of a constituency—do not properly constitute a rebellion. But because of the social background, the riots, while not *the rebellion* of the Negro people, are charged with manifestations of rebellion.

It is because of this background that the riots can set off a chain reaction, fan out from the slum proletariat and, as Detroit showed, involve people who ordinarily would not be found looting stores. It is because of this background that snipers and the most violent elements can feel that their actions are in some sense heroic. And it is because of this background that the riots have enormous implications for the future of all Negroes.

As Martin Luther King, A. Philip Randolph, Roy Wilkins and Whitney Young pointed out in their recent statement, the most severe and immediate damage has been to the Negro community itself. In addition to those who lost their lives, thousands lost their homes, food supplies, access to schools. There is danger of a counterreaction enlisting the most bigoted, vigilante-minded elements in the white community. Ammunition has been given to the reactionaries in an already backlash-dominated Congress. Many whites sincerely in favor of integration will be silenced out of fear and confusion. Riots do not strengthen the power of black people; they weaken it and encourage racist power.

But why, asks white America, do the Negroes riot now—not when conditions are at their worst but when they seem to be improving? Why now, after all of the civil-rights and antipoverty legislation? There are two answers.

First, "progress" has been considerably less than is generally supposed. While the Negro has won certain important legal and constitutional rights (voting, desegregation of public accommodations, etc.), his relative socio-economic position has scarcely improved. There simply has not been significant, visible change in his life.

Second, if a society is interested in stability, it should either not make promises or it should keep them. Economic and social deprivation, if accepted by its victims as their lot in life, breeds passivity, even docility. The miserable yield to their fate as divinely ordained or as their own fault. And, indeed, many Negroes in earlier generations felt that way.

Today, young Negroes aren't having any. They don't share the feeling that something must be wrong with them, that they are responsible for their own exclusion from this affluent society. The civil-rights movement—in fact, the whole liberal trend beginning with John Kennedy's election—has told them otherwise.

Conservatives will undoubtedly seize the occasion for an attack on the Great Society, liberalism, the welfare state and Lyndon Johnson. But the young Negroes are right: the promises made to them were good and necessary and long, long overdue. The youth were right to believe in them. The only trouble is that they were not fulfilled. Prominent Republicans and Dixiecrats are demanding not that the promises be fulfilled, but that they be revoked.

What they and the American people absolutely must understand now is that the promises cannot be revoked. They were not made to a handful of leaders in a White House drawing room; they were made to an entire generation, one not likely to forget or to forgive. If Republican leaders Everett Dirksen and Gerald Ford, hand in glove with the die-hards of the Confederacy, continue their contemptible effort to exploit the nation's tragedy for partisan political advantage, they will sow the dangerous seeds of race hate and they will discredit themselves morally in the eyes of the coming generations and of history. This is not a wise policy for a party that only yesterday reduced itself to a shambles by catering to the most backward and reactionary elements in the country.

It is ironic that in a nation which has not undertaken a massive social and economic reform since the New Deal one now hears even liberal voices asking: "Don't the causes of the riots go deeper than economics, than jobs, housing, schools? Aren't there profound moral, cultural, psychological and other factors involved—powerlessness, an identity crisis?"

Of course, but in the present context such questions smack of a trend toward mystification which, if it gains ascendancy, will paralyze public policy. Then, too, I cannot help but suspect that they are rationalizations for the yearning of some white liberals to withdraw. "Obviously," they are saying "there seems to be nothing we can do. We're not even wanted. Why not give the ghettos over to the black power people?"

I have no hesitation in saying that this recommendation simply aids and abets the Congressional reactionaries, who would have no objection to letting Negroes run their own slum tenements, dilapidated schools and tax-starved communities. Isn't this in the best tradition of rugged self-help, Horatio Alger and all that? Haven't Barry Goldwater and William F. Buckley endorsed this notion of black power? Just so long as white people are left alone. Just so long as the total society is not forced to examine its own inner contradictions. Just so long as the Federal Government isn't challenged to launch radical and massive programs to rebuild our cities, end poverty, guarantee full employment at decent wages, clear our polluted air and water and provide mass transportation.

This is just the challenge posed by A. Philip Randolph's $185 billion "Freedom Budget for All Americans"—a carefully designed, economically feasible program for the obliteration of poverty in

10 years. Unless the nation is prepared to move along these lines —to rearrange its priorities, to set a timetable for achieving them and to allocate its resources accordingly—it will not be taking its own commitments seriously. Surely it cannot then turn amazedly to responsible Negro leaders, whose pleas for large-scale programs it has failed to heed, for an explanation of the consequences.

The present Administration has a grave responsibility. It is very well for it to proclaim that we can have guns *and* butter, that we can pursue our course in Vietnam and still make progress at home. We do have the economic capacity for both, as the Freedom Budget itself shows. But we are not doing both. Let us stop proclaiming that we *can* do what we *don't* do and start *doing* it.

If Administration actions are not to mock its own rhetoric, the President must now take the lead in mobilizing public opinion behind a new resolve to meet the crisis in our cities. He should now put before Congress a National Emergency Public Works and Reconstruction bill aimed at building housing for homeless victims of the riot-torn ghettos, repairing damaged public facilities and in the process generating maximum employment opportunities for unskilled and semiskilled workers. Such a bill should be the first step in the imperative reconstruction of all our decaying center cities.

Admittedly, the prospects for passage of such a bill in the present Congress are dismal. Congressmen will cry out that the rioters must not be rewarded, thereby further penalizing the very victims of the riots. This, after all, is a Congress capable of defeating a meager $40 million rat extermination program the same week it votes $10 million for an aquarium in the District of Columbia!

But the vindictive racial meanness that has descended upon this Congress, already dominated by the revived coalition of Republicans and Dixiecrats, must be challenged—not accommodated. The President must go directly to the people, as Harry Truman did in 1948. He must go to them, not with slogans, but with a timetable for tearing down every slum in the country.

There can be no further delay. The daydreamers and utopians are not those of us who have prepared massive Freedom Budgets and similar programs. They are the smugly "practical" and myopic philistines in the Congress, the state legislatures and the city halls who thought they could sit it out. The very practical choice now before them and the American people is whether we shall have a conscious and authentic democratic social revolution or more tragic and futile riots that tear our nation to shreds.

Suggested Reading

Lerone Bennett, *Before the Mayflower: A History of the Negro in America, 1619-1965,* Chicago, Johnson, 1966 (Penguin paperback).

Peter M. Blau and Otis Dudley Duncan, *The American Occupational Structure,* New York, Wiley, 1967.

John H. Bracey, Jr., August Meier, and Elliott Rudwick, *Black Nationalism in America,* New York, Bobbs-Merrill, 1970.

Leonard Broom and Norval Glenn, *Transformation of the Negro American,* New York, Harper & Row, 1965 (Torchbook paperback).

Claude Brown, *Manchild in the Promised Land,* New York, Macmillan, 1965 (Signet paperback).

Eldridge Cleaver, *Soul on Ice,* New York, McGraw-Hill, 1968 (Delta paperback).

Stanley Elkins, *Slavery: A Problem in American Institutional and Intellectual Life,* Chicago, University of Chicago Press, 2nd edition, 1968 (Phoenix paperback).

Ralph Ellison, *Shadow and Act,* New York, Random House, 1964 (Signet paperback).

Nathan Glazer and Daniel P. Moynihan, *Beyond the Melting Pot,* Cambridge, Mass., MIT Press, 1964 (MIT paperback).

Norval D. Glenn and Charles M. Bonjean, *Blacks in the United States,* San Francisco, Chandler, 1969.

Raymond W. Mack, *Race, Class, and Power,* New York, American Book Co., 2nd edition, 1968 (Van Nostrand paperback).

————, *Our Children's Burden: School Desegregation in Nine American Communities,* New York, Random House, 1968 (Vintage paperback).

————, *The Changing South,* Chicago, Aldine, 1970.

Edgar May, *The Wasted Americans,* New York, Harper & Row, 1964 (Signet paperback).

Gunnar Myrdal, *An American Dilemma,* New York, Harper & Row, new edition, 1962 (Torchbook paperback).

Thomas F. Pettigrew, *A Profile of the Negro American,* Princeton, Van Nostrand, 1965 (Van Nostrand paperback).

Report of the National Advisory Commission on Civil Disorders, New York, Bantam Books, 1968 (paperback).

Kenneth M. Stampp, *The Peculiar Institution,* New York, Knopf, 1956 (Vintage paperback).

Pierre Van Den Berghe, *Race and Racism,* New York, Wiley, 1967.

Arthur I. Waskow, *From Race Riot to Sit-in: 1919 and the 1960's,* Garden City, Doubleday, 1966 (Anchor paperback).

Index

A Note on the Editor

Raymond W. Mack is Professor of Sociology and Dean of Faculties at Northwestern University, and formerly president of the Society for the Study of Social Problems. Born in Ashtabula, Ohio, he studied at Baldwin-Wallace College and the University of North Carolina. His other books include *Transforming America, Our Children's Burden, Sociology and Social Life,* and *Race, Class, and Power*.

QUADRANGLE PAPERBACKS

Social Science

E. Digby Baltzell. *Philadelphia Gentlemen.* (QP236)
Milton L. Barron. *The Blending American.* (QP243)
Abraham S. Blumberg. *Criminal Justice.* (QP227)
James V. Cornehls. *Economic Development and Economic Growth.* (NYTimes Book, QP240)
Donald R. Cressey. *Crime and Criminal Justice.* (NYTimes Book, QP233)
Shalom Endleman. *Violence in the Streets.* (QP215)
Nathan Glazer. *Cities in Trouble.* (NYTimes Book, QP212)
William J. Goode. *The Contemporary American Family.* (NYTimes Book, QP223)
George and Eunice Grier. *Equality and Beyond.* (QP204)
F. William Howton. *Functionaries.* (QP232)
Morris Janowitz. *Political Conflict.* (QP226)
Michael B. Kane. *Minorities in Textbooks.* (QP231)
Kurt Lang and Gladys Engel Lang. *Politics and Television.* (QP216)
Charles O. Lerche, Jr. *Last Chance in Europe.* (QP207)
Raymond W. Mack. *Prejudice and Race Relations.* (NYTimes Book, QP217)
Harry T. Marmion. *The Case Against a Volunteer Army.* (QP234)
David Mitrany. *A Working Peace System.* (QP205)
Wilbert E. Moore. *Technology and Social Change.* (NYTimes Book, QP241)
Earl Finbar Murphy. *Governing Nature.* (QP228)
H. L. Nieburg. *In the Name of Science.* (QP218)
Martin Oppenheimer. *The Urban Guerrilla.* (QP219)
Martin Oppenheimer and George Lakey. *A Manual for Direct Action.* (QP202)
James Parkes. *Antisemitism.* (QP213)
Fred Powledge. *To Change a Child.* (QP209)
Lee Rainwater. *And the Poor Get Children.* (QP208)
The Rockefeller Report on the Americas. (QP214)
Edward Sagarin. *Odd Man In.* (QP242)
Ben B. Seligman. *Main Currents in Modern Economics.* (3 vols, QP237, 238, 239)
Ben B. Seligman. *Molders of Modern Thought.* (NYTimes Book, QP224)
Ben B. Seligman. *Permanent Poverty.* (QP229)
Clarence Senior. *The Puerto Ricans.* (QP201)
Harold L. Sheppard. *Poverty and Wealth in America.* (NYTimes Book, QP220)
Arthur L. Stinchcombe. *Rebellion in a High School.* (QP211)
Edward G. Stockwell. *Population and People.* (QP230)
Harry M. Trebing. *The Corporation in the American Economy.* (NYTimes Book, QP221)
Michael Walzer. *Political Action.* (QP235)
David Manning White. *Pop Culture in America.* (NYTimes Book, QP222)
Harold Wolozin. *American Fiscal and Monetary Policy.* (NYTimes Book, QP225)

Philosophy

F. H. Bradley. *The Presuppositions of Critical History.* (QP108)
E. M. Cioran. *The Temptation to Exist.* (QP119)
William Earle. *The Autobiographical Consciousness.* (QP121)
William Earle. *Objectivity.* (QP109)
James M. Edie, James P. Scanlan, Mary-Barbara Zeldin, George L. Kline. *Russian Philosophy.* (3 vols, QP111, 112, 113)
James M. Edie. *An Invitation to Phenomenology.* (QP103)
James M. Edie. *New Essays in Phenomenology.* (QP114)
James M. Edie. *Phenomenology in America.* (QP105)
R. O. Elveton. *The Phenomenology of Husserl.* (QP116)
Manfred S. Frings. *Heidegger and the Quest for Truth.* (QP107)
Moltke S. Gram. *Kant: Disputed Questions.* (QP104)
James F. Harris, Jr., and Richard Severens. *Analyticity.* (QP117)
E. D. Klemke. *Studies in the Philosophy of G. E. Moore.* (QP115)
Lionel Rubinoff. *Faith and Reason.* (QP106)
Stuart F. Spicker. *The Philosophy of the Body.* (QP118)
Pierre Thévenaz. *What Is Phenomenology?* (QP101)
Paul Tibbetts. *Perception.* (QP110)
Robert E. Wood. *The Future of Metaphysics.* (QP120)

American History

James Truslow Adams. *Provincial Society, 1690-1763.* (QP403)
Frederick Lewis Allen. *The Lords of Creation.* (QP35)
Lewis Atherton. *Main Street on the Middle Border.* (QP36)
Thomas A. Bailey. *Woodrow Wilson and the Lost Peace.* (QP1)
Thomas A. Bailey. *Woodrow Wilson and the Great Betrayal.* (QP2)
Charles A. Beard. *The Idea of National Interest.* (QP27)
Carl L. Becker. *Everyman His Own Historian.* (QP33)
Barton J. Bernstein. *Politics and Policies of the Truman Administration.* (QP72)
Ray A. Billington. *The Protestant Crusade.* (QP12)
Allan G. Bogue. *From Prairie to Corn Belt.* (QP50)
Kenneth E. Boulding. *The Organizational Revolution.* (QP43)
Robert V. Bruce. *1877: Year of Violence.* (QP73)
Roger Burlingame. *Henry Ford.* (QP76)
Gerald M. Capers. *John C. Calhoun, Opportunist.* (QP70)
David M. Chalmers. *Hooded Americanism.* (QP51)
John Chamberlain. *Farewell to Reform.* (QP19)
Arthur C. Cole. *The Irrepressible Conflict, 1850-1865.* (QP407)
Alice Hamilton Cromie. *A Tour Guide to the Civil War.*
Robert D. Cross. *The Emergence of Liberal Catholicism in America.* (QP44)
Richard M. Dalfiume. *American Politics Since 1945.* (NYTimes Book, QP57)
Carl N. Degler. *The New Deal.* (NYTimes Book, QP74)
Chester McArthur Destler. *American Radicalism, 1865-1901.* (QP30)
Robert A. Divine. *American Foreign Policy Since 1945.* (NYTimes Book, QP58)
Robert A. Divine. *Causes and Consequences of World War II.* (QP63)
Robert A. Divine. *The Cuban Missile Crisis.* (QP86)
Robert A. Divine. *The Illusion of Neutrality.* (QP45)
Elisha P. Douglass. *Rebels and Democrats.* (QP26)
Melvyn Dubofsky. *American Labor Since the New Deal.* (NYTimes Book, QP87)
Arthur A. Ekirch, Jr. *Ideologies and Utopias.* (QP89)
Harold U. Faulkner. *The Quest for Social Justice, 1898-1914.* (QP411)
Carl Russell Fish. *The Rise of the Common Man, 1830-1850.* (QP406)
Felix Frankfurter. *The Commerce Clause.* (QP16)
Lloyd C. Gardner. *Architects of Illusion.* (QP91)
Edwin Scott Gaustad. *The Great Awakening in New England.* (QP46)
Ray Ginger. *Altgeld's America.* (QP21)
Ray Ginger. *Modern American Cities.* (NYTimes Book, QP67)
Ray Ginger. *Six Days or Forever?* (QP68)
Evarts B. Greene. *The Revolutionary Generation, 1763-1790.* (QP404)
Gerald N. Grob. *Workers and Utopia.* (QP61)
Louis Hartz. *Economic Policy and Democratic Thought.* (QP52)
William B. Hesseltine. *Lincoln's Plan of Reconstruction.* (QP41)
Granville Hicks. *The Great Tradition.* (QP62)
Stanley P. Hirshson. *Farewell to the Bloody Shirt.* (QP53)
Dwight W. Hoover. *A Teacher's Guide to American Urban History.* (QP83)
Dwight W. Hoover. *Understanding Negro History.* (QP49)
Frederic C. Howe. *The Confessions of a Reformer.* (QP39)
Harold L. Ickes. *The Autobiography of a Curmudgeon.* (QP69)
William Loren Katz. *Teachers' Guide to American Negro History.* (QP210)
Burton Ira Kaufman. *Washington's Farewell Address.* (QP64)
Edward Chase Kirkland. *Dream and Thought in the Business Community, 1860-1900.* (QP11)
Edward Chase Kirkland. *Industry Comes of Age.* (QP42)
Herbert S. Klein. *Slavery in the Americas.* (QP84)
Adrienne Koch. *The Philosophy of Thomas Jefferson.* (QP17)
Gabriel Kolko. *The Triumph of Conservatism.* (QP40)
Aileen S. Kraditor. *Up from the Pedestal.* (QP77)
John Allen Krout and Dixon Ryan Fox. *The Completion of Independence, 1790-1830.* (QP405)
Walter LaFeber. *John Quincy Adams and American Continental Empire.* (QP23)
Lawrence H. Leder. *The Meaning of the American Revolution.* (NYTimes Book, QP66)
Jerome Levinson and Juan de Onís. *The Alliance That Lost Its Way.* (QP92)
David E. Lilienthal. *TVA: Democracy on the March.* (QP28)

American History (continued)

Arthur S. Link. *Wilson the Diplomatist*. (QP18)
Huey P. Long. *Every Man a King*. (QP8)
Gene M. Lyons. *America: Purpose and Power*. (QP24)
Neill Macaulay. *The Sandino Affair*. (QP82)
Ernest R. May. *The World War and American Isolation, 1914-1917*. (QP29)
Henry F. May. *The End of American Innocence*. (QP9)
Thomas J. McCormick. *China Market*. (QP75)
August Meier and Elliott Rudwick. *Black Protest in the Sixties*. (NYTimes Book, QP78)
George E. Mowry. *The California Progressives*. (QP6)
Allan Nevins. *The Emergence of Modern America, 1865-1878*. (QP408)
William L. O'Neill. *American Society Since 1945*. (NYTimes Book, QP59)
William L. O'Neill. *Everyone Was Brave*. (QP88)
William L. O'Neill. *The Woman Movement*. (QP80)
William L. O'Neill. *Women at Work*. (QP90)
Frank L. Owsley. *Plain Folk of the Old South*. (QP22)
Thomas G. Paterson. *Cold War Critics*. (QP85)
David Graham Phillips. *The Treason of the Senate*. (QP20)
Julius W. Pratt. *Expansionists of 1898*. (QP15)
Herbert I. Priestley. *The Coming of the White Man, 1492-1848*. (QP401)
C. Herman Pritchett. *The Roosevelt Court*. (QP71)
Moses Rischin. *The American Gospel of Success*. (QP54)
John P. Roche. *The Quest for the Dream*. (QP47)
Arthur Meier Schlesinger. *The Rise of the City, 1878-1898*. (QP410)
David A. Shannon. *The Socialist Party of America*. (QP38)
Andrew Sinclair. *The Available Man*. (QP60)
Preston W. Slosson. *The Great Crusade and After, 1914-1928*. (QP412)
June Sochen. *The Black Man and the American Dream*. (QP81)
John Spargo. *The Bitter Cry of the Children*. (QP55)
Bernard Sternsher. *Hitting Home*. (QP79)
Bernard Sternsher. *The Negro in Depression and War*. (QP65)
Ida M. Tarbell. *The Nationalizing of Business, 1878-1898*. (QP409)
Richard W. Van Alstyne. *The Rising American Empire*. (QP25)
Willard M. Wallace. *Appeal to Arms*. (QP10)
Norman Ware. *The Industrial Worker, 1840-1860*. (QP13)
Dixon Wecter. *The Age of the Great Depression, 1929-1941*. (QP413)
Albert K. Weinberg. *Manifest Destiny*. (QP3)
Bernard A. Weisberger. *They Gathered at the River*. (QP37)
Thomas J. Wertenbaker. *The First Americans, 1607-1690*. (QP402)
Robert H. Wiebe. *Businessmen and Reform*. (QP56)
William Appleman Williams. *The Contours of American History*. (QP34)
William Appleman Williams. *The Great Evasion*. (QP48)
Esmond Wright. *Causes and Consequences of the American Revolution*. (QP31)

European History

William Sheridan Allen. *The Nazi Seizure of Power*. (QP302)
Hans W. Gatzke. *European Diplomacy Between Two Wars, 1919-1939*. (QP351)
Nathanael Greene. *European Socialism Since World War I*. (NYTimes Book, QP309)
W. O. Henderson. *The Industrial Revolution in Europe*. (QP303)
Raul Hilberg. *The Destruction of the European Jews*. (QP301)
Raul Hilberg. *Documents of Destruction*. (QP311)
Gabriel Jackson. *The Spanish Civil War*. (NYTimes Book, QP313)
Richard N. Hunt. *German Social Democracy*. (QP306)
John F. Naylor. *Britain, 1919-1970*. (NYTimes Book, QP312)
Steven E. Ozment. *The Reformation in Medieval Perspective*. (QP350)
Percy Ernst Schramm. *Hitler: The Man and the Military Leader*. (QP308)
Telford Taylor. *Sword and Swastika*. (QP304)
John Weiss. *Nazis and Fascists in Europe, 1918-1945*. (NYTimes Book, QP305)